Biblical Wisdom and the Victorian Literary Imagination

New Directions in Religion and Literature

This series aims to showcase new work at the forefront of religion and literature through short studies written by leading and rising scholars in the field. Books will pursue a variety of theoretical approaches as they engage with writing from different religious and literary traditions. Collectively, the series will offer a timely critical intervention to the interdisciplinary crossover between religion and literature, speaking to wider contemporary interests and mapping out new directions for the field in the early twenty-first century.

Series editors: Emma Mason and Mark Knight

Also available in the series:

The New Atheist Novel, Arthur Bradley and Andrew Tate
Blake. Wordsworth. Religion, Jonathan Roberts
Do the Gods Wear Capes?, Ben Saunders
England's Secular Scripture, Jo Carruthers
Victorian Parables, Susan E. Colón
The Late Walter Benjamin, John Schad
Dante and the Sense of Transgression, William Franke
The Glyph and the Gramophone, Luke Ferretter
John Cage and Buddhist Ecopoetics, Peter Jaeger
Rewriting the Old Testament in Anglo-Saxon Verse, Samantha Zacher
Forgiveness in Victorian Literature, Richard Hughes Gibson
The Gospel According to the Novelist, Magdalena Mączyńska
Jewish Feeling, Richa Dwor
Beyond the Willing Suspension of Disbelief, Michael Tomko
The Gospel According to David Foster Wallace, Adam S. Miller
Pentecostal Modernism, Stephen Shapiro and Philip Barnard
The Bible in the American Short Story, Lesleigh Cushing Stahlberg and Peter S. Hawkins
Faith in Poetry, Michael D. Hurley
Jeanette Winterson and Religion, Emily McAvan
Religion and American Literature since the 1950s, Mark Eaton
Esoteric Islam in Modern French Thought, Ziad Elmarsafy
The Rhetoric of Conversion in English Puritan Writing, David Parry
Djuna Barnes and Theology, Zhao Ng
Food and Fasting in Victorian Religion and Literature, Lesa Scholl
The Economy of Religion in American Literature, Andrew Ball
Christian Heresy, James Joyce, and the Modernist Literary Imagination, Gregory Erikson
Jesus and the Victorian Novel, Jessica Ann Hughes
Marilynne Robinson's Worldly Gospel, Jessica Ann Hughes

Biblical Wisdom and the Victorian Literary Imagination

Denae Dyck

BLOOMSBURY ACADEMIC
LONDON • NEW YORK • OXFORD • NEW DELHI • SYDNEY

BLOOMSBURY ACADEMIC
Bloomsbury Publishing Plc, 50 Bedford Square, London, WC1B 3DP, UK
Bloomsbury Publishing Inc, 1385 Broadway, New York, NY 10018, USA
Bloomsbury Publishing Ireland, 29 Earlsfort Terrace, Dublin 2, D02 AY28, Ireland

BLOOMSBURY, BLOOMSBURY ACADEMIC and the Diana logo
are trademarks of Bloomsbury Publishing Plc

First published in Great Britain 2024
Paperback edition published 2025

Copyright © Denae Dyck, 2024

Denae Dyck has asserted her right under the Copyright, Designs and Patents Act, 1988,
to be identified as Author of this work.

For legal purposes the Acknowledgments on pp. viii–x constitute
an extension of this copyright page.

Cover design: Rebecca Heselton
Cover image: *When the Morning Stars Sang Together* from The Book of Job, William Blake,
1825 © Digital image, The Museum of Modern Art, New York/Scala, Florence

All rights reserved. No part of this publication may be: i) reproduced or transmitted in any form, electronic or mechanical, including photocopying, recording or by means of any information storage or retrieval system without prior permission in writing from the publishers; or ii) used or reproduced in any way for the training, development or operation of artificial intelligence (AI) technologies, including generative AI technologies. The rights holders expressly reserve this publication from the text and data mining exception as per Article 4(3) of the Digital Single Market Directive (EU) 2019/790.

Bloomsbury Publishing Plc does not have any control over, or responsibility for, any third-party websites referred to or in this book. All internet addresses given in this book were correct at the time of going to press. The author and publisher regret any inconvenience caused if addresses have changed or sites have ceased to exist, but can accept no responsibility for any such changes.

A catalogue record for this book is available from the British Library.

A catalog record for this book is available from the Library of Congress.

ISBN: HB: 978-1-3503-3537-0
PB: 978-1-3503-3540-0
ePDF: 978-1-3503-3538-7
eBook: 978-1-3503-3539-4

Series: New Directions in Religion and Literature

Typeset by Integra Software Services Pvt. Ltd.

For product safety related questions contact productsafety@bloomsbury.com.

To find out more about our authors and books visit www.bloomsbury.com
and sign up for our newsletters.

For those who search with all their hearts

Contents

Acknowledgments   viii

Introduction: Biblical Interpretation, Victorian Writers, and
Wisdom Literature   1

1   Wisdom's Call: Poetic Dialogue and the Echoes of Job in Elizabeth
    Barrett Browning's *A Drama of Exile*   31
2   Wisdom's Footsteps: Heuristic Pathways and Proverbial Aphorisms in
    George MacDonald's *Phantastes*   59
3   Wisdom's Turn: Historical Recovery, Narrative Possibility, and the
    Direction of Biblical Parables in George Eliot's *Romola*   87
4   Wisdom's Reach: Mythmaking, Incarnational Poetics, and Interpretive
    Limits in John Ruskin's *The Queen of the Air*   115
5   Wisdom's Breath: Revelation, Concealment, and the Energy of
    Ecclesiastes in Olive Schreiner's *The Story of an African Farm*   143

Coda   173

Bibliography   186
Index   201

Acknowledgments

Perhaps it is fitting that a book about wisdom as dialogue should owe so much to so many people. Their generosity exceeds what I can recount here, yet I am very glad to offer this brief thanks to those who have supported, encouraged, challenged, and inspired me.

The questions informing my inquiry emerged while I was an undergraduate student at Ambrose University and evolved during my time studying and teaching at Dalhousie University and the University of Victoria. I am deeply indebted to Marjorie Stone, who helped me to articulate the first inklings of these ideas and whose kind mentorship has continued from my early days as a graduate student until the present time. My scholarship owes very much to the excellent guidance of Lisa Surridge, who supervised my dissertation, as well as the keen insight of committee members Mary Elizabeth Leighton, Adrienne Williams Boyarin, and Lynne Marks. As external examiner, Joshua King provided generous commentary on an early version of this project, along with thoughtful suggestions about how it might be further developed. Stephen Ross offered helpful advice and kind support as this work evolved into a book. Many other people have had a significant influence on my development as a writer and teacher, and I sincerely thank Alison Chapman, Chris Douglas, Sara Humphreys, Erin Kelly, Gary Kuchar, Robert Miles, Andrew Murray, Nicole Shukin, and Yan (Amy) Tang. My doctoral work was supported by the Social Sciences and Humanities Research Council of Canada, the Centre for Studies in Religion and Society at the University of Victoria, and the Visiting Scholars Program of the Armstrong Browning Library at Baylor University. The holdings at the Armstrong Browning Library informed my chapter on Elizabeth Barrett Browning, and I am grateful to the library staff who shared their knowledge with me and made me feel welcome during my stay, including Jennifer Borderud, Melinda Creech, Christi Klempnauer, and Melvin Schuetz. Foundational work for several chapters was completed during my time as a graduate student fellow at the Centre for Studies in Religion and Society, where I benefited from Paul Bramadat's leadership as well as collegial input from associates including Sara Beam, Scott Dolf, Bill Israel, Graham Jensen, Francis Landy, Miles Lowry, Jessica Pratezina, Peter Scales, and Lycia Troughton.

The ideas in this book have been greatly strengthened by conversations at the annual conferences and virtual events hosted by the North American Victorian Studies Association, the British Women Writers Association, and the Victorian Studies Association of Western Canada. Collaborative work on the Crafting Communities project enriched my thinking about the forms that embodied wisdom and reflective practice might take in the classroom and beyond. Joining a working group of the Christian Poetics Initiative Scholars Network at the Rivendell Centre for Theology and the Arts has further added to my experiences of scholarly community, and I am grateful for the leadership and vision of Mark Knight and David Mahan. Taken together, these contexts have provided wonderful opportunities to learn from those I admire and respect, including Ilana Blumberg, Lori Branch, Amy Coté, Karen Dieleman, Joy Dixon, Richa Dwor, Kylee-Anne Hingston, Andrea Korda, Charles LaPorte, Diana Maltz, Emma Mason, Joe McQueen, Elizabeth Parker, Aubrey Plourde, Amanda Vernon, and Vanessa Warne.

I am grateful to have found a new academic home at Texas State University, where this project was completed. It is a privilege to work with such excellent colleagues, and I have especially benefited from the encouragement and support offered by Rebecca Bell-Metereau, Jennifer Dubois, Simon Lee, Dan Lochman, Cecily Parks, James Reeves, Teya Rosenburg, Nithya Sivashankar, Elizabeth Skerpan-Wheeler, Vicki Smith, Julie Weng, and Ruben Zecena. My students, both at Texas State and at the University of Victoria, have also been teachers to me, and I thank them for their enthusiasm and curiosity.

I have been very fortunate in working with Bloomsbury Academic. I would like to thank Ben Doyle and Laura Cope at Bloomsbury for their helpfulness throughout the publication process, as well as series editors Mark Knight and Emma Mason. Insightful reader feedback has made this book substantially more compelling and cohesive. An earlier version of Chapter 1 appeared as "Falling into Hope: Wisdom Poetry and the Reinterpretation of Suffering in Elizabeth Barrett Browning's *A Drama of Exile*," *Victorian Poetry* 58, no. 1 (2020): 27–51. Rights in the Authorized (King James) Version in the United Kingdom are vested in the Crown; all biblical quotations are reproduced by permission of the Crown's patentee, Cambridge University Press.

Finally, I would like to express my profound gratitude to my friends and family. I write these words in loving memory of Joe Burghardt and with warm thanks to Rose Burghardt. Melinda O'Neill and Jaime Traynor live forever in my heart as sources of courage and creativity. Jamila Douhaibi, Adam Holman, Dominic Plante, Carol Stevenson, Gwen van der Kamp, and Sam Wong brightened the darkest moments of the past seven years and never doubted that my work would someday see the light of day. As fellow scholars and true friends, Emily Banta and Janice Niemann have shared with me all manner of struggles and successes. Adrienna Dyck has been there for me for as long as I can remember. Finally, I thank my parents, David and Ann-Marie Dyck. My very first teachers, they have shaped my passion for lifelong learning and continue to teach me so much about perseverance, character, and hope.

Introduction: Biblical Interpretation, Victorian Writers, and Wisdom Literature

For a witty and entertaining overview of the intellectual and literary controversies that animated the Victorian era (1837–1901), it is hard to improve on Oscar Wilde's *The Critic as Artist* (1891). Wilde's essay, cast as a dialogue between the savant Gilbert and his interlocutor Ernest, both gives voice to his own aesthetic philosophy and positions it against the backdrop of a hundred years of dynamic thought. Gilbert reflects:

> [T]he nineteenth century is a turning point in history, simply on account of two men, Darwin and Renan, the one the critic of the Book of Nature, the other the critic of the Books of God. Not to recognise this is to miss the meaning of one of the most important eras in the progress of the world.[1]

This remark is striking because, despite what Gilbert claims, twentieth- and twenty-first-century scholars seldom recognize Ernest Renan's biblical scholarship as having anything like equal cultural weight with Charles Darwin's scientific findings. As indicated by examples such as Gillian Beer's *Darwin's Plots: Evolutionary Narrative in Darwin, George Eliot, and Nineteenth-Century Fiction* (1983), George Levine's *Darwin Loves You: Natural Selection and the Re-Enchantment of the World* (2006), John Holmes's *Darwin's Bards: British and American Poetry in the Age of Evolution* (2013), and Trenton B. Olsen's *Wordsworth and Evolution in Victorian Literature: Entangled Influence* (2020), a substantial and elaborate body of scholarship has focused on how the rise of evolutionary theory influenced nineteenth-century literature. However, as Wilde suggests, our critical accounts "miss the meaning" of this historical period if they neglect to consider the force exerted by biblical scholarship—and, moreover, if they overlook the subtleties and sophistication of Victorian religious culture at large.

Recent scholarship on religion and secularization makes it possible to return to Wilde's remarks with fresh insights. For a long time, the critical consensus has been to regard the Victorian era as an age of doubt, a time when scientific and philosophical developments led to a widespread "crisis of faith." But over the past two decades, conversations across the fields of sociology, anthropology, philosophy, history, and literary criticism have questioned once widely held assumptions about the overall decline of faith in the nineteenth century, uncovering instead the vitality, variety, and dynamism of the period's religious expressions. Studies including Suzy Anger's *Victorian Interpretation* and Charles LaPorte's *Victorian Poets and the Changing Bible* have begun to illuminate how biblical scholarship such as Renan's played an important role in shaping Victorian literature. Increasingly, scholars have been reflecting on the extent to which ostensibly secular methods of literary criticism find their roots in complex theological debates.

These debates intensified as a result of work by Renan and his contemporaries: the scholarship generally referred to as "the higher criticism," which originated in the work of eighteenth-century German scholars and made its way into English translation in Britain by the middle decades of the nineteenth century. Challenging received traditions about the Bible's divine inspiration and theological unity, this criticism emphasized instead its diverse historical contexts and composite authorship. Rather than presuppose a special revelatory status, the higher critics studied the Bible "*like any other book*," as the Anglican cleric and classical scholar Benjamin Jowett put it in "On the Interpretation of Scripture," the final piece in the collectively authored *Essays and Reviews* (1860).[2] A joint venture by seven liberally minded theologians and academics who were dubbed by their detractors *the septum contra Christum* (the seven against Christ), *Essays and Reviews* brought the basic principles of the German higher critics to a wide British readership. This volume incited strong protests from many Victorian Christians, all the more so because of the fact that six of its seven contributors were ordained Anglican ministers. Indeed, the reactions against *Essays and Reviews* within the periodical press, particularly among dissenting Protestants, were stronger and more vehement than what had been directed against Darwin's *Origin of Species* the previous year.[3]

At the heart of this controversy was the higher criticism's implication that what had long been regarded as the very words of God should rather be seen as a collection of unruly documents featuring divergent voices and conflicting ideological positions—that the Bible was a fragmentary and dialogic text, to put it in the terms of today's theoretical parlance.[4] This discussion provoked questions that begin in the realm of theology and extend to the practice of hermeneutics writ large. Does inspiration depend on divine origins, or might it instead result from a text's literary qualities? What is at stake in the experiences of revelation or epiphany? To what extent should authorial intent condition the reader's response? As the Victorian period witnessed increasing emphasis on scientific, empirical, and historical knowledge, it also saw renewed investment in the question attributed to Pontius Pilate in the gospel of John, *quid est veritas?* or, "what is truth?" (Jn. 18:37).[5]

This book reassesses the interpretive challenges and imaginative possibilities sparked by the advent of biblical higher criticism, demonstrating that a range of Victorian writers wrestled with these hermeneutic issues by creatively refashioning wisdom texts and traditions. Whereas previous accounts of the higher criticism's cultural impacts have emphasized the unsettling of biblical history and repurposing of prophecy, this study recovers wisdom literature as a vital and distinctive genre. Given that the impacts of the higher criticism were felt especially keenly among Victorian dissenters, I follow habits in both nineteenth- and twenty-first-century Protestantism by focusing my analysis of wisdom literature on the books of Job, Proverbs, and Ecclesiastes, along with the gospel parables.[6] This corpus of wisdom literature centers embodied metaphors and existential mysteries, rather than the unfolding of a collective redemptive history. Moreover, wisdom literature presents a strategic opportunity to explore the theory and practice of interpretation because so much of it is explicitly concerned with the search for order, purpose, and meaning.

Wisdom literature's poetic prospects have enduring appeal, yet this genre reached newfound heights of expression during the Victorian era, with its crisis of interpretation. The memorable wit of Wilde's *The Critic as Artist* arises from his adaptation of Socratic dialogue and his aphoristic turns of phrase, forms rooted in classical and biblical wisdom literatures. Wilde's writings on aestheticism advance a gospel of beauty that at once subverts and preserves the traditions it inherits, seeking "to discard damaged oracles and salvage from their ruin a fragment of wisdom worth transmitting to posterity," as W. David Shaw puts it.[7] Wilde was not alone. In a commentary that made a self-conscious effort to reconcile recent higher critical findings with long-standing exegetical traditions, the Anglican reverend and Oxford professor Thomas Kelly Cheyne went so far as to claim that biblical wisdom literature, the book of Ecclesiastes in particular, was entering into the cultural consciousness on an unprecedented scale. "Never so much as in our own time have this taste and this ear been so largely possessed," he declared, citing echoes of Ecclesiastes ranging from the prose of Thomas Carlyle to the poetry of Christina Rossetti.[8] Surprisingly few literary scholars, however, have followed Cheyne's lead in tracing these resonances—perhaps because debates about the higher criticism in the periodical press tended to concentrate on biblical history, and subsequent literary critics have typically seen the period's religious discourse primarily through the lens of prophecy.[9] The present study helps to correct this neglect. Drawing from the theoretical work of Paul Ricoeur, I argue that wisdom literature provided an especially rich resource for Victorian writers responding to the dilemmas posed by the spread of the higher criticism. These writers adapted wisdom literature's characteristic forms of questioning and dialogue to reframe their experiences of doubt and uncertainty.

To probe the latent potentialities of these biblical rewritings, I take up Ricoeur's work on hermeneutics, including his idea of "creative interpretation," articulated in the conclusion to *The Symbolism of Evil* and developed throughout his subsequent writings. Positioned as a *via media* between philosophical study and religious exegesis, this concept provides a useful lens for re-examining nineteenth-century debates about biblical scholarship. Ricoeur emphasizes that the philosophical approach, if taken by itself, remains incomplete. "Beyond the desert of criticism, we wish to be called again," he remarks, evoking the motifs of exile and return that permeate biblical traditions.[10] Extrapolating from Ricoeur, I suggest that a variety of Victorian writers turned to wisdom literature in what was essentially a twofold response to higher criticism. On the one hand, their creative work participated in the higher critical project of challenging canonical authority and questioning literalist exegesis. On the other hand, the artistic qualities of their creative work departed from and even resisted the higher criticism's dominant methodological emphasis on historical recovery, instead reasserting the value of poetic metaphor.

In what follows, I examine several case studies from Victorian literature that adapt biblical wisdom traditions as a means of thinking through newly galvanized interpretive issues. Focusing on the 1840s to the 1880s, the decades that witnessed the most debate about the higher criticism in the Victorian press, my analysis concentrates on texts that incorporate wisdom literature's characteristic forms: the dramatic poem, the aphorism, the parable, the hymn to personified wisdom, and the fragmentary autobiographical narrative. My chapters trace these forms throughout Elizabeth Barrett Browning's *A Drama of Exile* (1844), George MacDonald's *Phantastes* (1858), George Eliot's *Romola* (1862–3), John Ruskin's *The Queen of the Air* (1869), and Olive Schreiner's *The Story of an African Farm* (1883). Rather than claim either to hold or to disprove certain knowledge of divine activity, Victorian wisdom writers combine searching inquiry with reverence for mystery. By both responding to higher critical findings and returning to exegetical traditions focused on contemplation and application, they invite readers to participate in an ongoing work of forming wisdom—both as a textual experience and as an embodied practice. This work, in turn, helped to propagate a broad array of ideas for re-imagining a divine presence at work within an ostensibly secular arena.

Secularization Narratives and the Victorian Literary Imagination

With the advent of a larger theoretical turn to religion, the time is ripe for Victorian studies to reconsider the period's literary imagination. Such work includes attending to the variety of genres that the Victorians (re)discovered and developed in the wake of new approaches to biblical interpretation, as well as reassessing secularization narratives at large. As a result of work by Talal Asad, William McKelvy, Charles Taylor, and many other scholars, secularization has become increasingly understood in terms of the revision or transformation of religion, rather than its decline or lack.[11] On the whole, literary studies has been a latecomer to these interdisciplinary conversations, as Joshua King and Winter Jade Werner observe in the introduction to their collection *Constructing Nineteenth-Century Religion: Literary, Historical, and Religious Studies in Dialogue*.[12] This tardiness is not surprising, given that justifications for the discipline have often been embedded in narratives of religious decline. Even so, recent ventures have highlighted the distinct contributions that literary studies can make to this broader project, including providing insight into how changing religious ideas were mediated through narrative and poetic forms.[13] The novel, for instance, has long been held to be a predominantly secular mode of writing—"the epic of a world that has been abandoned by God," to quote Georg Lukács.[14] However, several recent studies including J. Russell Perkin's *Theology and the Victorian Novel*, Norman Vance's *Bible and Novel*, and Mark Knight's *Good Words: Evangelicalism and the Victorian Novel* have reexamined this story.

Although it is now becoming almost cliché to interrogate older concepts of secularization, forging an alternative paradigm remains a challenging project. Scholars have had a difficult time arriving at a consensus about the basic term *secular* and its derivatives. Taylor's widely influential *A Secular Age*, for one, uses it to mean not the disappearance of religious belief but the proliferation of many different belief positions—a concept akin to that which has been described as "postsecular," by Jürgen Habermas.[15] While the word *postsecular* comes with its own varieties and ambiguities, I follow Lori Branch and Mark Knight in using "postsecular studies" to denote the growing body of scholarship that aims to move beyond a reductive secular/religious binary.[16] As Branch summarizes it, this work seeks to demonstrate that "the *seculum* isn't secular in the sense of materially-determined and free-of-belief, and religion is neither mere morality nor the abstract assent to doctrines modern believers and nonbelievers have made it out to be."[17] The goal, then, is to get beyond an unhelpful dichotomy and develop a robust model for approaching the wide range of human experiences associated with belief, doubt, longing, disillusionment, and hope.

Importantly, the very concept of secularism has a complex history, including new social and political uses during the Victorian era. The newspaper editor George Jacob Holyoake began using the term *secularism* in 1851 to marshal support for a growing movement of anti-religious freethinkers. In 1866, the National Secular Society was formed under the leadership of Charles Bradlaugh, who in later years was initially denied his seat in the House of Commons because he refused to take the Religious Oath of Parliament. Even so, the word derives from the Latin noun *saeculum*, used in the Vulgate (the Latin Bible of the Roman Catholic Church) to translate the Greek *aion* (age) and employed in liturgical formulae to bridge earth and eternity.[18] This liturgical sense suggests that to be *secular* has less to do with outright resistance to religion and more to do with investment in how a sense of sacrality might be brought to bear on the here and now. Within a biblical context, wisdom literature offers a useful avenue for pursuing this line of inquiry. The wisdom writers, especially those of Proverbs and Ecclesiastes, are expressly concerned with practical matters and earthly experiences. As Victorian adaptations of this wisdom literature suggest, recognizing humankind's shared condition of limited, imperfect knowledge might become the starting point for articulating many-sided reading practices and cultivating a sense of scholarly hospitality more broadly.

Such expressions of hospitality seem to be all the more urgent at a moment when many scholars are recognizing the need to "undiscipline" Victorian studies: that is, to radically rethink their approaches to researching and teaching this period, particularly in response to the findings of critical race and ethnicity studies. The word *Victorian* itself underscores the extent to which this field's boundaries have been forged through an imperialist lens.[19] In using this terminology, my aim is not to perpetuate an exclusivist construction that centers English cultural production but, rather, to prompt critical reflection on how these texts and writers have been situated—and might be resituated.

The writers examined in this book evince varying degrees of complicity in and resistance to the British imperial project. As recent reassessments of Victorian religious discourse within global contexts have shown, the relationship between Christian rhetoric and the consolidation of empire was an uneasy one. While religious discourse was often put to nationalist uses, it was also employed to critique nationalist and imperialist agendas—and, as Winter Jade Werner has shown, nineteenth-century missionary movements helped to shape emerging ideas about cosmopolitanism.[20] My analysis of the latent pluralism within Victorian rewritings of biblical wisdom literature aims to help further this work of recontextualizing the period's religious expressions.

This book's contribution to the critical project of rethinking Victorian religion focuses less on large-scale societal patterns than on individual writers and texts. Because the higher criticism provoked a particularly strong reaction from dissenting Protestants, I am most interested in writers who were influenced by these communities, at least throughout their early years. The hostility that many dissenting Protestants felt toward the higher criticism can be seen, for instance, in William Gillespie's reactionary rebuttal *The Truth of the Evangelical History of Our Lord Jesus Christ: Proved, in Opposition to Dr. D. F. Strauss, the Chief of Modern Disbelievers in Revelation* (1856). Just a few years later, in 1859, the biblical scholar Samuel Davidson was forced to resign his position from Lancashire Independent College, a Congregationalist institution, for making even moderate concessions to higher critical scholarship.[21] Against this backdrop of heated resistance, the more complex responses to the higher criticism evident in works by Elizabeth Barrett Browning and George MacDonald, the writers examined in Chapters 1 and 2, deserve a second look, as do their seemingly more "secular" contemporaries such as George Eliot and Olive Schreiner, the subjects of Chapters 3 and 5. John Ruskin, discussed in Chapter 4, requires similarly careful consideration in his non-dogmatic yet still broadly Christian approach to ancient literature, art, and mythology.

The common ground among writers who arrived at what would appear to be rather different belief positions indicates that there is a critical imperative for literary scholars to rethink habitual classifications of Victorian writers as either "religious" or "irreligious." After all, the religious dimension of human experience is not a stand-alone category but necessarily embedded within wider social contexts. Rather than think in terms of faith or doubt, I propose that it would be more productive to focus on a broad continuum of religious discourse's uses and transformations. Again, Taylor's scholarship lays the groundwork for this kind of intervention, especially in his critique of "subtraction stories"—that is, cultural or critical narratives that characterize the advent of modernity in terms of religious decline.[22] Along similar lines, historians including Timothy Larsen and David Nash have proposed further refinements to the critical vocabulary customarily applied to the Victorian period. Challenging conventional accounts of nineteenth-century intellectual and literary history, Larsen turns the "crisis of faith" paradigm on its head, pointing out that many secularist leaders reconverted to some form of Christianity.[23] Nash recommends a different model altogether, proposing that the "restrictive characterization of 'crisis'" might be better replaced with attention to how many Victorian intellectuals demonstrate an "essential capacity as religious/philosophical *seekers*."[24] Following Nash's suggestion, this book brings together writers who self-identified as Christians but whose eclectic or heterodox ideas set them apart from their contemporaries, as well as those who moved away from Christianity but nonetheless engaged rigorously with biblical wisdom literature in their own writing. Taken together, these examples underscore that creative and innovative thought can arise not only from outside religious traditions but also from within them.

My study owes much to feminist criticism that has complicated simplistic equations between religious discourse and the oppression of women. Cynthia Scheinberg, F. Elizabeth Gray, Rebecca Styler, Karen Dieleman, Gail Turley Houston, and Richa Dwor, among others, have called attention to the innovative theology expressed throughout the work of many Victorian women writers, both Christian and Jewish.[25] In considering texts by writers across the gender spectrum, I hope to broaden this conversation, showing how various Victorians engaged with long-standing biblical traditions of personifying wisdom, typically portrayed as female. As subsequent chapters will show, these artistic personifications could be subject to patriarchal ideologies, but they also have the capacity to unsettle misogynistic ideas. In their search for wisdom, the Victorian writers in my study anticipated later developments in feminist theology, with its quest for the feminine face of God.

By making wisdom literature my conceptual basis, I seek to call attention to an important strain of religious discourse that, within criticism on nineteenth-century British literature, has often been overshadowed by a focus on prophecy. Take, for example, the critical category of Victorian sage writing, which has long defined scholarly understanding of biblical allusion and literary authority in the period. First theorized in John Holloway's *The Victorian Sage: Studies in Argument* and substantially developed in George P. Landow's *Elegant Jeremiahs: The Sage from Carlyle to Mailer*, this category centers non-fiction prose written by male authors who adapted the voice and stance of the biblical prophets for the purposes of social critique—key figures include John Ruskin, Matthew Arnold, and Thomas Carlyle. Subsequent scholarship has expanded sage writing's boundaries in terms of both gender and genre, beginning with the essays collected in Thaïs E. Morgan's *Victorian Sages and Cultural Discourse: Renegotiating Gender and Power*.[26] As Gavin Budge observed more than fifty years after the initial publication of Holloway's initial study, casual references to "the Victorian sage" have now become commonplace within "critical thinking about the nineteenth-century assertion of writerly authority."[27] Typically, Victorian sage writing follows what Landow calls "the prophetic pattern": claims of inspiration, forecasts of a divine plan, warnings for those who fail to heed the message, and blessings or promises for those who obey.[28] Effectively, this pattern shows how the Victorians adapted the model of the poet as prophet that they inherited from Romantic writers, especially William Blake. The poetry of Blake and his contemporaries, in turn, took shape within the context of developments in biblical scholarship that prompted them to put prophetic tropes to new, often surprising or subversive, purposes, as several recent studies have shown.[29] Although twentieth- and twenty-first-century criticism has foregrounded these new uses of prophetic discourse, Blake's religious revisionism ranges far and wide throughout wisdom literature, from his "Proverbs of Hell" (1790) to his illustrations of the book of Job (1826). Even as Blake attacked the cherished beliefs of Christian institutions and challenged religious authoritarianism, biblical symbols and metaphors remained vital elements of his artistic imagination. Complementing the long-standing focus on the prophetic pattern and uncovering another important aspect of how Victorian writers continued in a similar spirit, this book proposes that the spread of the higher criticism stimulated renewed engagement with yet another genre: wisdom literature.

While hard and fast lines between prophetic and wisdom literatures are difficult to draw, these genres have different theological emphases and employ distinctive literary tropes. Among biblical scholars today, some consensus has emerged regarding wisdom literature's characteristic features. In *The Wisdom Books*, the Hebrew Bible scholar Robert Alter begins by contextualizing this genre as a category of scholarship, variously constructed—other related groupings would include the Poetic Books (which would also include Psalms and Songs of Songs) and the Megilloth (the festival scrolls in the Jewish tradition, consisting of Ecclesiastes, Song of Songs, Lamentations, Ruth, and Esther). Even so, Alter proposes that the three books he selects (Job, Proverbs, and Ecclesiastes, or "Qohelet") have a "distinctive identity" arising from their "international" scope, highlighting their concern with "questions of value and of moral behaviour, of the meaning of human life."[30] James L. Crenshaw likewise describes wisdom literature's characteristic features as "non-revelatory address, concern for unraveling life's mysteries, and an absence of sacred traditions relating to Moses, David, or the patriarchs."[31] Ricoeur's explanation of biblical genres usefully distinguishes between prophecy and wisdom. According to Ricoeur, wisdom literature does not place the same emphasis on salvific history—or, for that matter, on the people of Israel as a nation—as do the historical and prophetic books. Furthermore, wisdom literature does not follow the prophetic formula, which he identifies as often reductively "taken as a referent" for revelatory discourse at large. Here, the prophet "presents himself not as speaking in his own name, but in the name of another, in the name of Yahweh." This double-authored formula "leads to the idea of scripture as dictated, as something whispered in someone's ear." Wisdom literature, by contrast, presents readers with a dialectical model of revelation-in-concealment and concealment-in-revelation based in "an unassignable design, a design that is God's secret."[32] Building on Ricoeur's claims and coordinating these insights with those of nineteenth-century writers, I suggest that wisdom literature's distinctive qualities took on new significance in light of the debates sparked by the higher criticism.

My analysis of how this wisdom literature helped to shape the Victorian literary imagination extrapolates from Ricoeur's approach to the Bible as literature. As Ricoeur acknowledges, his approach owes much to Northrop Frye's *The Great Code: The Bible and Literature*, though he pursues some different directions. While appreciative of Frye's magisterial work, Ricoeur suggests that focusing on the Bible's imaginative unity and typological patterning might risk obscuring its generic plurality. As Ricoeur puts it, the "variety of discourses" that permeates biblical texts might rather be understood as giving rise to "an order that is more polyphonic than typological."[33] In making this argument about the Bible's polyphonic ordering, Ricoeur turns to the rabbinic triad of the Law (Torah), the Prophets (Nevi'im), and the Writings (Ketuvim). This last category encompasses not only wisdom literature but also a wider array of poetic and historical books, yet still Ricoeur insists that these "other writings"—a label that he says "seems to suggest a certain disquiet"—provide a different orientation toward the self and toward God than that found within the Law and the Prophets.[34] Whereas Ricoeur outlines scripture's polyphony primarily in relation to these threefold categories, my analysis locates such dialogism within wisdom literature itself. As the following chapters show, this genre served important functions for Victorian writers who sought to respond creatively to higher critical ideas about inspiration, authority, and revelation.

Ricoeur's distinction between typological and polyphonic approaches to the Bible is especially useful in application to Victorian literature and culture because typological models have long been central to studies of biblical allusion, both in the verbal and visual arts, in this historical period. Typological exegesis presupposes the essential unity of Old and New Testaments, appropriating and subordinating Jewish traditions according to a Christocentric pattern. Events, rituals, and people recorded in the Hebrew scriptures are seen to anticipate, often incompletely or imperfectly, what was later fulfilled in the coming of Jesus.[35] As Landow claims, the Victorian typological imagination had its roots in "a non-canonical belief that God had dictated every word of the Bible"—that is, the doctrine of verbal inspiration.[36] Landow recognizes that this doctrine began to lose widespread credibility by the 1860s yet shows that typological habits of thought persisted long after its doctrinal precepts had been called into question. Without discounting typology's long-standing cultural influence, I seek to shed light on how writers revised, modulated, or departed from this typological patterning during a time of heated debate about biblical interpretation.

For Victorians from all manner of belief positions, from those staunchly committed to verbal inspiration to those who sought to refute all such doctrines, the Bible provided an "irreplaceable linguistic register," as Larsen has demonstrated in his wide-ranging study *A People of One Book: The Bible and the Victorians*.[37] My own more focused approach to Victorian literature and biblical interpretation responds to Larsen's concluding observation that the scholarly tendency to focus on higher critical methods has obscured the strength of the devotional reading practices that remained remarkably prevalent across cultural circles.[38] While the spread of the higher criticism and its impacts in dissenting Protestant communities serves as my starting point, my aim is ultimately to illuminate a more nuanced understanding of Victorian hermeneutics. Attending to the enduring influence of biblical wisdom in the wake of the higher criticism helps to show how thoughtful Victorian writers sought to combine scholarly rigor and personal reflection in their literary approaches to sacred texts.

The Advent of Biblical Higher Criticism

Although the higher criticism tends to be remembered primarily for its historicizing methods, nineteenth-century biblical scholars—and, of course, the creative writers who engaged with their ideas—had important things to say about the Bible's literary form. Wisdom literature's overtly poetic qualities made it less susceptible to what many believers saw as the more earth-shattering effects of the higher criticism—that is, the charges of inaccuracy that threatened literal readings of the historical and prophetic books. At the same time, metaphors derived from wisdom literature provided a fertile ground for nineteenth-century thinkers who sought to approach these texts less as unified divine dictation than as imperfect yet powerful human poetry.

The higher criticism traces its roots at least to the eighteenth century, but its effects were not felt on a broad scale in Britain until the mid-Victorian period. Coined by Johann Gottfried Eichhorn, the term *the higher criticism* (*die Höhere Kritik*) made its first appearance in the second edition of his *Einleitung in das Alte Testament* (*Studies in the Old Testament*) (1787). One of its earliest English uses is in the work of John Kendrick, a Unitarian biblical scholar who had studied at Göttingen under Eichhorn, in his essay "On the Mythical Interpretation of the Bible," published in 1827 in the *Monthly Repository*.[39] The term gets its meaning partly in distinction from "the lower criticism": whereas "the lower criticism" sought to determine which biblical manuscripts were the most reliable texts, the higher criticism aimed to develop methods for textual interpretation. These methods approached the Bible as a combination of history and mythology, rather than as a factual record. Johann Gottfried Herder, a contemporary of Eichhorn, described this methodological approach as a commitment to reading the Bible *menschlich* ("in the human way").[40] This "human way" went against the grain of readings that emphasized the Bible's special status as divine revelation.

New developments in textual scholarship, including source criticism, generated substantial debate about what it means for a text to be inspired. Pioneered in the work of the French physician and scholar Jean Astruc in 1753, source criticism highlighted the various written sources and oral traditions comprising individual books.[41] Coleridge positioned this theological issue front and center in the epistolary essays on the higher criticism that were posthumously published as *Confessions of an Inquiring Spirit*, which had been provisionally entitled "Letters on the Inspiration of the Scriptures" in manuscript form but were subsequently renamed by his nephew Henry Nelson Coleridge, in an effort to sound less confrontational to the readers of 1840.[42] In 1860, the year that *Essays and Reviews* brought higher critical principles to a wider reading public, Jowett remarked, "the word inspiration has received more numerous gradations and distinctions of meaning than perhaps any other in the whole of theology."[43] These refinements raised the question of whether every letter of the Bible should in itself be understood as the very words of God or whether the variety of discourses present within the Bible might in some way might bring about a divine message.

As it highlighted this composite authorship, the higher criticism also drew attention to contradictions and inaccuracies within canonical texts, findings that could be (and often were) used to heighten doubts about biblical authority. From the eighteenth century onwards, German scholars including Gotthold Ephraim Lessing and Hermann Samuel Reimarus rejected the supernatural claims of scripture, claiming them to be distorted superstitions.[44] Not all the higher critics—or those who were receptive to them—took such an adversarial stance, but questions about biblical history caused a significant stir among Victorian Christians. Arguably the most heated controversy concerned the scholarship of John William Colenso, Bishop of Natal and author of several mathematics textbooks. Colenso's *The Pentateuch and the Book of Joshua Critically Examined* (1862) applied a rigorous mathematical critique to these sources, showing that many of the dates, dimensions, and other figures given in these accounts could not be literally correct. His aim, as a bishop and a lifelong believer, was not to overturn biblical authority but to reform church dogmas that were based on a narrow commitment to scripture's exact words. But unfortunately for Colenso, these efforts went largely unappreciated: his book was widely condemned, and he himself was tried for heresy.[45] The uproar over Colenso underscores the degree to which literalism became a contested issue.

As made clear in Kendrick's 1827 review essay on the higher criticism, these innovations in biblical scholarship developed as part of an emerging study of comparative religions. Several of the higher critics were philologists who contributed to this orientalist endeavor—for instance, Ernest Renan, noted in Wilde's *The Critic as Artist* for his biblical scholarship, also wrote on the prophet Muhammad and the history of Islam. That this work upheld hierarchical categories indicative of imperialist, racist, and anti-Semitic ideologies is undeniable, yet these early forays into comparative religion also had the effect of displacing Christianity from its privileged cultural position. By the end of the century, the higher criticism had helped to fuel the rise of several new religious movements that drew from the spiritual teachings of many different traditions, an aspect of Victorian Britain's changing religious landscape that has lately received renewed critical attention.[46] While these developments in religious syncretism exceed the scope of this project, my focus on the higher criticism aims to show that nineteenth-century thinkers began to develop an understanding of wisdom literature as a genre that necessarily, if implicitly, invites inquiry beyond any single religion.

At the same time that the higher criticism situated Christianity within the context of other religions, it also challenged ideas about the divinity of Jesus.

While Renan's work as a philologist and historian of religion was wide ranging, he was best known in Victorian Britain for his *Vie de Jésus* (*Life of Jesus*) (1863), one of seven volumes in *Histoire des Origines du Christianisme* (*History of the Origins of Christianity*) (1863–90). Like his precursor David Friedrich Strauss, author of *Das Leben Jesu* (1835), Renan analyzed the gospels as historical documents and portrayed Jesus as human rather than divine. Both Strauss and Renan were tremendously controversial, provoking a series of "Lives of Christ" throughout the 1860s and 1870s.[47] These biographies ranged from devotional accounts that made mild concessions to the higher criticism to more heated reactions against Strauss and Renan. Toward the middle of the road was the anonymously published *Ecce Homo: A Survey of the Life and Work of Christ* (1865), which "edged its way quietly between the sceptical productions of continental criticism and the devotional, conservative works which prevailed in Britain," as Daniel L. Pals puts it.[48] Written by John Seeley, Professor of Latin at University College, London, *Ecce Homo* exemplified key features of the higher criticism. But instead of denying outright the doctrines of verbal inspiration and the divinity of Jesus—as some of the other higher critics did—Seeley offered little explicit theological commentary. The resulting ambiguity generated debate among British readers: was *Ecce Homo* the work of a heretic or an apologist? The verdict was unclear.

Literary texts informed by the higher criticism produce similarly complicated stories. Many of the higher critics, as well as those responding to them, expressed at least a qualified appreciation for the Bible's literary qualities. Consider, for example, George Eliot, the focus of my third and central chapter. Eliot played a key role in disseminating the higher criticism throughout Britain: her translations of Strauss's *Das Leben Jesus* and Ludwig Feuerbach's *Das Wesen Des Chrestentums* (*The Essence of Christianity*) were published in 1846 and 1854, respectively, and she commented on related scholarship in articles for the *Westminster Review*, the quarterly for which she worked as assistant editor from 1851 to 1854.[49] Even though Eliot had by this time self-consciously distanced herself from her religious upbringing, her writings suggest an ongoing esteem for the literary qualities of biblical texts. In 1842, shortly after she announced to her family her refusal to attend church, she wrote to her father explaining that while she rejected Christianity's "system of doctrines," she nevertheless held much admiration for "the moral teaching of Jesus himself."[50] More strikingly still, a letter dated February 14, 1846, and sent by her close friend Caroline Bray to their mutual acquaintance Sara Sophia Hennell reported that Eliot was "Strauss-sick," claiming that "dissecting the beautiful story of the crucifixion" had "made her ill."[51] These expressions suggest a visceral disquiet with higher critical methods of analysis. Eliot, along with the other writers in this book, combines an interest in higher critical approaches with a responsiveness to literary form that does not tidily align with this criticism's overarching emphasis on historical context.

Although the higher critics had insightful things to say about wisdom texts and traditions, this aspect of their work has been largely ignored. As indicated in the previous examples, what the Victorian public found most troubling was the higher criticism's critique of sacred texts that had been regarded as historical records. By contrast, their commentaries on books such as Job, Proverbs, and Ecclesiastes—more immediately legible as dramatic, witty, and introspective poetry—posed less of a threat to readers concerned about whether the Bible's narrative of salvific history could be taken literally. As a result, the vast and real influence of the wisdom books on Victorian literature and culture continues to be underestimated by scholars today. To broaden critical understanding, it is necessary to consider the texts and traditions that might not have received as much attention in the public debates about the higher criticism yet nevertheless had a demonstrable influence on Victorian literature. Considered carefully, with an eye to the Bible's variety of discourses, the division between the "historical" and "unhistorical" books is not always as stark as it would at first appear. The discovery of what would later be termed "the historical Jesus" necessarily, if indirectly, involves a reengagement with the wisdom corpus, given that Wisdom and Christ have been typologically linked at least since the thirteenth-century writings of St. Thomas Aquinas, as David Lyle Jeffrey observes.[52] Several of the higher critics who called attention to Jesus's humanity and his use of Jewish didactic traditions turned their hands to the wisdom books as well. Renan, for instance, published his own translations of Job (1858) and Ecclesiastes (1881). Moreover, some of the most controversial biographical accounts of Jesus, including those by both Renan and his precursor Strauss, feature brief but telling observations about how his teachings are structured as narratives. As will be discussed in subsequent chapters, these sayings and parables participate in the basic form of the Jewish *mashal*, the Hebrew word translated as *parabole* in the Septuagint. Derived from the word "to be like," *mashal* includes a range of tropes from metaphor to proverb to parable.[53] In subtle but significant ways, nineteenth-century critics began attending to the formal qualities that prompted later biblical scholars to consider these parables as part of the wisdom tradition.[54]

Any inquiry into Victorian uses of biblical wisdom literature faces significant challenges of delimitation. A study of wisdom literature and the poetry of Christina Rossetti, who is singled out in Cheyne's passing remarks about Victorian writers and Ecclesiastes, would merit a book unto itself.[55] As Emma

Mason has shown, Rossetti's poetry is inextricably interwoven with the Oxford Movement's doctrines of analogy and reserve—theological concepts that offer rich resources for thinking about wisdom literature.[56] These High Anglican frameworks place Rossetti at some remove from the dissenting Protestant communities on view in my study. Something similar might be said of Gerard Manley Hopkins, whose echoes of biblical wisdom throughout both the "Nature Sonnets" and the "Terrible Sonnets" must also be understood in relation to the theological ideas of the Oxford Movement, including the writings of John Henry Newman that prompted him to convert to Catholicism and enter the Jesuit priesthood. Victorian Christians of all denominational affiliations, as well as Victorian Jews, felt the impacts of biblical higher criticism; however, dissenting Protestantism's *sola scriptura* ethos made this criticism particularly contentious within these circles, generating both heated responses and creative experiments, as LaPorte has highlighted.[57] I follow his lead in concentrating my book accordingly.

Further orienting my approach is Mark Knight's *Good Words: Evangelicalism and the Victorian Novel*, especially his chapter on hermeneutics. Knight provides a nuanced account of evangelicalism as a dynamic theological movement stretching across Anglican and dissenting Protestant communities, reminding readers that this movement's rich traditions should not be reductively identified with twenty-first-century fundamentalism. He further observes that much of today's scholarship on Victorian literature proceeds from a "hermeneutics of suspicion" that seems diametrically opposed to the devotional, personal reading practices of these evangelical communities. And yet Knight concludes that the academic emphasis on reading with critical distance has its own problems, including its tendency to promote a false sense of superiority that "prevents us from thinking more fully about our participation in the stories that we tell."[58] I seek to continue this line of thought by probing Victorian responses to biblical higher criticism for their combination of rigorous critique and personal reflection. This twofold reading practice not only provides insight into the diversity of religious expressions in this historical period but also promises to speak into contemporary debates about literary criticism.

Creative Interpretation

Among literary scholars today, there is a rising interest in rethinking the discipline's investment in reading methods that privilege critical detachment and analytical distance. Rita Felski's influential *The Limits of Critique*, for one, advocates for a practice of "postcritical reading," whereby readers seek not simply to demystify, interrogate, or dissect the text—the actions typical of critique—but also to engage in more affective practices of self-reflection.[59] This emphasis on revitalizing approaches to interpretation that center the reader's emotional and often almost mystical experiences means that postsecular and postcritical methods are poised to intersect in promising ways, as several scholars have recently suggested.[60] Such intersections seem especially relevant for Victorian studies, given that the basic argument that studying literature fulfills a cultural and personal function that was once met through religious devotion finds expression in the work of several canonical Victorian writers, Matthew Arnold in particular. From "Dover Beach" (1867) to "The Study of Poetry" (1880), Arnold repeatedly suggested that religion was receding and predicted that it would be succeeded by a new cult of poetry—so much so that the claim that the fall of religion led to the rise of literary studies has sometimes been termed "the Arnoldian replacement theory."[61] Nevertheless, this seeming substitution is not as tidy as it might first appear. It may be neither possible nor desirable for literary studies to discard these religious roots. Indeed, the very word *hermeneutics* has distinctly religious origins: the activities of the Greek god Hermes, the messenger tasked with conveying divine secrets to the people of earth.[62]

Building on and responding to these developments in postsecular and postcritical scholarship, this book applies Ricoeur's theoretical writings in ways that recent studies have suggested but not fully pursued.[63] Although Ricoeur has been most often remembered for the "hermeneutics of suspicion" that he identifies as characteristic of the post-Marxist, post-Freudian, and post-Nietzschean world, he argues for the counterbalancing of a hermeneutics of suspicion and a hermeneutics of restoration.[64] His interpretive approach preserves several elements characteristic of Hans-Georg Gadamer's approach to hermeneutics, while also being responsive to Jürgen Habermas's critique of Gadamer.[65] With its reach across biblical criticism, philosophical hermeneutics, and literary form, Ricoeur's theoretical output yields many useful insights, including his claim that different biblical genres lend themselves to different models of religious revelation. I am especially interested in how his concept of "creative interpretation" might be brought to bear on literary engagements with biblical wisdom literature.

Ricoeur introduces "creative interpretation" as a response to the basic problem of the hermeneutic circle: the dilemma that "we must understand in order to believe, but we must believe in order to understand." His discussion explores ideas about the conflict—and, moreover, the potential rapprochement—of "religious" (i.e., theologically committed) and "philosophical" (i.e., doctrinally neutral) approaches to the interpretation of symbols. Between what Ricoeur identifies as the "two impasses" of philosophy and religion, he proposes to explore a third way, characterized as a mode of "creative interpretation" that combines rigorous critique and reverent reflection. As Ricoeur explains it, this model aims "to go beyond criticism by means of criticism, by a criticism that is no longer reductive but restorative."[66] This reading practice involves a renewed attention to metaphor's dynamic capacity, an idea encapsulated with aphoristic concision in the conclusion to *The Symbolism of Evil*, entitled "The Symbol Gives Rise to Thought." Ricoeur's subsequent work on parable and metaphor develops this line of inquiry, emphasizing that "the process of interpretation is not something superimposed from the outside of a self-contained expression; it is motivated by the symbolic expression which itself gives rise to the thought."[67] For Ricoeur, the particularities of literary form both initiate and shape the interpretive process. Within the nineteenth century, the higher critics, as well as those responding to them, articulated new ways of probing biblical texts for their symbolic potentials.

Even as the higher criticism emphasized historical approaches, it also prompted new understandings of the Bible's literary forms. To be sure, the higher criticism's focus on uncovering diverse historical contexts radically changed the way that eighteenth- and nineteenth-century readers understood themselves in relation to the biblical story, as Hans Frei's *The Eclipse of Biblical Narrative* has demonstrated.[68] Critical study of the Bible's literary genres tends to be dated as beginning later, with the advent of Hermann Gunkel's "form criticism" in the early twentieth century.[69] However, as Leo G. Perdue highlights, Gunkel's work is itself indebted to insights from the higher critics, especially Herder, who called attention to biblical poetry's complex patterning.[70] Even before Herder, Bishop Robert Lowth's *Lectures on the Sacred Poetry of the Hebrews* (1787) broke new ground in its study of this poetry's parallelism—a study with important implications for both prophetic and wisdom literatures. As Stephen Prickett has underscored, the higher criticism prompted a widespread shift away from narrower modes of typological exegesis, toward a more pluralistic understanding of biblical narrative among Romantic writers. Similarly, LaPorte has demonstrated that the higher criticism had a significant influence on the development of Victorian poetry.[71] My study shows that the higher criticism generated insights about the Bible's generic plurality in ways that included a renewed interest in the forms of wisdom literature.

Held up to careful examination, even some of the higher critics who seem at first to be emphatically concerned with history are, at times, quite thoughtful about literary form. The higher criticism's concern with uncovering a text's original situation, as well as recovering authorial intent, finds emphatic expression in the work of the prolific theologian and scholar Friedrich Daniel Ernest Schleiermacher, one of Strauss's instructors in biblical criticism. Most commonly known for his *On Religion* (1799), which countered narrower constructions of rationalism by reasserting the integral role of individual feeling in religious experience, Schleiermacher gave a series of lectures on hermeneutics which were widely influential following their posthumous publication in 1838. He posited a twofold attention to "grammatical" interpretation (linguistic content) and "psychological" interpretation (authorial intent). But even as these two aspects prompted Schleiermacher to focus on historical context, his discussion opens toward something more flexible. He suggests that "the insistence on historical interpretation is only the correct insistence on the connection of the writers of the N.T. [New Testament] with their age .... But this insistence becomes mistaken if it denies the new concept-forming power of Christianity and wants to explain everything from what is already there."[72] These remarks suggest his interest in the gradual development of religious expressions, and several of his contemporaries drew connections between such conceptual dynamism and literary form.

As a case in point, consider Benjamin Jowett, who adopted and defended Schleiermacher's ideas in his contribution to *Essays and Reviews*. On the whole, Jowett argues for a rigorous recovery of authorial intention; however, he too tempers his concern with history in ways that invite attention to the subtleties of literary form. Although Jowett generally insists that the meaning of the biblical text must be traced to "the mind of the prophet or evangelist who first uttered or wrote it," he concedes that "all that the Prophet meant may not have been consciously present to his mind; there were depths which to himself also were but half revealed."[73] Recognizing a variety of genres within the biblical canon, Jowett further suggests that Job and Ecclesiastes exhibit a "depth and inwardness" that "require a measure of the same qualities in the interpreter himself." Extending this commentary to the New Testament, he cautions that these qualities are all too often missed by the Bible readers of his day:

> But this inwardness of the words of Christ is what few are able to receive; it is easier to apply them superficially to things without, than to be a partaker of them from within. And false and miserable applications of them are often made, and the kingdom of God becomes the tool of the kingdoms of the world.[74]

Here, Jowett tempers the historicizing method affirmed elsewhere in his essay. Rather than situate "the words of Christ" (many of which took the form of parables) solely in relation to the original setting, he challenges his audience "to be a partaker of them from within"—that is, to read them with minds and hearts open to transformation. These remarks invite further attention to the formal qualities of wisdom literature that call forth such introspection. In the hands of Victorian writers, this literature provided the raw material for in-depth, imaginative engagement with inherited religious traditions.

Forming Wisdom

To highlight the formal characteristics of biblical wisdom literature, I turn to Ricoeur's work on poetics, a category that he distinguishes from rhetoric not based on literary kind but on linguistic use. For Ricoeur, rhetoric and poetics denote two "reciprocally inverse" functions: the former "aims at persuading men by giving to discourse pleasing ornaments," while the latter "aims at redescribing reality by the twisting pathway of heuristic fiction."[75] Subsequent biblical scholars have productively applied this distinction to wisdom literature. Leo G. Perdue draws from Ricoeur's work on metaphor to analyze the "world-building capacity" that he sees as integral to wisdom literature.[76] Similarly, Roland E. Murphy observes that the aim of wisdom literature's "dominant forms," which he identifies as "the saying, the admonition, and the wisdom poem," is "not so much to command" but to "provoke the reader into a reflective mood."[77] Rather than prescribe a fixed interpretation, wisdom literature invites the reader's participation in open-ended acts of making meaning. I seek to show how Victorian writers put this poetics to thought-provoking purposes.

Susan E. Colón's *Victorian Parables* opens the door for my inquiry into biblical wisdom, interpretive practice, and literary form. Whereas Colón concentrates on the specific form of the parable as it appears within Victorian realist novels, I analyze how wisdom literature as a broader genre allowed writers of both prose and poetry to participate creatively in higher critical debates. My approach focuses not on the interpretive work *depicted within* the text but that *performed by* the text. Put another way, my concern is not with fictional representations of Victorians being challenged by reading the higher criticism—as in James Anthony Froude's *The Nemesis of Faith* (1849) or Mary Augusta Ward's *Robert Elsmere* (1888)—but with how literary forms themselves might facilitate engagement with the conceptual issues resulting from the higher criticism. Adapting the cross-genre model that has characterized studies of Victorian sage writing since the 1990s, my selections span poetry, novels, and non-fiction prose. This approach does not attempt a survey of Victorian wisdom writing but instead offers more in-depth consideration of how a few strategically chosen writers imitated and developed wisdom literature's characteristic forms. Concentrating each chapter on a single author and text means that there are many roads not taken. And yet, wisdom literature itself seems to invite if not require such an intensive approach, given that this genre is designed to inculcate meditation. Wisdom literature, as Ben Witherington suggests, requires "patience and time" to understand: its reliance on "metaphors, similes, figures, images, and riddles" rather than "straightforward propositions" means that "one is obligated not merely to read the Wisdom material but also to ruminate on it."[78] Rather than be comprehensive, my aim is to be invitational.

As it appears in the religious traditions with which my study engages, wisdom is at once imaginative and corporeal in its formative power. The Hebrew word for wisdom, *hokmâ*, is used variously to refer to spiritual experience, ethical understanding, practical skill, and artistic craftsmanship.[79] For those writing in the wake of higher critical debates about the incarnation, wisdom literature provided a useful resource for reimagining Christ, the Wisdom of God, as well as renewing their perceptions of the natural world.[80] My own titles play with embodied metaphors to signal how these writers engaged with inherited traditions of personifying wisdom in order to revitalize their search for meaning. This metaphorical conceit is compellingly deployed in Coleridge's response to higher critical ideas in his *Confessions of an Inquiring Spirit*. Refuting narrowly conceived ideas of verbal inspiration—that is, the prescription to "believe the Scriptures throughout dictated, in word and thought, by an infallible Intelligence"—Coleridge declares:

> [T]he doctrine in question petrifies at once the whole Body of Holy Writ, with all its harmonies & symmetrical gradations; the flexible and the rigid; the supporting Hard and the cloathing Soft; the blood that is the life; the intelligencing Nerves; and the rudely woven but soft and springy Cellular, in which all are embedded and lightly bound together![81]

Combining tactile and auditory imagery, his comparison of scripture to a living organism is kinaesthetic, even synaesthetic, in its force. Pushing back against a dogmatic literalism, Coleridge revivifies the theological concept of a dynamic, living Word. Each of the writers discussed in this book differs with respect to their ideas about Christology, yet they all seek to bridge the gap between the textual accounts of the Jesus who lived in the first century and the ethical insights arising from attempts to live out these ideas in the present.

The following chapters illustrate five examples of how Victorian writers turned to wisdom literature to face the interpretive dilemmas intensified by the spread of the higher criticism. Chapter 1 analyzes how Elizabeth Barrett Browning repositions the book of Job's poetic dialogues in *A Drama of Exile* (1844), a masque-like revision of the biblical fall story. Responding to scholarship that emphasizes the feminist energies of EBB's religious work, I argue that her portrayal of Eve participates in widespread interpretive debates about the authority of biblical texts and the meaning of suffering in the Christian tradition. Her artistic approach shows her subtle but significant affinities with higher critics such as Robert Lowth and Johann Gottfried Herder, providing a reverent yet innovative engagement with biblical poetry as poetry. Chapter 2 examines George MacDonald's uses of wisdom literature in his fairytale romance *Phantastes* (1858), an allegorical story that draws on both the themes and forms of the book of Proverbs, from tropes of wayfinding to aphoristic expressions. My discussion puts *Phantastes* into conversation with MacDonald's essays on the imagination, which were, in turn, informed by Coleridge's writings on the higher criticism. Like Coleridge, MacDonald reframes the concept of inspiration beyond limiting ideas of divine dictation, while also engaging thoughtfully with devotional reading practices.

Chapter 3 considers George Eliot's turn to wisdom literature in *Romola* (1862–3), a historical novel that reflects Eliot's work as both a translator and practitioner of higher critical hermeneutics. By engaging with the narrative patterns of the biblical parables, Eliot offers a thoughtful response to historical criticism on the gospels, including the work of David Friedrich Strauss and Ludwig Feuerbach. *Romola* engages with nineteenth-century debates about incarnation theology, fashioning its heroine into an imperfect type of the suffering servant and using the language of "the kingdom of God" to explore an expansive vision of human sympathy and fellowship. Chapter 4 analyzes John Ruskin's portrait of wisdom in *The Queen of the Air* (1869), a series of lectures on Athena that are at once an exposition of Greek mythology and an innovative act of mythmaking that combines classical, apocryphal, and biblical traditions as it offers its own hymn to personified wisdom. His approach partakes in the higher criticism's work of challenging literalism but departs from this criticism's emphasis on historical recovery. Complementing and complicating critical approaches that foreground Ruskin's characteristically authoritarian voice as Victorian sage, my discussion reconsiders how Ruskin speaks as a sage in dialogue—with himself, as well as with his audiences and readers. Chapter 5 focuses on Olive Schreiner's creative recourse to biblical wisdom literature in *The Story of an African Farm* (1883), a semi-autobiographical account informed by her experiences growing up on a Wesleyan mission station near Wittebergen, South Africa. Schreiner's novel at once satirizes religious institutions and unfolds a range of dynamic possibilities for repurposing religious discourse, especially as refracted through the tropes of Ecclesiastes. Although skeptical of prophetic authority, Schreiner uses wisdom literature's forms to advance a self-reflexive commentary on the art of making meaning. As Ricoeur's theoretical insights help to illuminate, all five writers turn to wisdom literature as a means of reimagining religious revelation as a participatory experience, one that requires the reader's active engagement.

In a brief coda, I reflect on what Victorian studies stands to gain by attending to biblical wisdom literature's varied uses and transformative potentials. As developments in postsecular and postcritical scholarship have shown, contemporary debates in literary criticism can trace their roots to nineteenth-century controversies surrounding religious texts. Literary engagements with biblical wisdom traditions offer useful models of many-sided reading practices that not only deconstruct authoritarian abuses of religious discourse but also appreciate this discourse for its variety, dynamism, and latent possibilities. Returning to the hermeneutic questions woven throughout the book, this closing discussion considers how wisdom literature's images, tropes, and forms invite and challenge readers to take up interpretive practices that are both generative and generous.

Notes

1 Oscar Wilde, "The Critic as Artist," in *The Artist as Critic: Critical Writings of Oscar Wilde*, ed. Richard Ellmann (New York: Random House, 1969), 407.
2 Benjamin Jowett, "On the Interpretation of Scripture," in *Essays and Reviews: The 1860 Text and Its Reading*, ed. Victor Shea and William Whitla (Charlottesville: University Press of Virginia, 2000), 504.
3 On the reception of *Essays and Reviews*, see Mark Knight and Emma Mason, *Nineteenth-Century Literature and Religion: An Introduction* (Oxford: Oxford University Press, 2006), 130–4. The seven contributors to *Essays and Reviews* were Frederick Temple, Rowland Williams, Baden Powell, Henry Bristow Wilson, Mark

Pattison, Charles Wycliffe Goodwin, and Jowett. Goodwin, the geologist, was the only one who was not ordained.

4   This terminology arises from Mikhail Bakhtin's influential concept of dialogism, theorized in relation to the hybrid form of the novel, as well as to the broader concept of language as a social phenomenon. See Mikhail Bakhtin, *The Dialogic Imagination: Four Essays*, ed. Michael Holquist, trans. Caryl Emerson and Michael Holquist (Austin: University of Texas Press, 1981), 259–75.

5   *The Bible: Authorized King James Version with Apocrypha* (Oxford: Oxford University Press, 2008). All biblical quotations are cited parenthetically in text. Rights in the Authorized (King James) Version in the UK are vested in the Crown. Reproduced by permission of the Crown's patentee, Cambridge University Press.

6   The following studies all highlight the trend of focusing on Job, Proverbs, and Ecclesiastes within Protestant concepts of the wisdom books: James L. Crenshaw, *Old Testament Wisdom: An Introduction* (Louisville: John Knox Press, 2010); Leo G. Perdue, *Wisdom and Creation: The Theology of Wisdom Literature* (Nashville: Abingdon Press, 1994); and William P. Brown, *Wisdom's Wonder: Character, Creation, and Crisis in the Bible's Wisdom Literature* (Grand Rapids: William B. Eerdmans, 2014). Roman Catholic and orthodox traditions would recognize two additional books in this vein: Ecclesiasticus (or Ben Sira) and the Wisdom of Solomon.

7   W. David Shaw, *Secrets of the Oracle: A History of Wisdom from Zeno to Yeats* (Toronto: University of Toronto Press, 2009), 246.

8   Thomas Kelly Cheyne, *Job and Solomon, or the Wisdom of the Old Testament* (New York: Thomas Whittaker, 1889), 246, 242.

9   Shaw's book, cited above, is a notable exception, as its discussion features several prominent Victorians, not only Wilde but also Alfred Tennyson, Robert Browning, and George Eliot. However, as underscored by its subtitle (*A History of Wisdom from Zeno to Yeats*), Shaw's temporal, geographical, and religious parameters reflect a wide lens.

10 Paul Ricoeur, *The Symbolism of Evil*, trans. Emerson Buchanan (New York: Harper and Row, 1967), 349.

11 Talal Asad, *Formations of the Secular: Christianity, Islam, Modernity* (Stanford: Stanford University Press, 2003); William McKelvy, *The English Cult of Literature: Devoted Readers, 1774–1880* (Charlottesville: University of Virginia Press, 2007); and Charles Taylor, *A Secular Age* (Cambridge: Harvard University Press, 2007).

12 Joshua King and Winter Jade Werner. Introduction to *Constructing Nineteenth-Century Religion: Literary, Historical, and Religious Studies in Dialogue*, ed. Joshua King and Winter Jade Werner (Columbus: Ohio State University Press, 2019), 8–9.

13 See, for instance, Charles LaPorte and Sebastian Lecourt, "Introduction: Nineteenth-Century Literature, New Religious Movements, and Secularization," *Nineteenth-Century Literature* 73, no. 1 (2018): 147–60.

14 Georg Lukács, *The Theory of the Novel: A Historico-Philosophical Essay on the Forms of Great Epic Literature*, trans. Anna Bostock (London: Merlin, 1978), 88.
15 On the term "postsecular," see Jürgen Habermas's "Notes on Post-Secular Society," *New Perspectives Quarterly* 25, no. 4 (2008): 17–29.
16 Lori Branch and Mark Knight, "Why the Postsecular Matters: Literary Studies and the Rise of the Novel," *Christianity and Literature* 67, no. 3 (2018): 493–510.
17 Lori Branch, "Postcriticism and Postsecular: The Horizon of Belief," *Religion and Literature* 48, no. 2 (2016): 161.
18 For a helpful discussion of this etymology and of the history of secularism in Britain, see Norman Vance, *Bible and Novel: Narrative Authority and the Death of God* (Oxford: Oxford University Press, 2013), 17. On Charles Bradlaugh's activities with the National Secular Society, see Timothy Larsen, *A People of One Book: The Bible and the Victorians* (Oxford: Oxford University Press, 2011), 67–72.
19 Ronjaunee Chatterjee, Alicia Mireles Christoff, and Amy R. Wong. "Introduction: Undisciplining Victorian Studies," *Victorian Studies* 62, no. 3 (2020): 369–72.
20 Winter Jade Werner, *Missionary Cosmopolitanism in Nineteenth-Century British Literature* (Columbus: Ohio State University Press, 2020), 2–6.
21 Timothy Larsen, *Contested Christianity: The Political and Social Contexts of Victorian Theology* (Waco: Baylor University Press, 2004), 53–60.
22 Taylor, *A Secular Age*, 26–7.
23 Timothy Larsen, *Crisis of Doubt: Honest Faith in Nineteenth-Century England* (Oxford: Oxford University Press, 2006), 10–17.
24 David Nash, "Reassessing the 'Crisis of Faith' in the Victorian Age: Eclecticism and the Spirit of Moral Inquiry," *Journal of Victorian Culture* 16, no. 1 (2011): 70.
25 See Cynthia Scheinberg, *Women's Poetry and Religion in Victorian England* (Cambridge: Cambridge University Press, 2002); F. Elizabeth Gray, *Christian and Lyric Tradition in Victorian Women's Poetry* (New York: Routledge, 2009); Rebecca Styler, *Literary Theology by Women Writers of the Nineteenth Century* (Aldershot: Ashgate, 2010); Karen Dieleman, *Religious Imaginaries* (Columbus: Ohio State University Press, 2012); Gail Turley Houston, *Victorian Women Writers, Radical Grandmothers, and the Gendering of God* (Columbus: Ohio State University Press, 2013); and Richa Dwor, *Jewish Feeling: Difference and Affect in Nineteenth-Century Jewish Women's Writing* (London: Bloomsbury, 2015).
26 Thaïs E. Morgan, ed., *Victorian Sages and Cultural Discourse: Renegotiating Gender and Power* (New Brunswick: Rutgers University Press, 1900).
27 Gavin Budge, "Rethinking the Victorian Sage: Nineteenth-Century Prose and Scottish Common Sense Philosophy," *Literature Compass* 2, no. 1 (2005): 1.
28 George P. Landow, *Elegant Jeremiahs: The Sage from Carlyle to Mailer* (Ithaca: Cornell University Press, 1986), 41–71.
29 For a thoughtful study of how Blake's prophetic voice was informed by developments in biblical scholarship, see Stephen Prickett, *Words and the*

Word: Language, Poetics, and Biblical Interpretation (Cambridge: Cambridge University Press, 1986), 95–122; see also Chris Bundock, *Romantic Prophecy and the Resistance to Historicism* (Toronto: University of Toronto Press, 2016), 141–67.

30 Robert Alter, *The Wisdom Books: Job, Proverbs, and Ecclesiastes: A Translation and Commentary* (New York: Norton, 2010), xiii–xiv.

31 James L. Crenshaw, *Prophets, Sages, and Poets* (St. Louis: Chalice Press, 2006), 48.

32 Paul Ricoeur, "Toward a Hermeneutic of the Idea of Revelation," in *Essays on Biblical Interpretation*, ed. Lewis S. Mudge, trans. David Pellauer (Philadelphia: Fortress Press, 1980), 75–81.

33 Paul Ricoeur, "Experience and Language in Religious Discourse," in *Phenomenology and the Theological Turn: The French Debate*, ed. Dominique Janicaud (New York: Fordham University Press, 2000), 138.

34 Ibid., 143–4.

35 On typological thought in the Victorian era, see George P. Landow, *Victorian Types, Victorian Shadows: Biblical Typology in Victorian Literature, Art, and Thought* (New York: Routledge and Keagan Paul, 1980). For a discussion of typology's appropriation and subordination of Jewish traditions, see Scheinberg, *Women's Poetry and Religion*, 32–5.

36 Landow, *Victorian Types*, 55.

37 Larsen, *A People*, 4.

38 Ibid., 297.

39 On early nineteenth-century British responses to the higher criticism, see Vance, *Bible and Novel*, 81.

40 See Charles LaPorte, *Victorian Poets and the Changing Bible* (Charlottesville: University of Virginia Press, 2011), 6.

41 Hypotheses about these sources were developed throughout the century, most famously in the respective work of Hermann Hupfeld and Julius Wellhausen. For a useful overview of developments in biblical source criticism from the eighteenth through the twentieth century, see Richard S. Hess, *The Old Testament: A Historical, Theological, and Critical Introduction* (Grand Rapids: Baker Academic, 2016), 32–50.

42 On the publication and reception of *Confessions*, see Anthony John Harding, *Coleridge and the Inspired Word* (Kingston: McGill-Queen's University Press, 1985), 74–100.

43 Jowett, "On the Interpretation of Scripture," 485.

44 Daniel L. Pals, *The Victorian "Lives" of Jesus* (San Antonio: Trinity University Press, 1982), 8–9.

45 Larsen, *Contested Christianity*, 59–77.

46 See, for instance, the articles featured in the 2018 double special issue on "New Religious Movements and Secularization," ed. Charles LaPorte and Sebastian Lecourt, *Nineteenth-Century Literature* 73, nos. 2–3 (2018).

47 Pals, *The Victorian "Lives" of Jesus*, 80–94. The more conservative accounts produced in Victorian Britain include F. W. Farrar's *The Life of Christ* (1874), Henry James Coleridge's *The Public Life of Our Lord* (1874), G. S. Drew's *The Son of Man* (1875), and John Cunningham Geikie's *The Life and Words of Christ* (1877).

48 Ibid., 40–3. Since its publication in 1865, this book's title has incorporated this hybridization of Latin and English, though the work itself is written in English. "Ecce homo" (behold the man) refers to the Vulgate's translation of the words used by Pontius Pilate when presenting Jesus before the crowd (Jn. 19:5).

49 Eliot's translations were published by John Chapman. Contributions to the *Westminster Review* that reflect her knowledge of higher critical scholarship include her 1856 review of James Heywood's two-volume *Introduction to the Book of Genesis* (1855), an abridged translation of Peter Von Bohlen's *Die Genesis, historischkritisch erläutert* (1835).

50 George Eliot, *The George Eliot Letters*, ed. Gordon S. Haight, vol. 1. (New Haven: Yale University Press, 1954), 128.

51 Ibid., 1: 206.

52 David Lyle Jeffrey, "Wisdom," in *A Dictionary of Biblical Tradition in English Literature*, ed. David Lyle Jeffrey (Grand Rapids: William B. Eerdmans, 1992), 834.

53 See Susan E. Colón, *Victorian Parables* (London: Bloomsbury, 2012), 3.

54 See Ronald A. Piper, *Wisdom in the Q-Tradition: The Aphoristic Teaching of Jesus* (Cambridge: Cambridge University Press, 1989); Ben Witherington, *Jesus the Sage: The Pilgrimage of Wisdom* (Philadelphia: Fortress Press, 1994); and Charles W. Hedrick, *The Wisdom of Jesus: Between the Sages of Israel and the Apostles of the Church* (Eugene: Cascade Books, 2014).

55 Cheyne, *Job and Solomon*, 246. This commentary identifies Rossetti's poems "Vanity of Vanities" and "A Testimony" as examples of her engagement with Ecclesiastes. For more recent critical discussion of Rossetti's poetry and biblical allusion, including echoes of wisdom literature, see Elizabeth Ludlow, *Christina Rossetti and the Bible: Waiting with the Saints* (London: Bloomsbury, 2014); see also Ryan Sinni, "Wise Women and Strange Men: The Book of Proverbs in 'Goblin Market,'" *Victorian Poetry* 60, no. 1 (2022): 71–86.

56 Emma Mason, *Christian Rossetti: Poetry, Ecology, Faith* (Oxford: Oxford University Press, 2018), 37–44.

57 LaPorte, *Victorian Poets*, 16–17.

58 Mark Knight, *Good Words: Evangelicalism and the Victorian Novel* (Columbus: Ohio State University Press, 2019), 151–5.

59 Rita Felski, *The Limits of Critique* (Chicago: University of Chicago Press, 2015), 11–12.

60 See Charles LaPorte, "Romantic Cults of Authorship," in *Constructing Nineteenth-Century Religion: Literary, Historical, and Religious Studies in Dialogue*, ed. Joshua

King and Winter Jade Werner (Columbus: Ohio State University Press, 2019), 258–9; see also Winter Jade Werner and John Wiehl, "Chasing David Copperfield's Memory of a Stained Glass Window: Or, Meditations on the Postsecular and Postcritical," *LIT: Literature Interpretation Theory* 31, no. 1 (2021): 1–4.

61 Michael Kaufman, "The Religious, the Secular, and Literary Studies: Rethinking the Secularization Narrative in Histories of the Profession," *New Literary History* 38, no. 4 (2007): 616.

62 David Jasper, "Biblical Hermeneutics and Literary Theory," in *The Blackwell Companion to the Bible in English Literature*, ed. Rebecca Lemon et al. (Chichester: Wiley Blackwell, 2009), 37.

63 See, for instance, Stephen Best's incisive response to Felski's *The Limits of Critique*, wherein he proposes that Ricoeur's dialectic of trust-suspicion has much more to offer postcritical readings than has yet been recognized: "*La Foi* Postcritique, on Second Thought," *PMLA* 132, no. 2 (2017): 339. See also LaPorte, "Romantic Cults," 258.

64 Rita Felski's discussion notes and exemplifies the extent to which Ricoeur has been remembered primarily for his idea of the "hermeneutics of suspicion." See Felski, *The Limits*, 1–4.

65 For a useful overview of Ricoeur's theoretical interventions in the Gadamer-Habermas debate, see B. H. McLean, *Biblical Criticism and Philosophical Hermeneutics* (Cambridge: Cambridge University Press, 2012), 237–40.

66 Ricoeur, *The Symbolism*, 348–51.

67 Ricoeur, "Biblical Hermeneutics," *Semeia* 4 (1975): 133.

68 Hans Frei, *The Eclipse of Biblical Narrative: A Study in Eighteenth-and Nineteenth-Century Hermeneutics* (New Haven: Yale University Press, 1974), 64.

69 See for instance, the overview in Hess, *The Old Testament*, 38.

70 Leo G. Perdue, *Wisdom and Creation: The Theology of Wisdom Literature* (Nashville: Abingdon Press, 1994), 68.

71 Stephen Prickett, *Words and the Word: Language Poetics, and Biblical Interpretation* (Cambridge: Cambridge University Press, 1896), 40–3; LaPorte, *Victorian Poets*, 21–2.

72 Friedrich Schleiermacher, *Hermeneutics and Criticism and Other Writings*, trans. Andrew Bowie (Cambridge: Cambridge University Press, 1998), 15.

73 Jowett, "On the Interpretation of Scripture," 505–6.

74 Ibid., 493.

75 Ricoeur, "Biblical Hermeneutics," 88.

76 Perdue, *Wisdom and Creation*, 50–2.

77 Roland E. Murphy, *The Tree of Life: An Exploration of Biblical Wisdom Literature* (Grand Rapids: William B. Eerdmans, 1990), 7.

78 Witherington, *Jesus the Sage*, 3.

79 On this etymology, see Crenshaw, *Old Testament Wisdom*, 9.
80 For recent scholarship that highlights the breadth, depth, and dynamism of nineteenth-century ideas about Christology, see the essays collected within *The Figure of Christ in the Long Nineteenth-Century*, ed. Elizabeth Ludlow (London: Palgrave Macmillan, 2020).
81 Coleridge, *Collected Works*, 11.1133.

1

Wisdom's Call: Poetic Dialogue and the Echoes of Job in Elizabeth Barrett Browning's *A Drama of Exile*

The elemental themes that Paul Ricoeur identifies as characteristic of biblical wisdom literature—namely, "solitude, the fault, suffering, and death—where the misery and the grandeur of human beings confront each other"—figure prominently in the poetry of Elizabeth Barrett Browning (hereafter, EBB).[1] Her early work *The Seraphim* (1838) meditates on the crucifixion from the vantage point of two witnessing angels, and her later verse novel *Aurora Leigh* (1857) opens with a quotation from Ecclesiastes. Perhaps her most resonant echoes of biblical wisdom literature are those that reverberate throughout *A Drama of Exile*. EBB claimed in the preface to her widely reviewed volume *Poems* (1844) that this piece was the "most important work" that she had "ever trusted into the current of publication" (*WEBB* 2: 567).[2] Originally issued in two installments in the July and August 1844 issues of the *United States Magazine and Democratic Review*, *A Drama of Exile* featured as the lead work in this collection, which appeared only a few months later in America as *A Drama of Exile: And Other Poems*. These widely reviewed books had the effect of making her "England's most internationally recognized poet," as Marjorie Stone observes.[3] By the end of the nineteenth century, EBB had become one of the most highly regarded female poets to have written in English—Oscar Wilde, for one, celebrated her as the only English poetess who could be named "in any possible or remote conjunction with Sappho," and when George Eliot turned her hand to writing poetry she looked to EBB as a poetic model.[4] Although it was initially the sonnets and other shorter poems from the 1844 volume that garnered the most attention, EBB's continued revisions to *A Drama of Exile* for its republication in subsequent collections (in 1850, 1853, and 1856) underscore this poem's primacy in her imagination and its pivotal role in her artistic development.[5]

This grandly ambitious poem offers a sustained engagement with the experience of both limitation and aspiration. Beginning where the third chapter of Genesis concludes, *A Drama of Exile* reinterprets the story of humankind's expulsion from Eden. This innovative starting point distinguishes EBB's work from its many literary precursors, John Milton's *Paradise Lost* (1674) the most obvious among them.[6] Rather than simply retell the biblical fall narrative, *A Drama of Exile* reflects on what might rather be termed "the fallout of the fall," taking up challenging questions about the order of the cosmos and the meaning of suffering. EBB thus extends her revisionary engagement with biblical texts beyond the opening chapters of Genesis, turning to the topics and forms of wisdom literature, especially the book of Job. Just as the dialogues in Job engage with radically different moral imaginations, so too *A Drama of Exile* gives voice to competing and conflicting ideas. Over the course of some 2,270 lines, its many speakers call into question the distinction between prelapsarian and postlapsarian states, the place of humankind in relation to the cosmos, and the idea that all suffering is punitive.

To analyze the scope of EBB's ambition, my argument situates *A Drama of Exile* in relation to the interpretive debates sparked by the dissemination of biblical higher criticism. Originating in the work of German scholars including Gotthold Ephraim Lessing, Johann Gottfried Eichhorn, and Johann Gottfried Herder, this criticism challenged accepted ideas about the Bible's divine inspiration and doctrinal unity, emphasizing instead its diverse historical contexts, theological inconsistencies, composite authorship, and generic plurality. This approach complements the growing body of scholarship that highlights the feminist energies of *A Drama of Exile*, from Dorothy Mermin's hailing of *A Drama of Exile* as "Eve's story" in 1989 to subsequent studies including those by Stone, Linda Lewis, Alexandra M. B. Wörn, Terence Allen Hoagwood, and Karen Dieleman.[7] Building on Hoagwood's discussion of EBB's recourse to "the symbolic terms of the [biblical fall] myth for representation of contemporary social themes," I add that her engagement with what the Victorians called "the Woman Question" issues from her response to widespread interpretive debates about biblical authority.

EBB herself hinted, if obliquely, at these contexts in a letter to her friend R. H. Horne dated December 29, 1843, explaining the twofold emphasis of *A Drama of Exile* as follows: "the peculiar anguish of Eve" and "the first steps of Humanity into the world-wilderness, driven by the Curse" (*BC* 8: 116). This description signals her investment not only in the Woman Question as represented in Eve, the original sinner blamed throughout centuries of Christian exegesis, but also in the theological concerns explored throughout the book of Job. As *A Drama of Exile* unfolds, it complicates the creation narratives of Genesis 1–2, the first of which culminates in the divine decree that Adam and Eve rule over all created things. Rather than emphasize dominion, this dramatic poem evokes the alternative cosmology suggested by the book of Job's divine speeches. EBB puts into the mouths of her Earth spirits the rebuking message and even some of the very words of these speeches, which open with the decentering question "Where wast thou when I laid the foundations of the earth?" (Job 38:4) and emphasize both the wildness and the majesty of the natural world.[8] Through its layered biblical intertexts, *A Drama of Exile* highlights the formal and theological plurality of the sources it engages, qualities that were brought into relief with the advent of the higher criticism. While resistant to the higher critics's more skeptical claims, EBB avoided reactionary extremism. The Baptist preacher Charles Spurgeon, a staunch defender of verbal plenary inspiration and opponent of modern biblical scholarship, claimed that "the higher criticism" might be better termed "the Profaner Cavilling."[9] If this derisive slur dismisses the higher criticism as trivial, the uproar within the periodical press indicates that many other dissenting Protestants regarded this criticism as a forceful, dangerous foe.[10] By contrast, EBB's poetic practices indicate that she saw in higher critical concepts of the Bible as poetry and mythology opportunities to discard literalist readings and pursue a broader array of interpretive possibilities. As EBB's creative meditation would have it, the shutting of Eden's gates does not foreclose on a divine fullness that follows humankind into the wilderness.

A Drama of Exile thus performs what Ricoeur identifies as one of the "fundamental functions" of the book of Job's wisdom poetry—that is, "to bind together *ethos* and *cosmos*, the sphere of human action and the sphere of the world" by establishing "the *pathos* of actively assumed suffering." This wisdom poetry, in Ricoeur's words, "places suffering into a meaningful context by producing the active quality of suffering."[11] So too, *A Drama of Exile* seeks to make painful experiences meaningful. Drawing on a range of biblical texts from the survey of nature in Job to the personification of Wisdom in Proverbs to the hymn on Christ's *kenosis* (self-emptying) in Philippians, EBB expresses a poetic theology that valorizes willing acts of self-limitation. She thereby offers a powerful reinterpretation of suffering, figured not as victimization but as a pathway to experiencing divine immanence. This theology reflects her thoughtful study of biblical interpretation, from nineteenth-century developments to much older exegetical traditions, as well as her conviction that poetry and theology illuminate each other.

In what follows, I analyze EBB's adaptation of wisdom poetry in conjunction with specific developments in biblical scholarship, including higher critical studies of biblical poetry's parallel patterning, the rise of source criticism, and changing concepts of Christology. These contexts show that *A Drama of Exile* participates in a significant moment in the history of biblical interpretation: the paradigm shift whereby the Bible became widely understood "not as the product of dictation by the Holy Ghost but as the work of men," as E. S. Shaffer summarizes it.[12] Through her reverent yet innovative engagement with biblical poetry as poetry, EBB questions the idea that religious revelation consists of a single and authoritative divine pronouncement. Instead, *A Drama of Exile* suggests a flexible concept of revelation as a dynamic process—a model that aligns in prescient and compelling ways with the work of later exegetical and hermeneutic thinkers such as Ricoeur.

"Poetry Glorified": EBB and Higher Critical Studies of Biblical Poetry

The transformative hope expressed in *A Drama of Exile* issues from EBB's understanding of the Bible less as unified divine revelation than as incomplete human poetry, an understanding that suggests her subtle but significant affinities with the higher critics. Until the turn of the twenty-first century, most literary scholarship on EBB tended to remember her as a pious devotional poet; however, this portrayal obscures the eclectic range of her religious vision, from her fascination with Swedenborgian mysticism to her interest in spiritualist seances.[13] As Stone observes, this critical neglect results from a reductive (and gendered) binary that privileges the so-called "skeptical" poetry of Robert Browning over that of his so-called "orthodox" wife.[14] Such oversimplification fails to recognize EBB's thoughtful and, at times, quite searching responses to Christian texts and traditions. Since Stone's early recovery work, other studies have offered more nuanced accounts of EBB as a religious thinker, including Dieleman's recovery of her writings on the Greek Christian poets, which demonstrate a sophisticated knowledge of patristic traditions as well as an articulate response to nineteenth-century ideas about religion and poetry, from the theology of the Oxford Movement (Tractarianism) to higher critical scholarship.[15]

As early as 1842, EBB expressed her clear conviction that "Christ's religion is essentially poetry—poetry glorified" (*BC* 5: 220); about a year later, she developed this claim by asserting that "the *poetry of Christianity* will one day be developed greatly & nobly—& that in the meantime we are as wrong poetically as morally, in desiring to restrain it" (*BC* 7: 21). Even as EBB celebrated "the poetry of Christianity," she distanced her ideas from the Oxford Movement's understanding of religious poetry, expressed in John Keble's widely influential *Lectures on Poetry* (1831–41). As Kirstie Blair observes, both Brownings's understanding of religion as "the *sine qua non* of poetry" took up the religious ideals of dissenting Protestant communities in ways that offered "perhaps the strongest alternative current" to the Oxford Movement's poetics.[16] In emphasizing Christianity's ongoing development, EBB has more in common with Samuel Taylor Coleridge, whom she admired as a writer of great "genius" (*BC* 6: 75, 7: 123), and the ideas about biblical interpretation that he advanced in his posthumous *Confessions of an Inquiring Spirit* (1840). Coleridge's epistolary essays portrayed scripture as a living corpus, best interpreted in "the light of the Spirit in the mind of the believer."[17] Much like Coleridge, who sought to navigate a *via media* between what he saw as the extremes of both the higher criticism and literalist schools of exegesis, EBB adopted a nuanced stance regarding developments in biblical interpretation.

A brief survey of her correspondence demonstrates that EBB's response to biblical higher criticism is difficult to classify. On the one hand, she had a few choice words about David Friedrich Strauss, whose controversial *Das Leben Jesu* (*Life of Jesus*) (1835) portrayed Jesus as human, not divine, and discredited accounts of prophecies and miracles—in an 1851 letter, she denounced "that villainous Strauss," deeming his work both "dull and wicked together" (*BC* 17: 5). On the other hand, her description of the Bible as "a worthy *myth*" advances distinctly Straussian terms of analysis (*BC* 10: 135). As Charles LaPorte demonstrates, the ostensible resistance to the higher criticism in some of EBB's letters stands in tension with the higher critical principles evident in her own creative practices, which he discusses in relation to François René Auguste de Chateaubriand's "articulation of Christianity as a fundamentally poetical religion" in *Le Génie du Christianisme* (*The Genius of Christianity*) (1802).[18] While LaPorte's illuminating analysis does not consider the particular case of *A Drama of Exile*, his analysis invites further examination of EBB's deep and multifaceted engagement with other studies by eighteenth and nineteenth-century biblical critics.

Chief among these studies are Robert Lowth's *De sacra poesie hebraeorum* (*Lectures on the Sacred Poetry of the Hebrews*), originally delivered in Latin in 1747 and widely disseminated in Britain following their English translation in 1787, and Johann Gottfried Herder's *Vom Geist der Erbräischen Poesie* (*The Spirit of Hebrew Poetry*) (1782–3; translated in 1833). These studies broke new ground in their attention to biblical poetry's parallel form, as well as in their efforts to historically contextualize this poetry. This work contributed to what Stephen Prickett identifies as a broad scale shift from typological to narrative readings of the Bible, whereby the Bible became understood less as "a timeless compendium of divinely inspired revelation" than as "a work of literature within the context of ancient Hebrew life."[19] In their discussion of the Bible as literature, both Lowth and Herder focused on the opening chapters of Genesis and the divine speeches in Job as exemplifying its poetic qualities. Lowth remarked that biblical poetry is animated by the tropes of "the Chaos and the Creation," initially advanced in the first chapter of Genesis.[20] He similarly privileged Job, the final book examined in his lectures, by deeming it "single and unparalleled in the Sacred Volume" and discussing its "sublimity of style" (2: 347, 431). Herder's subsequent study concurred about Job's sublimity and even more directly connected this book to Genesis, claiming that the imagery from the natural world in Job provides the reader with "the eyes to perceive and contemplate the works of creation"—in other words, with a powerful perceptual awakening or renewal.[21]

Although EBB does not mention reading Herder in her letters, she was, at the very least, familiar with Lowth's work through his *Select Psalms in Verse* (1811) and Chateaubriand's references to *Lectures on the Sacred Poetry of the Hebrews*.[22] Furthermore, her own biblical study emphasized the very poetic passages prized by Lowth and Herder. Already adept in Greek, EBB began teaching herself Hebrew in 1832, reading the Hebrew Bible with the aid of a grammar and lexicon.[23] In a letter dated June 9 of that year, she outlined her plan of study to H. S. Boyd, her friend and scholarly mentor: "I have been reading thro' the first eight chapters of Genesis in Hebrew, & after I have read the whole of that book, I mean to begin Job" (*BC* 3: 25). By the time she began composing *A Drama of Exile*, EBB referred to having "read the Hebrew Bible from Genesis to Malachi right through," though this statement obscures the fact that, as evident in her diaries and letters, her reading schedule departed from canonical sequencing to privilege the books of poetry (*BC* 8: 118). Early in her study, she expressed ambitions to put her skills as translator and exegete to creative uses: in November 1832, she told Boyd that she hoped to write a "poetical version of the Psalms" by the next spring (*BC* 3: 62). While no evidence remains of her having attempted this project, her own poetry clearly demonstrates her knowledge of and appreciation for biblical poetry's parallel patterning.

Within *A Drama of Exile*, EBB's composite portrayal of postlapsarian life evokes what Herder described as some of the most distinctive features of the book of Job's poetry. Remarking the divine speeches of chapters 38–41, Herder claimed that even as this survey of creation presents "the world of monsters"—that is, the fierce creatures Behemoth and Leviathan—it remains "full of natural feeling, full of the universal providence and goodness of God in his wide empire" (1: 77–8). EBB similarly combines wildness and providence in her depictions of the cosmos. This combination emerges in the opening dialogue between the fallen angel Lucifer and the gatekeeper Gabriel, just outside Eden. This exchange initiates the poem's work of questioning the distinction between fallen and unfallen states:

> *Luc*: Get thee to thy Heaven,
> And leave my earth to me.
> *Gab*: Through Heaven and earth
> God's will moves freely, and I follow it
> As colour follows light. He overflows
> The firmamental walls with deity. (ll. 112–16)

Whereas Lucifer's possessive pronouns and end-stopped imperatives emphatically sunder heaven from earth, Gabriel's enjambed lines gather them as common places of divine activity. His speech puts heaven and earth on the same line, following this unpunctuated combination with a spondaic foot ("God's will") that emphasizes divine omnipresence. The terminal placement of "overflows" intensifies this fullness, distancing the verb from its object and accelerating the reader's progression toward the following line. With their subtle play on the separation of the waters from the firmament as described in Gen. 1:6-7, these lines portray the Creator as exceeding the boundaries of creation. This image of plenitude clarifies Gabriel's previous simile about his obedience to the divine will: "I follow it as colour follows light" (ll. 114–15). Just as light includes all colors, so God's will encompasses Gabriel's movement. In *A Drama of Exile*, heaven and earth are not containers of divine activity but contained by divine activity—and thus EBB's poem invites a perceptual shift akin to what Herder identified as the renewed contemplation of "the works of creation" achieved by Job's wisdom poetry (1: 95).

Forming *A Drama of Exile:* Fragmented Sources and Interpretive Dialogue

Without directly questioning the seven-day creation account in Genesis, this pre-Darwinian reinterpretation accords with the higher criticism's approach to the Bible as a composite, fragmentary, and literary document. More particularly, the source criticism that began with the respective studies of Jean Astruc and Alexander Geddes in the late eighteenth century drew attention to the plurality of oral and written traditions comprising the Pentateuch. Based on differing lexical styles and differing names for God, this criticism distinguished, for instance, between the first creation account (Gen. 1:1–2:3), which uses "Elohim," and the second creation and fall narratives (Gen. 2:3–3:24), which use "Yahweh."[24] Later studies extended these principles and applied them to books beyond the Pentateuch, Job included. Herder, for instance, acknowledged the stylistic differences between this book's frame story—where God grants "the Adversary" permission to test the righteous man Job to his limits—and its central dramatic poem, where Job, his friends Eliphaz, Bildad, Zophar, and Elihu, as well as God himself, participate in an unruly debate about the meaning of suffering (1: 110–11). By the end of the Victorian period, biblical criticism had revised this analysis considerably: a commentary by the Anglican minister T. K. Cheyne, for example, dates the poem as belonging to the exilic or postexilic periods and identifies the prologue, the epilogue, the interpolated hymn to wisdom in chapter 28, and the speeches of Elihu as late additions.[25] Twenty-first-century biblical scholarship has further highlighted Job's dialogism, including Carol A. Newsom's examination of Job as a "polyphonic text," in a study that adapts Mikhail Bakhtin's work to theorize this book's refusal to privilege a single authorial voice and its resistance to closure.[26]

These interpretive models find important precedents within nineteenth-century biblical criticism. Herder structured *On the Spirit of Hebrew Poetry* as a dialogue between two speakers, the fictitious orientalists Alciphron and Euthyphron, and called attention to the reciprocal and flexible qualities of dialogue as a form: "Here two individuals speak, and whoever will, may listen, improve what they have to say, and be either teacher or learner" (1: 21). The prolific theologian and scholar Friedrich Schleiermacher further highlighted dialogue as a vital means of catalyzing the search for meaning. Schleiermacher's esteem for this model becomes clear in his *Introduction to the Dialogues of Plato* (1804; trans. 1836), a volume that EBB herself acquired sometime after her marriage to Browning in 1846. Marginal pencil strokes in this book, now held at the Armstrong Browning Library at Baylor University, underscore specific passages pertaining to Schleiermacher's discussion of Plato's objectives and methods. Even though it is impossible to determine the identity of the hand in question and even though these markings certainly post-date the composition of *A Drama of Exile*, they usefully illuminate related developments in nineteenth-century hermeneutics. Marked passages include Schleiermacher's identification of "the consciousness of ignorance" as the necessary starting point for the pursuit of wisdom, as well as his assertion that embarking on this quest requires "that the final object of the investigation not be directly enunciated ... but that the mind be reduced to the necessity of seeking and put into the way by which it may find it."[27] Schleiermacher thus conceptualizes dialogue as arising from awareness of the limits of one's own knowledge, a concept developed by Hans-Georg Gadamer in his discussion of Schleiermacher's hermeneutics. As Gadamer puts it, "To reach an understanding in a dialogue is not merely a matter of putting oneself forward and successfully asserting one's own point of view but being transformed in a communication in which we do not remain what we were."[28] Genuine intellectual exchange requires openness to mutual change.

EBB herself prized such dialogic energy, and the composition history of *A Drama of Exile*, like so many of her poems, reflects a collaborative, incremental process. Although some of EBB's letters present the poem's development in terms reminiscent of the Romantic model of the individual, inspired genius, closer examination shows that this piece developed gradually and as the result of consultation. Corresponding with Boyd on December 12, 1843, EBB described the poem tentatively entitled "The First Day of Exile" as a subject that had "siezed [*sic*] on [her] and wd. not let [her] go until [she] wrote on it"; a few weeks later, she used similar language in a letter to Horne (*BC* 8: 83, 8: 17). More than two years earlier, however, she told her friend Mary Russell Mitford that she had been "haunted for a long while" by a poem provisionally entitled "*A Day from Eden*" (*BC* 5: 146). This letter appears to refer to an unpublished manuscript entitled "Adam's Farewell to Eden in His Age." Although cast as a dramatic monologue, this piece evinces some of the anaphoric patterns, trochaic rhythms, and variant refrains that EBB later developed through the songs of the Eden and Earth spirits in *A Drama of Exile*. The extensive editorial advice that she received from her cousin John Kenyon during the latter stages of writing this poem further complicates the notion of individual genius. As she recounted to Boyd on March 22, 1844, not long after her initial "exultation & boldness of composition" she fell into despair about the poem and would have burned her manuscript had it not been for her cousin's intervention (*BC* 8: 267). Unpublished and undated letters from Kenyon to EBB further reveal Kenyon's hand in shaping the poem. At the same time as Kenyon assured his cousin that he admired the poem, he questioned her archaic diction choices and suggested substantive edits regarding characterization.[29] For her part, EBB thanked Kenyon for his "unspeakable kindness," going so far as to say of the two-volume *Poems* (1844), "isn't it '*our* book?'" (*BC* 9: 51). This epistolary exchange underscores the dynamism of EBB's composition and revision practices, which accord with the dialogism of the poems themselves.

Her recourse to biblical wisdom texts throughout *A Drama of Exile* further aids in shaping an authorial mode that does not foreground the writer's interpretive superiority but unfolds as a process of dialogue. Dialogue occupies a crucial place within EBB's imagination, as Dieleman has shown in her analysis of EBB's poetic adaptation of the "dialogic and democratic" figure of the Congregationalist preacher, a role sometimes extended to women and one that depended on support from the entire congregation. Dieleman's analysis usefully highlights EBB's participation in Congregationalist gatherings during her formative years, arguing that Congregationalist approaches to worship, scripture, and preaching influenced her development of a model of poetic authority that departed from the authoritarian prophetic stance asserted by Victorian sages such as Thomas Carlyle.[30] This line of argument can be further extended by considering the many biblical genres informing EBB's revision of prophetic sage writing. Her use of wisdom literature's dialogic forms effectively enacts one of her drama's animating motifs: attentive listening as a means to insight. She thereby departs from what both John Holloway and George P. Landow identify as prophetic sage discourse's characteristic reliance on visual metaphors to express authority.[31] This movement from visual to auditory metaphors reinforces her refiguring of the sage's authorial positioning. For EBB, sages distinguish themselves not by virtue of their superior vision but through their ability to discern harmony, even within the cacophony of a chaotic world.

Clashing Cosmologies: Genesis, Job, and the Earth in Exile

As *A Drama of Exile* unfolds, EBB reinterprets the fall narrative by drawing from a variety of texts that together display the formal and theological plurality of biblical traditions—the very plurality that came into sharp relief as a result of the higher criticism. A comparison of subtle differences between the autograph manuscript of *A Drama of Exile* and its published texts reveals the careful development of her biblical rewritings.[32] Her revisionary work emerges in the first conversation between Adam and Eve, as well as in the chorus of Eden spirits that precedes this dialogue and accompanies humankind's departure from Paradise. When Adam and Eve speak for the first time, the manuscript compares the angelic songs that they hear in the wilderness to a "healing rain" (p. 25). Conversely, the text as published in 1844 and onwards, likens this music to a "watering dew" (l. 533), a simile that brings prelapsarian imagery into the wilderness.[33] Eve's wondering response to Adam's statements that he would rather be cast out with her than alone in Paradise becomes intensified from "is it but a dream of thee I hear?" (p. 22) to "Where is loss? / Am I in Eden?" (ll. 487–8). These changes accord with the alterations that EBB made to the refrain of the Eden chorus: while the manuscript emphasizes what the spirits of the trees, rivers, birds, and flowers alike shall no longer "give" (pp. 12–16) to Adam and Eve, the published text repositions subject and object to call attention to what Adam and Eve "shall hear nevermore" (ll. 302, 328, 354, 389), emphasizing not the diminishment of the earth's majesty but the hardening of humankind's perception.

This perceptual hardening, however, stands in tension with the hopeful possibilities evoked by the Eden chorus's kinesthetic and synaesthetic language. Sung at the threshold of Paradise, the songs of the Eden spirits begin with an exhortation to attentive listening that echoes the words used in the book of Proverbs to describe personified Wisdom, who calls out at the gates of the city, "hearken unto me, O ye children" (Prov. 8:32). The Eden chorus cries, "Harken, oh harken! let your souls behind you / Turn, gently moved! / Our voices feel along the dread to find you / O lost, beloved" (ll. 227–30). By following the motion of the soul with embodied language that is both auditory and tactile, the spirits present the heeding of this call as a fully corporeal process that brings together spiritual and somatic action.

In addition to this joining of body and soul, the songs of the Eden spirits bridge heaven and earth as they describe the "divine impulsion" (l. 285) in their midst:

Dropt, and lifted, dropt, and lifted
In the sunlight greenly sifted,—
In the sunlight and the moonlight
Greenly sifted through the trees (ll. 287–90)

Insofar as the adverb "greenly" modifies the activity of the sunlight and moonlight, these lines combine visual and tactile experiences in ways that prepare for the subsequent synaesthetic description of "a ruffling of green branches / Shaded off to resonances" (ll. 294–5). This passage offers yet another instance where variations between manuscript and published text show the gradual refinement of EBB's ideas. In place of "shaded off," the manuscript has "riffling into" (p. 12), a phrase that emphasizes motion but lacks the sensory combination of color and sound that appears in the published text. The incantatory cadence of these tetrameter lines heightens the contrast between the blank iambic pentameter speeches of the human characters, on the one hand, and, on the other, the songs of the Eden spirits, with their varied, intricate play of rhythm and rhyme. Remarking the chorus's resistance to metrical classification, Donald S. Hair suggests that its range evokes the divine creator's "exuberant variety."[34] This variety not only betokens divine exuberance but also assigns to the natural world a wildness that resists human attempts to contain it. *A Drama of Exile* thereby advances a cosmological patterning akin to what Ricoeur identifies in the divine speeches of the book of Job: "inscrutable order, measure beyond measure, terrifying beauty."[35]

Within EBB's poem, these paradoxical combinations find their most intense expression in the cries of the Earth spirits who confront Adam and Eve in the wilderness. These spirits turn what begins as a sorrowful lamentation into a series of threatening denunciations. The first spirit's mournful exclamations over the loss of paradisiacal splendor—"deep waters, cataract and flood," as well as "mountain-summits, where the angels stood" (ll. 1099, 1101)—give way to forceful, even predatory assertions of power, as the spirit declares to Adam and Eve, "Alp and torrent shall inherit / Your significance of will" (ll. 1529–30). Their anaphoric catalogue of natural wonders and wild creatures from "storm-wind" to "owlet" employs patterns of repetition and images that recall the series of questions with which God rebukes Job (ll. 706–18).[36]

While both EBB and the Job poet use nature's untamable power to question humankind's assumed position as the pinnacle of creation, *A Drama of Exile* lets the earth and animal spirits speak for themselves. Subverting the rule that humans exert through language, the spirits declare, "Your bold speeches, our Behemoth / With his thunderous jaw shall wield" (ll. 1539–40). This pointed allusion to the description of the Behemoth in Job chapter 40 evokes the beast's physical strength. By portraying this creature as master of the logocentric order, *A Drama of Exile* suggests that human attempts to exert dominion over the natural world through language, as in Adam's act of naming the animals in the second creation narrative, are futile.[37] In representing the Behemoth as an emissary of the Earth spirits, EBB's interpretation of Job chapter 40 accords with Herder's understanding of these creatures as natural beings, rather than spiritual figures. Departing from the allegorical tradition of reading Behemoth and Leviathan as Satan and the Anti-Christ, Herder discussed these creatures as physical animals, likening them to the hippopotamus or elephant and claiming that the very name *behemoth* derives from an Egyptian term (1: 106–7).[38] At the same time, an element of the older allegorical tradition seems to survive in

EBB's poem, insofar as these Earth spirits are goaded by curses directed toward humankind by none other than Lucifer.

Lucifer's role in *A Drama of Exile* is telling of EBB's Romantic revisionism, as well as her efforts to reframe concepts of fallenness. Her portrayal of Lucifer responds both to Milton's *Paradise Lost* and to Byron's *Cain* (1821), as Stone observes: even as EBB figures Lucifer as fallen and mistaken, she also offers a sympathetic representation of him as the former Morning Star.[39] In her preface to *Poems* (1844), she described her anthropomorphic Lucifer as "an extreme Adam," meant "to represent the ultimate tenderness of sin and loss" (*WEBB* 2:567). This preface displays EBB's efforts to renegotiate inherited literary traditions through an innovative use of the trope of exile, as Cynthia Scheinberg observes.[40] Anticipating that *A Drama of Exile* would be unfavorably compared with *Paradise Lost*—as indeed it was by both *The Atlas* and *Blackwood's Edinburgh Magazine*—EBB distinguished her poem by foregrounding its setting:

> I had promised my own prudence to shut close the gates of Eden between Milton and myself, so that none might say I dared to walk in his footsteps. He should be within, I thought, with his Adam and Eve unfallen or falling,—and I, without, with my EXILES,—*I* also an exile! (*WEBB* 2: 567–8)

In addition to revealing her consciousness of her place as a woman writer on the margins of a literary tradition dominated by men, these terms evoke the biblical language used to describe the expulsion of humankind from Eden, as well as Israel's exile in Babylon. She provided further commentary on her understanding of this concept in a letter to Boyd, explaining that her drama's title "refers to Lucifer's exile, and to that other mystical exile of the Divine Being"— that is, Christ's incarnation (*BC* 8:267). Encompassing everything from the fall of Lucifer to the divine *kenosis*, this capacious concept of exile brings together pain and promise within the postlapsarian world.

A Drama of Exile shows that to blur the distinction between prelapsarian and postlapsarian states is necessarily to raise issues of theodicy. If, as EBB's Adam tells Eve when first attempting to assuage her trepidation about the spirits they encounter in the wilderness, "the circle of God's life / Contains all life beside" (ll. 909–10), then this circle must somehow encompass destructive forces. It is on this issue that the book of Job and the opening chapters of Genesis converge. EBB's interpretation sees the fall as, if not exactly a *felix culpa* in the traditions of St. Ambrose or St. Augustine, then certainly a moment of possibility. Elsewhere in the drama, Adam and Eve declare that their enduring love for each other makes the fallen world almost as if it were unfallen: Eve marvels, "Where is loss? / Am

I in Eden?" (ll. 477–8), and Adam declares, "Because with *her*, I stand / Upright, as far as can be in this fall" (ll. 489–90). In bringing together standing and falling, EBB echoes and revises the words of Raphael in Milton's *Paradise Lost*, who emphasizes that angelic beings "stand or fall" by their own choice and likewise admonishes Adam that "to stand or fall" lies within his own power.[41] Her Lucifer further contests this model when he suggests, "Is it not possible, by sin and grief / (To give the things your names) that spirits should rise / Instead of falling?" (ll. 726–8). While it would be overstating the point to suggest that EBB is "of the devil's party without knowing it," as William Blake famously said about Milton, she nonetheless opens debate about received ideas of fallenness.[42] For EBB, transgression may be educative: as Eve puts it, she has been "schooled by sin to more humility"—a statement that finds in the fall a transformative effect (l. 1178).

Taking Tradition to Task: Eve's Role in *A Drama of Exile*

By reconsidering the fall for both its curses and its blessings, *A Drama of Exile* interrogates Christian exegetical and literary traditions that associate Eve with sin. As EBB reflected in a letter to Horne shortly prior to the poem's publication, "*[f]irst in the transgression* has been said over & over again, because of the tradition,—but *first & deepest in the sorrow*, nobody seems to have said" (*BC* 8: 117).[43] Even though EBB construed herself as alone in the struggle against patriarchal exegesis—in another, often-cited letter, she claimed, "I look everywhere for Grandmothers & see none" (*BC* 10: 14)—readers today might, thanks to the interventions of feminist scholars, identify several potential "Grandmothers" in the preceding centuries, from Julian of Norwich to Aemilia Lanyer. Within the nineteenth century alone, EBB appears to have had, if not grandmothers, then at least some daring older sisters. Such women include the historian Lucy Aikin, whose *Epistles on Women* (1810) offered a feminist rewriting of Western culture from Eve to the eighteenth century, and the Owenite socialist Eliza Sharples, who in 1832 gave an address that celebrated Eve's eating of the forbidden fruit: "Well done, woman! LIBERTY FOR EVER."[44]

Held up against such radical feminism, *A Drama of Exile* seems remarkably mild: indeed, there are moments when EBB's Eve seems as condemning of her sin as any of the church fathers. Consider, for instance, the initial exchange between Adam and Eve, where Eve prostrates herself before Adam and implores,

"Strike, my lord! / *I* also, after tempting, writhe on the ground" (ll. 435–6).⁴⁵ This exhortation attests to EBB's sense of both the weight and the potential richness of the traditions she sought not merely to invert but, rather, to engage productively. Contesting misogynistic interpretations of the biblical fall narrative while still reworking elements of inherited ideas, she ultimately renders Eve both a penitential figure and an insightful one. EBB's nuanced, labored engagement with patriarchal exegesis is again evident in her composition process: the manuscript of *A Drama of Exile* contains two variants of the initial conversation between Adam and Eve, revealing her gradual revisions. In one variant, the hypocatastasis of the lines quoted above appears as an explicit, if clumsy, simile: "I writhe here likest what I tempted like" (p. 20). In the other, Eve goes so far as to ask Adam to apply the curse that God offers the serpent in Genesis to herself, crying, "Bruise my head," and repeating, "My head lies at thy foot, my serpent head" (p. 19). Subsequent lines in both the manuscript and the published text, however, show EBB's departure from this reading. In what appears to be the later draft, Eve follows her self-abasing statement with a more confident assertion: "since I was the first in the transgression, with my little foot / I will be the first to tread from this sword-glare / Into the outer darkness of the waste" (p. 25). Marginal commentary by EBB shows her lingering dissatisfaction with these lines; the following notation in her own hand appears in pencil at the bottom of the page: "I do not like 'little'—it is almost coquettish—with my firm foot?" (p. 25). The line in the poem as published in 1844 reads "with a steady foot," a revision that both sustains the speech's iambic meter and emphasizes Eve's strength (l. 547).

By depicting Eve as the first to venture out into the wilderness, *A Drama of Exile* at once counters misogynistic readings of the fall narrative and emphasizes the shared position of man and woman in relation to the rest of the universe. This emphasis has lately received attention in several ecotheological readings of the poem.⁴⁶ Importantly, EBB's exploration of Eve's place as *"first & deepest in the sorrow"* (*BC* 8: 117) does not define Eve's anguish solely—or even primarily—in terms of the curse offered in Genesis, "in sorrow shalt thou bring forth children" (Gen. 3:16). Beyond the labor of childbirth, Eve does the work of seeking restoration with the newly fallen world. This work is initiated by her responses to the Earth spirits and solemnized through the blessing Adam gives to Eve later in the poem. Adam extols the many "lofty uses" and "noble ends" to which Eve will "aspire" (ll. 1829–31), including "comforting for ill, and teaching good / And reconciling all that ill and good / Unto the patience of a constant hope" (ll. 1845–7). By claiming for herself "this high part / Which lowly shall be counted,"

Eve affirms that the "Noble work" she will hold "in place of garden-rest" operates from a principle of harmony rather than hierarchy (ll. 1899–1900).

A Drama of Exile thus looks beyond the contest of power that the Earth spirits suggest and toward a radical embrace of limitation. In this way, EBB underscores and further develops the sense of human finitude the higher critics found in the sublime poetry of Job. Lowth, for instance, claimed that this book's "design" contrasts the "corruption, infirmity, and ignorance of human nature" with the "infinite wisdom and majesty of God" (2: 83). Similarly, Herder argued that, of all biblical texts, the book of Job "furnishes the clearest proof" of humankind's "comparative weakness" in relation to God's "incomprehensible power" (1: 52). Both Lowth and Herder, then, drew attention to the diminishment of the human subject in the divine speeches, which, in their emphasis on the unfathomed mysteries of the natural world, complicate the model of human dominion often derived from the opening chapters of Genesis.[47]

EBB similarly questions anthropocentric models of the cosmos: Eve responds to Adam's assertions of dominion by identifying mutuality among all forms of life. Even as the Earth spirits threaten to crush humankind under their scorn, Adam declares, "we may be overcome by God / But not by these" (ll. 1549–50). Eve's rejoinder "By God, perhaps, in these" (l. 1551) questions the separation that Adam presumes. At the same time, EBB effectively reworks what may be, for feminist critics, one of the most vexing lines in all of *Paradise Lost*: "He for God only, she for God in him" (4.297). In *A Drama of Exile*, Eve's statement reflects a theology of immanence: whereas Adam separates God and the Earth spirits, Eve finds continuity between the divine presence and the forces of nature. Moreover, in response to Adam's classification of the Earth spirits as "Inferior creatures" (l. 1163), Eve admonishes, "Let us not stand high / Upon the wrong we did to reach disdain" (ll. 1175–6). In effect, she flattens Adam's hierarchical language by not only recalling the fall but also, in the lines that follow, making sorrow the means of restoring their relationship with the earth. Eve beseeches the Earth spirits, "let my tears fall thick / As watering dews of Eden, unreproached" (ll. 1220–1) and "let some tender peace, made of our pain, / Grow up betwixt us, as a tree might grow" (ll. 1307–9). Her sorrow makes possible a renewal of organic connections between human and nonhuman life. The imagery of the restorative "watering dews of Eden" at once recalls the tears of the Eden spirits, described as falling "purely" while Adam and Eve hearken to their song (ll. 249–50), and looks forward to Christ's words about the "tears" of his "clean soul," which he declares will "set a holy passion / to work clear absolute consecration" (ll. 1976, 1977–8).

Eve proceeds both to intensify the dynamic qualities of her suffering and to give it roots, emphasizing the transformative qualities of this humility:

And I am prescient by the very hope
And promise set upon me, that henceforth
Only my gentleness shall make me great,
My humbleness exalt me. (ll. 1273–9)

By making limitation the grounds of aspiration, she figures herself as falling into hope. This reclamation of humility puts Eve in the position of the self-sacrificing Christ who appears later in the drama. The first to respond to Christ's proclamation of "the Love, which is [himself]" (l. 1820), she immerses herself in this love by declaring that, regardless of any blessing given specifically to her, she is "blessed in harkening" to him (l. 1822). Moreover, Christ's description of the work Adam and Eve must do echoes Eve's acceptance and reclamation of her postlapsarian position. Exhorting the humans to live, love, and work "nobly, because lowlily" (l. 1996), Christ effectively echoes Eve's previous statement that she will accept her own work as a "high part, which lowly shall be counted" (l. 1898). EBB continued to develop this idea throughout her later poetry—the final book of *Aurora Leigh*, incorporates what appears to be a revised version of Eve's lines and attributes them to Christ. Reflecting on the ethics advanced in the gospels, the poet Aurora remarks, "My humbleness, said One, has made me great" (*WEBB* 3: 263). Throughout her poetic theology, EBB dismantles hierarchies of high and low to advance a wider vision of greatness.

In associating Eve and Christ, EBB participates in the long-standing tradition of feminizing Christ that Julie Melnyk identifies as experiencing a resurgence with the rise of evangelicalism in eighteenth- and nineteenth-century British Christianity, especially in the religious writings of Low Church Victorian women. Melnyk contends that, even though this portrayal of Christ allowed women "to claim spiritual and moral authority as representatives of a new order," its "indissoluble connection between Christ's power and his suffering undercut any attempt to turn spiritual authority into secular power."[48] Yet whereas this reading conceptualizes suffering as the result of oppression, *A Drama of Exile* invites readers to see suffering as part of an all-encompassing gesture of love. As the poem continues, EBB suggests that the acceptance of limitation exemplified by Eve finds a powerful theological counterpart not only in the willing descent of God the Son but also in the very act of creation by God the Father. As Emma Mason has shown in her analysis of Christina Rossetti's poetry, a renewed emphasis on *kenosis* allowed nineteenth-century thinkers to revive their theology of the incarnation in response to contemporary debates about evolution.[49] The parallel development traceable in *A Drama of Exile* reflects EBB's knowledge of both patristic theology and higher critical developments.

From Humility to Hope: Kenotic Self-emptying and Creative Self-limitation

A Drama of Exile introduces this theology through an innovative turn, bringing "*a vision of* CHRIST" into the wilderness (*WEBB* 1: 56). Occurring as the Earth spirits reach the height of their ferocity, this vision both recalls and repositions the theophany in the book of Job, when God appears out of the whirlwind. While Job's divine speeches employ sublime descriptions of nature that foreground the Creator's ineffable otherness, EBB's Christ restores harmony between humankind and nature in ways that emphasize divine immanence. At first, Christ's rebuke of the Earth spirits seems simply to reinscribe a model of anthropocentric dominion: he subdues the Earth spirits by enjoining them, "Receive man's sceptre" and further claims, "This regent and sublime Humanity / Though fallen, exceeds you!" (l. 1798). Though such affirmation of anthropocentric dominion is at odds with the poem's ecotheological elements, this model of kingship undergoes an important metamorphosis in subsequent lines: Christ closes his rebuke by dignifying the Earth spirits's service (ll. 1815–20) and then models servitude himself.

In a striking reversal of the gospel accounts of Jesus's transfiguration into glory before Peter, James, and John, EBB describes Christ as "*gradually transfigured*" into "*humanity and suffering*" (p. 60).[50] She thus recalls the Pauline hymn on Jesus's humility, which lauds the one who "made himself of no reputation, and took [on] ... the form of a servant, and was made in the likeness of man: and being found in fashion as a man ... humbled himself and became obedient to death, even the death of a cross" (Phil. 2:6-8). What the authorized version renders as "made himself of no reputation" appears in the Greek text as ἑαυτὸν ἐκένωσεν (*heaton ekenosen*), literally "emptied himself," a phrase that appears to have fascinated EBB.[51] In a letter to Mitford written shortly after the publication of *A Drama of Exile*, she alluded to "that 'emptying' of the Saviour's soul from Deity, which is a scriptural doctrine," noting emphatically, "[i]t is said that *He emptied Himself*" (*BC* 9: 101). Her words highlight the magnitude of Christ's *kenosis*: more than a demotion of stature, this statement suggests a forceful corporeal action. EBB's emphasis on this willing acceptance of limitation aligns with the kenotic Christology advanced by German theologians, beginning with Gottfried Thomasius in his *Christi Person und Werk* (1845) and developed by Wolfgang Friedrich Gess closer to the end of the century. Revising the Lutheran account of Christ's self-emptying as pertaining only to his human nature, these kenotic theologians argued for a limitation of Christ's divinity as well.[52] Much as they sought to bridge theology and anthropology through an expanded understanding of *kenosis*, so EBB portrays this act of self-limitation as radiating throughout the entire universe.

Her allusion to the hymn on Christ's humility thickens the wisdom poetry that animates *A Drama of Exile*. As Ben Witherington observes, the "servant song" in Philippians adapts the hymns of praise to personified Wisdom in other texts, such as the eighth chapter of Proverbs. This passage finds yet another precedent, Witherington notes, in the description of the suffering servant in the book of Isaiah, particularly in the portrait of this servant as one who "hath borne our griefs and carried our sorrows" (Isa. 53:3-4).[53] By figuring Christ as suffering servant, EBB engages with a long-standing typological reading of Job as prefiguring Christ. As Ricoeur observes, Job is often identified with the suffering servant, a figure that he identifies as having the potential "to make of suffering, of the evil that is undergone, an *action* capable of redeeming the evil that is committed." Such action demands a radical selflessness, and this selflessness explains why Job, an imperfect type of this figure, must repent at the end of the book. As Ricoeur sees it, the divine speeches prompt Job to surrender both "the demand for retribution" and "the claim to form by oneself a little island of meaning in the universe."[54] Through this repentance, Job models the soul's growth from a false sense of privilege to a humbled participation in a vast cosmos that far exceeds any one individual.

Within *A Drama of Exile*, Adam and Eve undergo a similar process: Christ's suffering servitude becomes the paradigm for their own spiritual development. Christ declares that he will "tread earth" and that the "tears of [his] clean soul" will "set a holy passion to work clear / Absolute consecration" (ll. 1971, 1976, 1977–8). Eve's affirmation "We worship in thy sorrow, Saviour Christ" (l. 1926) further emphasizes the continuity between divine and human suffering. While EBB's Christology stands at some remove from the demythologized paradigm of Ludwig Feuerbach, who suggested in *Das Wesen des Christentums* (*The Essence of Christianity*) (1841) that "love makes God man and man God," *A Drama of Exile* appears broadly in agreement with Blake's similarly chiastic formulation, "God becomes as we are that we may be as he is."[55] Moreover, EBB extends this redemptive work throughout creation: her Christ assigns a cosmological significance to his suffering when he lists the reasons for his coming to earth: "For all the world in all its elements, / For all the creatures of earth, air, and sea, / For all men in the body and in the soul" (ll. 1963–5).

A *Drama of Exile* intensifies this cosmic interconnectivity when the Earth spirits speak again toward the close of the poem. Addressing Adam and Eve, these spirits declare, "our God's refracted blessing in our blessing shall be given" (l. 2029). This assertion claims the Creator as the God of human and nonhuman life alike, thus recalling the Eden spirits's hailing of "divine impulsion" in their midst (l. 285). Moreover, their reference to this blessing as "refracted" suggests not only mediation but also accommodation, evoking the concept of creation as divine self-limitation that Jürgen Moltmann highlights as finding expression in select Christian theologians beginning with the work of Nicholas of Cusa in the fifteenth century. Moltmann further traces this model to the Jewish concept of *shekinah*, the indwelling presence of God that remains with his people even into exile. As Moltmann sees it, this concept effectively diffuses the problem of evil by portraying God as one who does not "rule the world like an autocrat or dictator" but rather "waits and awaits."[56] A *Drama of Exile* similarly depicts the divine presence as growing and changing with the entire created order.

As the poem builds toward its final lines, EBB amplifies her theology of immanence by foregrounding the active state of waiting. Her exilic scene is a place of expectation where joy and sorrow coexist. Even as the Earth spirits echo the seven-day structure and refrain of the creation story in the first chapter of Genesis, declaring that "the evening and the morning / Shall re-organise in beauty / A sabbath day of sabbath joy" (ll. 2012–14), they acknowledge the "melancholy" of the present, mortal state (l. 2015). Yet within this sadness, the Earth spirits anticipate renewal: they will "leap up in God's sunning / To join the spheric company" (ll. 2048–9). By putting this expectation into the mouths of the Earth spirits, EBB evokes the Pauline idea that all creation groans while awaiting redemption.[57] The chorus of invisible angels—the very last voices to speak in the poem—heightens this expectation by echoing the earlier words of the Eden spirits. Taking note of these echoes, Herbert Tucker correlates the "melancholia" of the Eden spirits's statement "In all your music, our pathetic minor / Your ears shall cross" (ll. 255–6) with the transfigured sorrow expressed in the angel chorus's drawing Adam and Eve "into the full chant divine," where "the human in the minor / Makes the harmony diviner" (ll. 2082, 2084–5). As Tucker explains, these lines exemplify the role of the "diminutive"—that is, the elements of aphoristic concision present within EBB's otherwise exuberant, sprawling poetry—in providing a "fit register at once of experiential loss and of visionary promise."[58] Even as the Eden spirits and angel chorus underscore Adam and Eve's smallness, they raise the prospect that fallen humankind might perceive and participate in a harmony that exceeds them.

Fittingly, *A Drama of Exile* culminates with a call to hear and respond to the music of both the heavens and the earth. Its initial exhortation to "harken," as the Eden spirits put it (l. 227), reaches a crescendo in the repeated command of the angel chorus: "Listen to our loving" (ll. 2068, 2100, 2114, 2127). This chorus urges, "Listen, through man's ignorances, / Listen, through God's mysteries, / Listen, down the heart of things" (ll. 2068). By presenting this act as occurring in the absence of clarity and knowledge, EBB embraces epistemic limitation at the same time that she makes this limitation the source of an indefinable wonder. In lines added to the poem as published in 1850, she further intensifies this pattern: "Listen, man, through life and death, / Through the dust and through the breath, / Listen down the heart of things" (ll. 2187–9).[59] Gathering together life, death, dust, and breath, the chorus implies that attentive ears may discern, within creation's many voices, the sounds of an ongoing divine revelation.

These echoes demonstrate EBB's subtle adaptation of biblical poetry's parallel patterning, which was brought into sharper relief as a result of the studies by Lowth and Herder. Although Lowth's account of parallelism as occurring when poets "express the same thing in different words, or different things in a similar form of words" emphasized similarity (1: 68–9), Herder drew attention to parallelism's function of intensifying meaning. Herder observed that parallel lines "strengthen, heighten, empower each other," an observation that Robert Alter cites as a useful corrective to the widespread misconception of parallelism as based merely in synonyms.[60] In subtle ways, Herder's remarks anticipate Alter's analysis of the "narrative impulse" evident in the poetry of the prophetic and wisdom books, an analysis that builds on his earlier work on biblical narrative.[61] As Alter demonstrates, the repetitive techniques of the biblical writers and editors "produce a certain indeterminacy of meaning," wherein "[m]eaning, perhaps for the first time in narrative literature, was conceived as a *process*, requiring continual revision."[62] Similar patterns underlie *A Drama of Exile*: its many voices echo, amplify, or invert the words of other speakers in ways that not only revise the biblical and literary texts with which the poem engages but, ultimately, put *A Drama of Exile* in dialogue with itself.

Accordingly, the poem concludes with the promise of continuation. Once all speech has passed into silence, EBB's stage directions outline the drama's final motions, images, and sounds as follows: "*The stars shine on brightly while*

ADAM *and* EVE *pursue their way into the far wilderness. There is a sound through the silence, as of the falling tears of an angel*" (*WEBB* 1: 71). Exactly how this extravagant scene would be staged remains unclear, as Edgar Allan Poe highlighted in an incisive review: "How there can be sound during silence, and how an audience are to distinguish, by such sound, angel tears from any other species of tears, it may be as well, perhaps, not too particularly to inquire."[63] Logical and practical problems aside, these stage directions return to the overarching motif of tears, including those of the Eden spirits (ll. 248–50), Eve (ll. 1220–1), and Christ (l. 1976). Even as its theological and cosmological concerns remain—at times spectacularly—unresolved, *A Drama of Exile* opens new interpretive possibilities for the biblical fall story. These possibilities favor plurality over unity, continuity over separation, and questions over answers, as the poem's fragmentary and dialogic form performs its own meditation on the art of falling short.

Such dialogic openness accords with EBB's sense of "truth" as something only imperfectly grasped by any single religious tradition or institution. Writing in early January 1844, she explained her ecumenical concept of a "Universal Church of Christ" in terms that affirm variety, emphasizing that "the *churches* of Christ are *many*—and the ministrations of the one spirit are *many*—and the aspects of Truth to the human mind are many indeed" (*BC* 8: 149). EBB herself moved across several religious and political communities throughout the course of her lifetime, as a British writer who frequently published in American periodicals and spent much of her poetic career living as an expatriate in Florence. Studies by both Christopher M. Keirstead and Alison Chapman have called attention to her contributions to religiously inflected ideas of cosmopolitanism.[64] As her poetic engagement with Christianity's sacred texts demonstrates, EBB's pluralist outlook arises from a nuanced approach to biblical hermeneutics. She incorporates higher critical insights about the literary qualities of biblical texts, without becoming threatened by this criticism's challenge to received traditions.

In her ecumenical Christianity, EBB shares much in common with George MacDonald, the subject of my next chapter. Like EBB, MacDonald emerged from a Congregational Christian context but expressed substantial reservations with any single denominational affiliation. Furthermore, both EBB and MacDonald distinguished themselves from their dissenting Protestant contemporaries through their comparatively greater degree of receptiveness to ideas emerging from German biblical scholarship, with which they engaged both critically and creatively in their letters and published writings. As Chapter 2 will show, MacDonald goes a step further in his openness not only to questioning but also to a form of productive doubt. Whereas *A Drama of Exile* portrays wisdom as resulting not from attaining a singular transcendent vision but from attending to a plurality of voices, MacDonald continues this trajectory by turning self-reflexively toward the reader's interpretive efforts.

Notes

1. Paul Ricoeur, "Toward a Hermeneutic of the Idea of Revelation," in *Essays on Biblical Interpretation*, ed. Lewis S. Mudge, trans. David Pellauer (Philadelphia: Fortress Press, 1980), 85.
2. All references to Elizabeth Barrett Browning's published works come from the following source: *The Works of Elizabeth Barrett Browning*, 5 volumes, ed. Sandra Donaldson, Rita Patteson, Marjorie Stone, and Beverly Taylor (London: Pickering & Chatto, 2010); they are cited parenthetically as *WEBB*. References to *A Drama of Exile* are cited by line numbers for precision; the full text of the poem appears in *WEBB* 1: 3–74. Following the conventions used by this edition's editors, I refer to the poet as EBB, the initials she used as her poetic signature both before and after her marriage to Robert Browning on September 12, 1846.
3. Marjorie Stone, "Lyric Tipplers: Elizabeth Barrett Browning's 'Wine of Cyprus,' Emily Dickinson's 'I taste a liquor,' and the Transatlantic Anacreontic Tradition," *Victorian Poetry* 54, no. 2 (2016): 123.
4. Oscar Wilde, "English Poetesses," in *The Complete Works of Oscar Wilde*, vol. 14, ed. Robert Ross (London: Dawsons of Pall Mall, 1969), 111. For a discussion of EBB's influence on Eliot, see Charles LaPorte, *Victorian Poets and the Changing Bible* (Charlottesville: University of Virginia Press, 2011), 190–1.
5. This trend in the book's reception is evident in the *Atlas*, the *John Bull*, the *Sun*, the *Examiner*, *Blackwood's Edinburgh Magazine*, the *Critic*, and the *Westminster Review*. These reviews are reprinted in full in *The Brownings' Correspondence*, 9: 319–80. See *The Brownings' Correspondence*, 28 volumes to date, ed. Philip Kelley et al. (Winfield, Kans.: Wedgestone, 1984–2023). Subsequent references to this collection are cited parenthetically as *BC*.
6. In addition to *Paradise Lost*, important precursors include George Gordon Byron's *Cain* (1821), Robert Pollok's *The Course of Time* (1827), and Robert Montgomery's *The Messiah* (1832). See Stone, "A Heretic Believer: Victorian Religious Doubt and New Contexts for Elizabeth Barrett Browning's 'A Drama of Exile,' 'The Virgin Mary,' and 'The Runaway Slave at Pilgrim's Point,'" *Studies in Browning and His Circle* 26, no. 2 (2006): 19–24.
7. Dorothy Mermin, *Elizabeth Barrett Browning: The Origins of a New Poetry* (Chicago: University of Chicago Press, 1989), 88; Stone, *Elizabeth Barrett Browning*

(Hampshire: Macmillan, 1995), 80; Linda Lewis, *Elizabeth Barrett Browning's Spiritual Progress: Face to Face with God* (Columbia: University of Missouri Press, 1998), 54; Alexandra M. B. Wörn, "'Poetry Is Where God Is': The Importance of Christian Faith and Theology in Elizabeth Barrett Browning's Life and Work," in *Victorian Religious Discourse: New Directions in Criticism*, ed. Jude V. Nixon (New York: Palgrave Macmillan, 2004), 245–8; Terence Allan Hoagwood, "Biblical Criticism and Secular Sex: Elizabeth Barrett Browning's *A Drama of Exile* and Jean Ingelow's *A Story of Doom*," *Victorian Poetry* 42, no. 2 (2004): 165–80; Karen Dieleman, *Religious Imaginaries: The Liturgical and Poetic Practices of Elizabeth Barrett Browning, Christina Rossetti, and Adelaide Procter* (Athens: Ohio University Press, 2011), 87–91; Karen Dieleman, "Ecotheological Relationships in Elizabeth Barrett Browning's *A Drama of Exile*," *Christianity and Literature* 69, no. 3 (September 2020): 418–38.

8   *The Bible: Authorized King James Version with Apocrypha* (Oxford: Oxford University Press, 2008). All biblical quotations are cited parenthetically in text. Rights in the Authorized (King James) Version in the United Kingdom are vested in the Crown. Reproduced by permission of the Crown's patentee, Cambridge University Press.

9   Charles Spurgeon, qtd. in Timothy Larsen, *A People of One Book: The Bible and the Victorians* (Oxford: Oxford University Press, 2011), 268.

10 For relevant discussions in the periodical press, see Mark Knight and Emma Mason, *Nineteenth-Century Religion and Literature: An Introduction* (Oxford: Oxford University Press, 2006), 130–4.

11 Ricoeur, "Toward a Hermeneutic of the Idea of Revelation," 86.

12 E. S. Shaffer, "The Hermeneutic Community: Coleridge and Schleiermacher," in *The Coleridge Connection: Essays for Thomas McFarland*, ed. Richard Gravil and Molly Lefebure (New York: Macmillan, 1990), 2000.

13 For one of the earliest studies to call attention to EBB's wide-ranging spiritual vision, see Lewis, *Elizabeth Barrett Browning's Spiritual Progress*, 140–65. Other important early recovery work on EBB as a complex religious thinker includes Cynthia Scheinberg, *Women's Poetry and Religion in Victorian England* (Cambridge: Cambridge University Press, 2002), 62–105. For more recent work on EBB and spiritualism, see Alison Chapman, *Networking the Nation: British and American Women's Poetry and Italy, 1840–1870* (Oxford: Oxford University Press, 2015), 168–98.

14 Stone, "A Heretic Believer," 12.

15 Karen Dieleman, "A Politics of Just Memory: Elizabeth Barrett and the Greek Christian Poets," *The Journal of Browning Studies*, vol. 3 (December 2012): 5–28.

16 Kirstie Blair, *Form and Faith in Victorian Poetry and Religion* (Oxford: Oxford University Press, 2010), 122–5.

17 Samuel Taylor Coleridge, *Confessions of an Inquiring Spirit*, in *The Collected Works of Samuel Taylor Coleridge*, vol. 11. no. 2, ed. H. J. Jackson and J. R. de J. Jackson (Princeton: Princeton University Press, 1995), 11.2: 1167.

18 LaPorte, *Victorian Poets*, 38.
19 Stephen Prickett, *Words and the Word: Language, Poetics, and Biblical Interpretation* (Cambridge: Cambridge University Press, 1986), 196, 105.
20 Robert Lowth, *Lectures on the Sacred Poetry of the Hebrews*, 2 volumes (Hildesheim, Germany: Georg Olms Verlag, 1969), 1: 187. Subsequent references to this text are cited parenthetically by volume and page numbers.
21 Johann Gottfried Herder, *The Spirit of Hebrew Poetry*, 2 volumes, trans. James Marsh (Burlington, Vermont: Edward Smith, 1833), 1: 95. Subsequent references to this text are cited parenthetically by volume and page numbers.
22 EBB mentions reading "Lowth's version" of the Psalms in a letter to Hugh Stuart Boyd dated November 19, 1846 (*BC* 14: 44). References in other letters to Hugh Blair's work indicates that EBB would also have very likely been familiar with Blair's summation of Lowth's ideas in his *Lectures on Rhetoric and Belles Letters*, first published in 1783 (*BC* 10: 113).
23 For a thoughtful discussion of EBB's study of Hebrew, see Scheinberg, *Women's Poetry and Religion*, 67–76.
24 Hypotheses about these sources were developed throughout the century by scholars including Hermann Hupfeld and Julius Wellhausen. For a useful overview of source criticism, see Roland Kenneth Harrison, *Introduction to the Old Testament* (Grand Rapids: William B. Eerdmans, 1969), 12–13.
25 Thomas Kelly Cheyne, *Job and Solomon; or, The Wisdom of the Old Testament* (New York: Thomas Whittaker, 1889), 42–7, 71–5, 85.
26 Carol A. Newsom, *The Book of Job: A Contest of Moral Imaginations* (Oxford: Oxford University Press, 2003), 21.
27 F. D. E. Schleiermacher, *Introduction to the Dialogues of Plato*, trans. William Dobson (London: John William Parker, 1836), 5, 17. X BL 184 S341s, Brownings' Library, Armstrong Browning Library of Baylor University.
28 Hans-Georg Gadamer, *Truth and Method*, 2nd edn., trans. Joel Weinsheimer and Donald G. Marshall (New York: Continuum, 1975), 371.
29 See John Kenyon to EBB, n.d., Criticism on EBB's *A Drama of Exile*. L0128.1, Browning Collections, Armstrong Browning Library of Baylor University. See also John Kenyon to EBB, n.d. [1844], Criticism on EBB's *Poems* (1844). L0128.2, Browning Collections, Armstrong Browning Library of Baylor University.
30 Dieleman, *Religious Imaginaries*, 23–4, 49–50.
31 John Holloway, *The Victorian Sage: Studies in Argument* (London: Macmillan, 1953), 296; George P. Landow, *Elegant Jeremiahs: The Sage from Carlyle to Mailer* (Ithaca: Cornell University Press, 1986), 51.
32 EBB, A Drama of Exile, 1844, MS D0216, Browning Collections, Armstrong Browning Library of Baylor University. Subsequent references to this manuscript are cited parenthetically by page numbers.

33 See Gen. 2:16.
34 Donald S. Hair, *Fresh Strange Music: Elizabeth Barrett Browning's Language* (Montreal: McGill-Queen's University Press, 2015), 95.
35 Ricoeur, *The Symbolism of Evil*, trans. Emerson Buchanan (New York: Harper and Row, 1967), 321.
36 See Job 38:4-25.
37 See Gen. 2:19.
38 This tradition finds its roots in Gregory the Great's influential *Moralia in Job* (AD 595) and remained the dominant interpretation until Thomas Aquinas in the thirteenth century. See Susan Schreiner, *Where Shall Wisdom Be Found: Calvin's Exegesis of Job from Medieval and Modern Perspectives* (Chicago: University of Chicago Press, 1994), 49-72.
39 Stone, *Elizabeth Barrett Browning*, 83.
40 Scheinberg, *Women's Poetry and Religion*, 71.
41 John Milton, *Paradise Lost*. In *John Milton: Complete Poems and Major Prose*, ed. Merritt Y. Hughes (Indianapolis: Hackett, 2003), 5.540, 8.640. Subsequent references to Milton's epic poem come from this edition and are cited parenthetically in text.
42 William Blake, *The Marriage of Heaven and Hell*, ed. Michael Phillips (Oxford: Bodleian Library, 2011), 65.
43 The biblical precedent for this interpretation appears in the following passage: "For Adam was formed first, then Eve. And Adam was not deceived, but the woman being deceived was in the transgression" (1 Tim. 2:13-14).
44 See Lucy Aikin, *Epistles on Women, Exemplifying Their Character and Condition in Various Ages and Nations with Miscellaneous Poems* (London: J. Johnson & Co, 1810); see also Eliza Sharples qtd. in Barbara Taylor, *Eve and the New Jerusalem: Socialism and Feminism in the Nineteenth Century* (London: Virago Press, 1983), 146.
45 See, for example, the statements about Eve made by Tertullian, "The Apparel of Women," in *Disciplinary, Moral, and Aesthetical Works*, trans. and ed. Rudolph Arbesman, Sister Emily Joseph Daly, and Edwin A. Quain (New York: Fathers of the Church, 1959), 117; see also Augustine, *The Confessions, The City of God, On Christian Doctrine*, trans. J. F. Shaw (Chicago: William Benton, 1952), 628.
46 See Dieleman, "Ecotheological Relationships," 424-46. See also Melissa J. Brotton, "'Lost Angel in the Earth': Ecotheodicy in Elizabeth Barrett Browning's 'A Drama of Exile,'" in *Ecotheology in the Humanities: An Interdisciplinary Approach to Understanding the Divine and Nature*, ed. Melissa J. Brotton (Minneapolis: Lexington Books, 2015), 209-28.
47 See Kathyrn Schifferdecker, *Out of the Whirlwind: Creation Theology in the Book of Job* (Cambridge: Harvard University Press, 2008); see also Richard Bauckham, *The Bible and Ecology: Rediscovering the Community of Creation* (Waco: Baylor

University Press, 2010). Bauckham contextualizes the book of Job's divine speeches within a wider array of biblical traditions with ecotheological models.
48 Julie Melnyk, "'Mighty Victims': Women Writers and the Feminization of Christ," *Victorian Literature and Culture* 31, no. 1 (2003): 132.
49 Emma Mason, *Christina Rossetti: Poetry, Ecology, Faith* (Oxford: Oxford University Press, 2018), 183–7.
50 See Mt. 17:1-13; see also Lk. 9:26–38.
51 *The Greek New Testament*, ed. Kurt Aland et al., 3rd edn. (Stuttgart, West Germany: United Bible Societies, 1983); See also William F. Arndt and F. Wilbur Gingrich, *A Greek-English Lexicon of the New Testament and Other Early Christian Literature*, 2nd edn. (Chicago: University of Chicago Press, 1979), 428.
52 For a helpful summary of this kenotic Christology, see Wolfhart Pannenburg, *Jesus, God and Man*, trans. Lewis L. Wilkins and Duane A Priebe (Louisville: Westminster Press, 1977), 309–10.
53 See Ben Witherington, *Jesus the Sage: A Pilgrimage of Wisdom* (New York: Fortress Press, 1994), 259–60. The description of the suffering servant appears powerfully in Isa. 53:3-4.
54 Ricoeur, *The Symbolism of Evil*, 321–4.
55 Ludwig Feuerbach, *The Essence of Christianity*, trans. George Eliot (New York: Harper and Row, 1957), 61; William Blake, "Appendix to the Prophetic Books," in *Poetical Works*, ed. John Sampson (Oxford: Oxford University Press, 1913), 426.
56 Jürgen Moltmann, "God's Kenosis in the Creation and Consummation of the World," in *The Work of Love: Creation as Kenosis*, ed. John Polkinghorne (Grand Rapids: William B. Eerdmans, 2001), 142, 146, 149.
57 Rom. 8:22.
58 Herbert Tucker, "An Ebbigrammar of Motives; or, Ba for Short," *Victorian Poetry* 44, no. 4 (2006): 454.
59 On EBB's revisions, see the editorial note in *WEBB* 1: 68.
60 Herder, quoted in Robert Alter, *The Art of Biblical Poetry* (New York: Basil Books, 1985), 11.
61 Alter, *Biblical Poetry*, 28–9.
62 Alter, *The Art of Biblical Narrative* (New York: Basil Books, 1981), 12.
63 Edgar Allan Poe, Review of *A Drama of Exile and Other Poems*, in *The Broadway Journal* (January 4, 1845): 4–8. Reprinted in *The Brownings' Correspondence* vol. 10, ed. Philip Kelley and Scott Lewis (Winfield: Wedgestone, 1991), 349–57.
64 Christopher M. Keirstead, *Victorian Poetry, Europe, and the Challenge of Cosmopolitanism* (Columbus: Ohio State University Press, 2011), 65–89; Alison Chapman, *Networking the Nation: British and American Women's Poetry and Italy, 1840-1870* (Oxford: Oxford University Press, 2015), 91–115.

2

Wisdom's Footsteps: Heuristic Pathways and Proverbial Aphorisms in George MacDonald's *Phantastes*

Today, George MacDonald is most often remembered for his influence on the cluster of fantasy writers known as the Inklings—C. S. Lewis, in particular, singled out MacDonald as both a literary model and spiritual guide.[1] In his own time, MacDonald's writings circulated within a variety of Christian contexts, making them difficult to classify along denominational lines. Influenced by F. D. Maurice, MacDonald joined the Church of England in 1860, yet his frequent contributions to *Good Words* throughout the following decade, along with his subsequent editorship of *Good Words for the Young* (November 1869 to September 1872), place him within a more ecumenical context.[2] Moreover, his literary career began after he resigned from the pastorate of a Congregational church in Arundel (1851–3): the deacons charged him with heresy because of his reservations with the doctrine of hell, his speculations that animals might enter heaven, and his receptiveness to German biblical scholarship.[3] MacDonald's *Unspoken Sermons*, a series of spiritual reflections never delivered from the pulpit, display his sustained commitment to the discourse of preaching, as well as his conviction that religious teaching might be accomplished through other forms. Much as Elizabeth Barrett Browning's *A Drama of Exile* adapts the book of Job's poetic dialogues to awaken new ways of perceiving the postlapsarian world, as discussed in Chapter 1, so also MacDonald's sermon on "The Voice of Job" (1885) uses biblical wisdom poetry as a means of reframing the experience of religious revelation. In his reading of this book's divine speeches, MacDonald emphasizes that they appeal not to the "logical faculty" but "to the revealing, God-like imagination."[4] This distinction between the intellect and the imagination, informed by MacDonald's broadly Romantic philosophy, accords with the emphasis on wonder and creativity that distinguishes his own didactic voice.

MacDonald's ideas about creative wisdom emerge in nascent yet telling ways in his early work *Phantastes* (1858), a densely allusive story about the education of the imagination and the first of his fairy tales written for an adult audience. Published in October 1858 by Smith, Elder, and Company, *Phantastes* participates in the *bildungsroman* tradition of German Romanticism while also revising the medieval quest narrative. The story follows its first-person narrator, the aspiring poet Anodos, on a journey into fairyland, where he attempts to win his ideal lady, defeat the darkness within himself, and gain the honor of knighthood. MacDonald's use of aphoristic chapter epigraphs, many of which take the form of prudential maxims, puts his didactic tale within a broad tradition of wisdom writing, one that extends from the biblical Proverbs to Samuel Taylor Coleridge's *Aids to Reflection in the Formation of a Manly Character on the Several Grounds of Prudence, Morality, and Religion* (1825, hereafter, *Aids to Reflection*). Coleridge's volume consists of a series of sayings from English theologians, primarily the seventeenth-century thinkers Archbishop Robert Leighton and Dr. Henry More. Like Coleridge, whose writings on the imagination MacDonald very much admired, MacDonald makes extensive use of the aphorism, a form rooted in the proverbial wisdom tradition. And, like Coleridge, MacDonald engages intensively and self-reflexively with hermeneutical questions.

Building on previous scholarship that highlights the rich literary genealogy of *Phantastes*, my approach aims to illuminate MacDonald's interpretive model.[5] As much as *Phantastes* is a story about character formation, it is also a story about becoming an attentive reader. The book's chapter epigraphs foreground its dense intertextuality, including quotations from sources such as Percy Bysshe Shelley and Friedrich Schleiermacher—quotations that reflect MacDonald's eclectic engagement with British and German Romanticism. A similar emphasis on reading sustains the story's plot. The journey begins with a wish that Anodos voices while listening to a fairy tale read aloud, and his subsequent adventures are punctuated by encounters with other books. Midway through his quest, he discovers a library, where he reads a story that both foreshadows and catalyzes his own intellectual and spiritual development. As I propose, the many acts of reading that animate *Phantastes* anticipate the theoretical ideas that MacDonald later articulated in his essays "The Imagination: Its Functions and Its Culture" (1867) and "The Fantastic Imagination" (1893).[6] To unfold these connections, I put MacDonald into dialogue with Coleridge's writings on the higher criticism. As this context demonstrates, MacDonald's ideas about the right reading of fairy tales participate in consequential debates resulting from the advent of modern biblical scholarship. MacDonald follows Coleridge in reframing the concept of inspiration beyond limiting ideas of divine dictation. In so doing, they attempt to navigate a *via media* between devotional approaches to scripture and higher critical ideas.

For both Coleridge and MacDonald, the path to this middle way runs through biblical wisdom literature. Coleridge's *Confessions* challenges narrowly literalist modes of exegesis by citing the dialogic poetry of Job, as I have noted in this book's introduction. His earlier *Aids to Reflection* makes extensive use of the forms characteristic of Proverbs: its many sayings from British theologians range from pithy statements to narrative vignettes, intertwined with Coleridge's own commentary. Throughout *Phantastes*, MacDonald adapts these aphoristic forms not only to foreground intertextual dialogue but also to respond creatively to received wisdom traditions. These traditions are pointedly masculine, as underscored by Coleridge's titular reference to *"the Formation of a Manly Character,"* yet MacDonald's representations of wisdom in *Phantastes* ultimately suggest a more androgynous model of both humanity and divinity. Not unlike EBB, MacDonald responds to nineteenth-century debates about Christology in ways that portray Christ, the wisdom of God, as fully human in a sense that unsettles gender binaries. Yet whereas EBB's statements in her letters about the ongoing development of "the *poetry of Christianity*" outline the participatory model of religious revelation implicit in her creative work (*BC* 7:21), MacDonald explicitly theorizes such participation.

By situating *Phantastes* in relation to higher critical debates and analyzing its connections to biblical wisdom literature, I aim to provide a new context for understanding MacDonald's departure from Scotch Calvinism and embrace of German Romanticism. Recent scholarship has located MacDonald within and across the nineteenth-century's dynamic theological movements, demonstrating the need for renewed scholarly inquiry into work that has been oddly marginalized within mainstream literary studies, despite his high standing in the eyes of the Inklings.[7] In his spiritual autobiography *Surprised by Joy* (1955), Lewis championed *Phantastes* as the book that "baptized" his imagination, a sacramental metaphor that is at once deeply personal and richly suggestive of MacDonald's own ideas about reading as a pathway to redemption.[8] My discussion returns to *Phantastes* to reconsider the intellectual touchstones and literary styles that together inform MacDonald's invitational, even provocative, didactic fiction.

This chapter coordinates *Phantastes* with MacDonald's discussions of imagination and interpretation in subsequently published essays, along with relevant insights from his letters. MacDonald departs from the emphasis on recovering authorial intent prevalent in nineteenth-century hermeneutics, focusing instead on the reader's active and co-creative work. His uses of wisdom literature demonstrate his commitment to what Paul Ricoeur theorizes as language's "poetic function," which aims to "resdescrib[e] reality by the twisting pathway of heuristic fiction."[9] MacDonald works self-reflexively with motifs of wayfinding, signaled in his protagonist's very name. Derived from the Greek, *Anodos* may be translated as either "pathless" or "an upward path"—a fitting ambiguity, given his perambulatory yet productive travels, and a playful twist on the pathways metaphor used throughout Proverbs to signify character formation.[10] MacDonald's interpretive model at once recovers longstanding exegetical traditions about contemplative reading and responds to changing ideas about Christology catalyzed by the higher criticism. Far from advancing a fixed path to perfection, MacDonald highlights the need for ceaseless efforts to move insight into application.

From Letter to Spirit: MacDonald's Imaginative Responses to Biblical Higher Criticism

MacDonald's writings on the imagination take shape against the backdrop of a widespread Romantic recovery of wonder and mystery, as well as more specific theological controversies about biblical inspiration. In 1851, while still in the pastorate at Arundel, MacDonald published a privately printed translation of the *Spiritual Songs* (1802) of Novalis (Philipp Friedrich Freiherr von Hardenberg). Like many Romantics, Novalis turned to the fairy-tale form as a means of critiquing enlightenment rationalism, a pattern evident in eighteenth-century writers such as Johann Wolfgang von Goethe, Friedrich de la Motte Fouqué, and E. T. A. Hoffman. Nineteenth-century Britain was introduced to much of this literature through Thomas Carlyle's translations, beginning in the early 1820s and culminating in *German Romance: Specimens of Its Chief Authors with Biographical and Critical Notices* (1827). In his essay on "The Fantastic Imagination," MacDonald identified Fouqué's *Undine* (1811) as "the most beautiful" fairy tale (313), and his earlier essay on "The Imagination" expresses his admiration for Carlyle, whose translation of Hoffman's *The Golden Pot* (1814) has been identified by MacDonald's son and biographer Greville as an important influence on *Phantastes*.[11] While MacDonald and Carlyle share substantial common ground in their attempts to renegotiate their shared intellectual heritage of Calvinist theology, they differ significantly in their authorial voice.

As G. K. Chesterton put it in his introduction to MacDonald's biography, Carlyle retained "a touch of the bully" in his authoritarian temper and thus "could never have said anything so subtle and simple as MacDonald's saying that God is easy to please but hard to satisfy."[12] By alluding to this memorable aphorism, Chesterton calls attention to MacDonald's enchanting use of what Robert Alter, in his commentary on Proverbs, terms "a poetry of wit."[13]

MacDonald's use of wisdom literature constitutes a significant literary innovation. Carlyle's characteristic mode of prophetic utterance has been seen as paradigmatic for the model of Victorian sage writing that has long defined scholarly understanding of biblical allusion and literary authority in this period.[14] However, this model risks overshadowing the variety of biblical genres that Victorian writers transformed. Prophetic and wisdom literatures have distinctive formal qualities and differing theological emphases that took on new significance in light of higher critical debates about inspiration and revelation, as outlined more fully in this book's introduction. Even as MacDonald frequently uses the adjective "prophetic" to describe the poet's work, his biblical quotations in his essay on "The Imagination" reach beyond the prophetic tradition. To underscore the point that "a wise imagination, which is the presence of the spirit of God, is the very best guide that Man or woman can have," his essay on "The Fantastic Imagination" invokes the books of both Proverbs and Ecclesiastes to emphasize the hiddenness of divine things (41–2).[15] These books are often regarded as emerging from two distinct camps within the biblical wisdom tradition, one conservative and the other skeptical.[16] However, MacDonald's quotations underscore their shared dialectical model of revelation-in-concealment and concealment-in-revelation.

This use of proverbial aphorisms for creative, even ironic, ends puts MacDonald in the company of Romantic writers such as William Blake, whose "Proverbs of Hell" from *The Marriage of Heaven and Hell* (1790) underscores this form's subversive potentials. Blake's enigmatic statements such as "Shame is Pride's cloak" and "Prisons are built with stones of Law, Brothels with bricks of Religion" recall the images and inverted parallelism of the sayings in Proverbs, even as they challenge institutional religion. Moreover, Blake's insistence that "without contraries is no progression" intensifies the provocative qualities that later scholars such as Peter Hatton have identified as characteristic of the biblical Proverbs.[17] As Hatton contends, this book is far from a "complacent mouthpiece" for a conservative wisdom tradition but rather "crafted to encourage readers to question traditional wisdom and to develop their critical faculties."[18] Throughout his critical and creative writings, MacDonald adapts the form of the Hebrew *mashal*, which includes a range of utterances from proverbs to riddles to parables, to generate a didactic mode that relies less on authorial pronouncement than on readerly participation.

MacDonald similarly defies classification as either "orthodox" or "heterodox" in his complex attitude toward biblical interpretation. He retained traditional ideas about the authorship of the synoptic gospels and the authenticity of miracles, even as these ideas became widely questioned throughout the latter decades of the nineteenth century.[19] While MacDonald, unlike EBB, makes no mention throughout his correspondence or diaries of reading specific works of higher critical scholarship such as *Essays and Reviews* or *Das Leben Jesu*, he clearly engaged with the broader interpretive debates sparked by these controversial studies. His letters demonstrate a pronounced aversion to narrower models of inspiration upheld by many dissenting Protestants in defiance of higher critical claims. In a letter composed in 1866, he went so far as to say that "the common theory of the inspiration of the [Bible's] words" was "degrading and evil," claiming that this theory made believers into "idolaters of the Bible instead of disciples of Jesus."[20] This surprisingly vehement language echoes Coleridge's condemnation of the "indiscriminate Bibliolatry" that gives rise to "forced and fantastic interpretations," including "arbitrary Allegories and mystic explanations of Proper Names."[21] Against a literalist commitment to scripture's very words, Coleridge argues, "it is the spirit of the Bible, and not the detached words and sentences, that is infallible and absolute."[22] Both Coleridge and MacDonald advance a letter/spirit distinction reminiscent of the Pauline phrase in the second epistle to the Corinthians, ultimately affirming that the Word of God resides less in written testaments than in the living testimony of changed hearts.[23] Gisela H. Kreglinger effectively summarizes MacDonald's nuanced position regarding developments in biblical scholarship by characterizing him as "not opposed to historical-critical inquiry as such" but as one who "questioned an uncritical embrace of a scientific approach without considering its limitations in leading to knowledge of the transcendent."[24] This descriptor aligns with the distinctions between reason and imagination that MacDonald himself outlines in "The Imagination." He asserts that the imagination is "nourished by facts" but "refuses to regard science as the sole interpreter of nature, or the laws of science as the only region of discovery" (2). As this expansive construction implies, MacDonald, who had earned prizes in chemistry at Aberdeen University in 1845, aimed not to overturn scientific reason but to reposition it as one of many modes of apprehension. Citing both Novalis and Francis Bacon, he claims in this essay that reason operates in the "scientific region" of inquiry that produces "intellectual truth," whereas poetry reaches a "higher sphere" of "truth in beauty" (14–15). MacDonald describes this elevated sphere in terms that recall Coleridge's concepts of primary and secondary imagination as outlined in his *Biographia Literaria*. Coleridge explains that the primary imagination constitutes "a repetition in the finite mind of the eternal act of creation in the infinite I AM"; the secondary imagination is an act of human creation that is different in degree but not in kind.[25] So, too, MacDonald finds "the inspiration of the Almighty" at work in all human art, claiming that true art has "a larger origin than man alone," as it participates in a divine act of creation (25).

This model of the imagination helps to account for MacDonald's pointed reservations with the category of allegory, despite his appreciative recourse to several allegorical texts throughout *Phantastes*. In his later essay on "The Fantastic Imagination," MacDonald emphasizes that, though a fairy tale may include allegorical elements, it is itself "not an allegory" and claims that a "strict allegory" produces "a weariness to the spirit." According to MacDonald, "a genuine work of art must mean many things; the truer its art, the more things it will mean" (317). Read in the context of MacDonald's wider engagement with nineteenth-century hermeneutic debates, these remarks can be understood not as censuring a particular genre but as calling into question ideas about authorial intent. MacDonald's fairy tales depart from the explicit, controlled, and unitary model of allegory exemplified in John Bunyan's *Pilgrim's Progress* (1678)— though this particular model should hardly be conflated with all allegory. Indeed, MacDonald's emphasis on symbolic polysemy as integral to artistic excellence prizes the very playful, dynamic, and plastic qualities that Erich Auerbach traces in the etymology of both *typos* and *figura*. As Auerbach shows, a similar emphasis on plenitude characterized figural interpretation from Tertullian through Augustine. Auerbach explains that the allegorical interpretation practiced by many of the church fathers gave equal emphasis to historical and figurative qualities, though he notes that later exegetical schools aimed to "spirit away" the "historical character" of scriptural texts.[26] In nineteenth-century Britain, tensions between historical and figurative approaches to interpretation were exacerbated by the spread of biblical higher criticism.

MacDonald's comments underscore the extent to which *allegory* became a contested term in the wake of such interpretive debates. For instance, in the preface to *Das Leben Jesu*, Strauss emphatically sundered the "allegorical view" that he identifies with traditional Christian exegesis from his own "mythic method." He claims that "the allegorical view attributes the narrative to a supernatural source, whereas the mythical view ascribes it to that *natural* process by which legends are originated and developed."[27] Prior to Strauss, Coleridge had protested against the allegorical readings that he regarded as emptying the Bible of its imaginative power, albeit in different terms. *The Statesman's Manual* (1816) distinguishes between allegory and symbolism: in Coleridge's words, an allegory offers "but a translation of abstract notions into a picture language," whereas a symbol "always partakes of the Reality which it renders intelligible."[28] Another layer of complexity emerges by taking into account the distinction between fabulism and figuralism as allegorical modes. Fabulism, as Deborah L. Madsen explains it, restricts "the signifying capacity of words to a single meaning," presuming "a one-to-one semantic correspondence." By contrast, figuralism presents "a continuity among signs" that implies "the existence of a providential scheme" but "cannot make that scheme present to human knowledge" and thus allows for "a polyvalence of significance."[29] As this analysis shows, debates about allegorical interpretation pertain not only to ideas of intrinsic versus extrinsic meaning, as emphasized by Strauss and Coleridge, but also to singular versus plural meanings.

Perhaps most prominent among MacDonald's many allegorical intertexts is Edmund Spenser's *The Faerie Queene* (1590). As John Docherty highlights, MacDonald's turn to Spenser begins with his book's opening epigram, taken from Phineas Fletcher's *The Purple Island* (1633), an allegorical poem about the human body and mind, wherein "Phantastes" personifies the imagination: "Phantastes from 'their fount' all shapes deriving, / In new habiliments can quickly dight."[30] Fletcher's source, in turn, is Book 2 Canto 9 of *The Faerie Queene*, where King Arthur, Sir Guyon, and squire Palmer meet Phantastes in the castle of Alma. One of Alma's three counsellors, Phantastes, "could things to come foresee," yet despite possessing "a sharp foresight and working wit," he is also described as keeping the company of "idle thoughts and fantasies, / Devices, dreames, opinions unsound."[31] By contrast, MacDonald does not personify Phantastes but leaves the connection between the story's title and its content oblique. His few direct references to "phantasy" occur in conjunction with the protagonist's ardent desire for his ideal lady. As MacDonald's protagonist gradually relinquishes his narrower desires in favor of an expanded understanding of love, *Phantastes* traces the maturation of a more capacious imaginative faculty.

Responses to *Phantastes* from the British periodical press frequently drew attention to issues of narrative design and authorial intent, which MacDonald further addressed in his essays. While *Phantastes* contributed to the growth of MacDonald's literary reputation and attracted favorable attention from Charles Dodgson (Lewis Carroll), with whom he later became close friends, most reviews were mixed at best. The reviewer for the *Athenaeum* concluded that MacDonald had "attempted an allegory" but failed, claiming that whereas "allegory shows us life moving with its shadow," MacDonald's work "has given us the shadow without the life."[32] Deeming *Phantastes* "a riddle that will not be read," this reviewer implies that an allegory should unfold according to two levels of meaning, connected via a single and stable interpretive key—that is, in a narrowly fabulistic mode. Likewise, a reviewer for the *Spectator* who commented that parts of MacDonald's story "appear to be allegorical" yet cannot be interpreted "satisfactorily" presumes that an allegory should be easily decipherable.[33] The *British Quarterly Review* similarly highlights the book's enigmatic qualities and lack of an explicit narrative code, observing that the reader must "dimly interpret" the protagonist's adventures "without feeling at all sure that Mr. MacDonald or Anodos himself saw them in the same light."[34] According to the interpretive model advanced in "The Fantastic Imagination," such ambiguity is not accidental but essential. Anticipating the reader's query "how am I to assure myself that I am not reading my own meaning into it, but yours out of it?" MacDonald responds, "It may be better that you should read your meaning into it. That may be a higher operation of your intellect than the mere reading of mine out of it: your meaning may be superior to mine" (316–17).

This emphasis on readerly agency takes the interpretive model suggested in Coleridge's *Confessions* to its logical conclusion. Coleridge identifies the disposition of "seek[ing] truth ... with humble spirit" as a precondition for a true encounter with "the Word of God." At the same time, he emphasizes that the reader's work of searching must be guided by the divine spirit that imbues "the organ and instrument of all the gifts, powers, and tendencies, by which the individual is privileged to rise above himself—to leave behind, and lose his individual phantom self, in order to find his true self in that distinctness where no division can be—in the Eternal I AM, the ever-living WORD."[35] Similarly, MacDonald claims that because the raw material of all human expression consists of "God's things, his embodied thoughts," a writer "cannot help his words and figures falling into such combinations in the mind of another as he himself had not foreseen" (320). Unlike Schleiermacher, who both acknowledges the difficulty of recovering authorial intent and maintains its paramount importance, MacDonald repositions both author and reader in relation to a divine significance that infuses all symbolic language yet remains imperfectly grasped.[36] For MacDonald, then, the goal of interpretation is not to retrieve a text's original significance but to participate in a heuristic process of readerly self-discovery.

Readerly Self-discovery in *Phantastes*

MacDonald's readiness to affirm the potential superiority of other interpretations, over and against his authorial intent, reflects the epistemic humility and disposition of openness he regarded as integral to wisdom writing. Throughout "The Imagination," MacDonald privileges the reader's ongoing, exploratory activity. This heuristic process is encoded in his very literary forms, from the Socratic dialogue embedded within his essays to the aphorisms and interpolated narratives incorporated throughout *Phantastes*. Evoking a range of sources from Coleridge's *Aids to Reflection* to Francis Bacon's *The Advancement of Learning* (1605), MacDonald prioritizes wonder as both the origin and the purpose of human thought. These sources underscore the dialogism inherent in aphoristic expressions. According to Bacon, the form of the aphorism itself resists intellectual hubris: whereas methods "dress up the sciences into bodies, and make men imagine that they have them complete," aphorisms "carry with them an invitation to others for adding and lending their assistance."[37] Or, to put it in Ricoeur's words, "the aphorism suggests at the same time that everything has already been said enigmatically and yet that it is always necessary to begin everything and to begin it again in the dimension of thinking."[38] MacDonald's use of aphoristic forms, which open toward the reader, accords with his overall emphasis on cultivating wonder.

Wonder emerges as a unifying theme throughout the loosely connected episodes comprising *Phantastes*. Anodos describes himself as experiencing "a chronic condition of wonder" that renders him "like a child" as he takes his first steps in this magical realm, but his sojourn soon requires him to confront threats of disenchantment from without and within (24). Although he receives repeated warnings about the destructive forces seeking to ensnare him, he maintains a cavalier and unfounded confidence in his ability to protect himself. The story's main events are set in motion by his discovery of a beautiful marble statue of a woman, whom he sings into life—a clear echoing of the Pygmalion and Galatea story of classical mythology, which MacDonald signals in this chapter's opening epigraph from Thomas Lovell Beddoes's "Pygmalion" (1825), a retelling of this myth. The more ardently Anodos pursues his ideal lady, the more obscured his judgment becomes. He is seduced by the maid of the Alder tree, who deceives him in the guise of his sought-after woman, and he only narrowly escapes destruction by the Ash, thanks to an unknown knight. For much of the remaining story, Anodos is haunted by the Shadow, a darkness presented as both a moral consequence of his succumbing to these destructive forces and a perceptual deadening to the beauty around him.

Anodos discovers the "dark figure" that becomes his shady companion when he enters a cottage in the forest, finds a mysterious door, and follows his irresistible desire "to see what was beyond it," despite clear warnings against doing so. As a menacing ogre tells him, anyone who has "met one in the forest" such as Anodos has met is sooner or later likely to be found by his Shadow. While this remark about Anodos's encounter with the Alder associates the Shadow with sexual transgression, the Shadow's domain is both sensual and intellectual. As Anodos continues his journey, he finds himself depending on the Shadow's capacity "to disenchant," deceiving himself into believing that it "does away with all appearances and shows [him] things in their true colour and form" (64). Subsequent events, however, show that it functions not to reveal but to destroy. Not long afterwards, Anodos meets a young girl, described as being on the threshold of womanhood, who carries a magical and musical globe. He befriends her and becomes intrigued by the globe, though she cautions him that he must be gentle with it. Incited by the Shadow, Anodos seizes the globe, repeatedly and forcibly touching it until it breaks in his hands and the maiden flees in tears. Literary critics tend to read this incident primarily as a moment of sexual violation, underscoring its clear erotic overtones. Yet Anodos's words about his irresistible desire "to know about the globe" suggest something in addition to carnal passion: they recall the avaricious curiosity that led to his discovery of the Shadow in the first place (66). The destruction of the maiden's musical globe by the clumsy and all-too-analytical Anodos anticipates MacDonald's remarks about how not to handle fairy tales in "The Fantastic Imagination." Reflecting on his own poetics, he remarks, "If there be music in my reader, I would gladly wake it," and concludes that such awakening requires a gentle hand: "The best way with music, I imagine, is not to bring the forces of our intellect to bear on it, but to be still and let it work on that part of us for whose sake it exists. We spoil countless precious things by our intellectual greed" (328).

As the story progresses, Anodos finds freedom from the Shadow—and leaves behind the intellectual greed it betokens—through an encounter with a book. Following the incident with the girl and the globe, he discovers an abandoned boat and drifts away until he arrives at the uninhabited palace of the Fairy Queen, where his Shadow is unable to follow him. He spends several days immersed in the palace library, where he "read, and read, until weary; if that can be designated a weariness, which was rather the faintness of rapturous delight" (79). As Anodos explains, this delight emerges from an oddly immersive experience, wherein he finds himself inside whatever text he picks up: "I took the place of the character who was most like myself, and his story was mine" (80). MacDonald thus offers a fascinating twist on Schleiermacher's imperative that the interpreter put himself "in the place of the author."[39] By putting the reader in the place not of the author but of the character, MacDonald shifts attention from textual origins to readerly experiences. Right interpretation, then, requires more than simply discerning accurate information: it is a transformative process. MacDonald dramatizes this model of interpretation when Anodos recounts in detail one particular book: the story of Cosmo von Wehrstahl, the Princess von Hohenweiss, and an enchanted looking glass. In addition to foreshadowing the events to come, this story prompts Anodos to see himself anew. Much like *Phantastes* itself, this interpolated narrative is a story of magic and maturation. Cosmo, a poor but noble university student in Prague, purchases a beautiful mirror from an antique shop. When he takes it home, he discovers its capacity to beautify his chamber: rather than offering "mere representation," the mirror transfigures the things that it reflects "out of the region of fact into the realm of art" (96). Gazing into its depths, Cosmo sees "the graceful form of a woman, clothed all in white," though he is unable to communicate with her (96). He becomes fascinated by this figure and begins to regard the mirror as his "secret treasure," likened to a miser's "golden hoard" (99). He learns incantations that allow him to speak with the woman, who tells him that she is under a spell and implores him to set her free by breaking the mirror. Cosmo hesitates, unwilling to give up his only means of contact with the princess. When he attempts to destroy the mirror with his sword, the glass simply vanishes. He then searches for the mirror, ultimately succeeding in breaking it but becoming fatally wounded in the process. Just before his death, he reunites with the princess, and they affirm their love for each other.

Without directly remarking the similarities between Cosmo's desire for the Princess von Hohenweiss and his own yearning for the white lady, Anodos seems, albeit dimly, to perceive these connections. He calls it "a simple story of ordinary life … wherein two souls, loving each other and longing to come nearer, do, after all, but behold each other as in a glass darkly" (91). In addition to evoking the first epistle to the Corinthians (1 Cor. 13:12 "For now we see through a glass darkly; but then face to face"), Anodos echoes Cosmo's remarks about his inability to approach the princess: "how many who love never come nearer than to behold each other as in a mirror; seem to know and yet never know the inward life?" (101). Taken together, these images suggest that the mirror in the story pertains not just to limited knowledge but also to a limiting idea of love.

Some time after Anodos leaves the library, he effectively recapitulates Cosmo's act of the breaking the mirror. Resolving to shatter his own illusions, he ceases to speak of the lady as if she were his, remarking, "I no longer called her to myself *my* white lady" (127). The magic mirror, then, both reflects the alluring power of the imagination and reveals the error of conflating possession with intimacy.

In addition to the more obvious psychodynamic readings invited by this symbolism, MacDonald's magic mirror suggests his commitment to an interpretive model focused on illuminating the reader's inner life. This method of reading has much in common with the *lectio divina* tradition as practiced by St. Ignatius of Loyola, as Daniel Gabelman has shown.[40] Broadly speaking, MacDonald might be situated within the long-standing scripture-as-mirror tradition that Jean Louis Chrétien identifies as informing exegetes from St. Augustine to Karl Barth. According to this tradition, "one discovers Revelation only by being discovered by Revelation."[41] Similarly, Anodos in *Phantastes* experiences himself less as reading than as being read: he explains that the book "glowed and flashed the thoughts upon the soul, with such a power that the medium disappeared from the consciousness" (90). These images align with MacDonald's later description of his own fairy stories as a flashing firefly, a delicate creature that invites those who behold it "not to bring the forces of our intellect to bear on it, but to be still and let it work on that part of us for whose sake it exists" ("The Fantastic Imagination" 328). A similar reversal of subject / object positions informs Coleridge's interpretive theory. The analogy of looking in a mirror underpins both the title and content of *Aids to Reflection*, and the later *Confessions* develops this metaphor in relation to biblical exegesis. Coleridge emphasizes that it is readers who are discovered by the truth, and not the other way around: as Coleridge puts it, "in the Bible there is more, *that finds me*" than "in all other books put together."[42] In addition to these Coleridgean influences, another useful point of comparison for MacDonald's model of revelation can be found in the work of Søren Kierkegaard. Though untranslated and unknown to MacDonald, Kierkegaard's work engages with overlapping philosophical and mystical contexts, as Stephen Prickett has noted.[43] More specifically, Kierkegaard's recourse to the scripture-as-mirror tradition to defend a subjectivist model of reading usefully illuminates MacDonald's parallel emphasis on application as a hermeneutic principle.

Kierkegaard's *For Self-Examination* (1851) meditates on the first chapter of the Epistle of James, which exhorts readers to meaningful action. The apostle declares, "if any be a hearer of the word, and not a doer, he is like unto a man beholding his natural face in a glass: for he beholdeth himself, and goeth his way, and straightway forgetteth what manner of man he was" (Jas. 1:23-24).[44] Working with this comparison, Kierkegaard calls attention to the imperative to see oneself in the mirror, as opposed to simply looking at the mirror as an object.[45] As Chrétien explains, Kierkegaard's commitment to such self-reflective reading does not reject higher critical scholarship altogether but rather "inaugurates a doctrine of the 'double truth' of the Bible" as both "a historical and literary document" and "the timeless and living Word of God."[46] Kierkegaard underscores the imperative for this approach to reading by recalling the parable told by the prophet Nathan to King David, following his adultery with Bathsheba and murder of Uriah. Kierkegaard argues that David's initial response, to condemn the actions of the man in the parable, indicates that he has understood Nathan's tale merely in an objective way; it is only upon hearing Nathan's rebuking words that he himself is that man that his understanding truly begins.[47]

In *Phantastes*, Anodos appears at first to be rather like the man described in the book of James, who gazes at himself and then immediately forgets what he looks like. Only after experiencing multiple moments of recognition does he undergo the kind of transformation that Kierkegaard theorizes. After the story of Cosmo concludes but before Anodos leaves the Fairy Queen's palace, he comes face to face with his own Princess von Hohenweiss—the white lady he has been pursuing. This time, she appears as one of many marble statues in the palace's music hall. He sings to her of his longing love and, in defiance of a prohibition inscribed near the statues ("TOUCH NOT!"), embraces her; she then springs to life, rebukes him, and flees. Anodos pursues her, only to find himself abruptly transported to a desolate hill. Through a series of uncanny returns, he is given additional opportunities to relinquish his possessive hold on his ideal—that is, to do what Cosmo did in the story when he broke the mirror. Anodos thereby grows into a greater understanding of love, one that allows him not only to abide with his longing for the unattainable lady but also to reframe this desire less as lack than as fullness.

Surprised by Love: MacDonald's Incarnational Theology

Following the interpolated narrative, the remaining episodes in *Phantastes* show the protagonist's incremental, imperfect attempts to manifest this greater love. Expelled from the fairy palace for his disobedience, Anodos moves through desolation to consolation. He descends a rocky chasm into a "pandemonium of fairy devils," beset by goblin-like creatures who taunt him, "you shan't have her; you shan't have her; he! he! he! She's for a better man." This "battery of malevolence" ignites "a spark of nobleness" within Anodos, who responds, "Well, if he is a better man, let him have her"—and immediately the goblins fall silent (128). After he leaves the subterranean realm, he learns that the woman he adores does indeed love someone else, none other than unknown knight who had rescued him from the Ash and the Alder. This discovery challenges his erotic impulses, though he still describes himself as "loving the white lady as [he] had never loved her before" (150). He gains the honor of knighthood through bravery in battle but again becomes overtaken by his Shadow, who imprisons him in a high tower. In an unexpected turn, he is rescued by the very maiden whose globe he had broken—now a mature woman and an artist in her own right. Humbled, the newly freed Anodos offers himself as a squire to the white lady's knight, devoted to him "because she loved him" (179). Ultimately, Anodos dies to protect him, thus ending his adventures in fairyland and beginning his return to everyday life.

As MacDonald presents it, this romantic quest is at once fanciful and profound. Anodos continues to narrate even after he dies, effectively attending his own funeral, where he observes, "the knight, and the lady I loved, wept over me. Her tears fell on my face" (189). It is difficult to interpret this scene as anything other than "a comic parody of an adolescent fantasy," to use Docherty's words—an excessive pathos that overflows into bathos.[48] What might otherwise be presented as a noble self-sacrifice becomes tinged with irony and even absurdity. Even so, the protagonist's subsequent reflections achieve a noteworthy gravitas:

> I knew now, that it is by loving, and not by being loved, that one can come nearest the soul of another; yea, that where two love, it is the loving of each other, and not the being loved by each other, that originates and perfects and assures their blessedness. I knew that love gives to him that loveth, power over any soul beloved, even if that soul know him not, bringing him inwardly close to that spirit; a power that cannot be but for good; for in proportion as selfishness intrudes, the love ceases, and the power which springs therefrom dies. Yet all love will, one day, meet with its return. All true love will, one day, behold its own image in the eyes of the beloved, and be humbly glad. (191)

Departing from his habitual narrative voice, Anodos offers what is almost a homily on the virtues of love, both as foreshadowed in the book he read in the library and as realized in his own experiences. His adventures resemble those from the story, with one striking discrepancy: unlike Cosmo, Anodos never gets the satisfaction of hearing the lady say that she returns his love. Still, what he experiences is not a tidy progression from *eros* to *agape*. His words imply the continuation of romantic desire, reframed in relation to a love that encompasses and exceeds it.

MacDonald's archaisms ("loveth" and "yea") approximate the diction of the King James Bible, recalling not only the first epistle to the Corinthians, with its hopeful affirmation that the imperfect state of seeing "through a glass, darkly" will ultimately be replaced by the clarity of beholding "face to face" (1 Cor. 13:12), but also the statements in the Johannine Epistles about the power of perfect love: "Beloved, let us love one another: for love is of God; and every one that loveth is born of God, and knoweth God. He that loveth not knoweth not God; for God is love .... No man hath seen God at any time. If we love one another, God dwelleth in us, and his love is perfected in us" (1 Jn 4:7-8, 12). MacDonald's sustained reflections on this passage emerge in his letters, as he invokes this passage even more directly to articulate a distinctly relational theology:

> Blessed be the God that makes us love each other. Is that not part of the meaning of the God of Love? It is the one thing he cares about. I see more and more into the religion there is in our relation to our fellow-men. I come nearer to understanding that if a man does not love his brother he cannot love God.

MacDonald sees divine presence as realized through human fellowship—more, loving human fellowship becomes a prerequisite for spiritual understanding. Once again, his theology follows that found in Coleridge's *Confessions*, which opens by entreating readers to proceed "without the servile fear that prevents or overclouds the free honor that cometh from Love" and cites the same biblical source text.[49] For Coleridge, as for MacDonald, divine wisdom is inextricable from divine love.

These intertexts help to illuminate MacDonald's incarnational theology. During the nineteenth century, the doctrine of the incarnation achieved new prominence, a theological trend that Timothy Larsen explains as contributing to the Victorian fascination with Christmas.[50] MacDonald's interest in this holiday can be seen, for instance, in his review of Robert Browning's *Christmas-Eve and Easter-Day: A Poem*. Despite this review's springtime publication (May 1853 in the *Monthly Christian Spectator*), it focuses exclusively on the Christmas element. "Christmas-Eve" features a speaker who goes on a supernatural nocturnal journey from a British dissenting chapel to a Roman basilica and finally to a German lecture-hall—a journey not utterly unlike that of Ebenezer Scrooge in Charles Dickens's *A Christmas Carol* (1843). In this process, Browning's speaker moves from a satirical rejection of what he sees as misguided exegesis to a more sympathetic recognition of all interpretations as imperfect or incomplete, from the allegorical readings advanced by the preacher who finds in the Baker's "dream of Baskets Three" in Genesis chapter 40 proof of "the doctrine of the Trinity" to the historical claims advanced by "the hawk-nosed high-cheek-boned Professor," an obvious caricature of the German higher critics.[51] What prompts this recognition is the speaker's surprising discovery of Jesus everywhere he goes. MacDonald's review calls attention not only to the pathos that Browning accomplishes through his comic style but also to Browning's ideas about the incarnation. Extrapolating from Browning, MacDonald insists, "the only proof of Christ's divinity is his humanity. Because his humanity is not comprehended, his divinity is doubted; and while the former is uncomprehended, an assent to the latter is of little avail."[52] His reflections express what he had privately suggested in more emphatic terms in a letter composed the very same month that this review saw publication: "the first thing is to know Jesus as a man, and any theory about him that makes less of him as a man—with the foolish notion of exalting his divinity—I refuse at once." He continues, "far rather would I be such a Unitarian as Dr. Channing than such a Christian as by far the greatest number of those that talk about his Divinity are."[53] Such remarks underscore the extent to which MacDonald's ideas about divine immanence esteemed the full humanity of Jesus.

While these theological contexts stand at some remove from *Phantastes*, MacDonald's reference to his story as a fairy tale for the Christmas season, as he described it in a subsequent letter to his father, places it in proximity to the holiday that inspired Browning's dramatic monologue.[54] Even more than "Christmas-Eve," *Phantastes* presents its epiphanic moments as part of an ongoing process. MacDonald's fairy tale depicts several instances in which Anodos meets an incarnation of Wisdom or Sophia, all of them female. Perhaps the most striking of these representations is the maiden with the globe, whom Bonnie Gaarden characterizes as MacDonald's representation of the "God within" that Anodos himself realizes in greater depth as he grows into a greater understanding of love.[55] In an uncanny and surprising return to what might have initially seemed to be a thinly veiled sexual conquest, the young girl whose treasure Anodos destroyed becomes his deliverer. Imprisoned by his Shadow in a high tower, Anodos is startled by "the sound of a woman singing," a sound likened to "an incarnation of Nature," and this melody shows him the way out of prison. His rescuer recalls their prior meeting, but instead of rebuking him for shattering her globe, she declares that she owes him "many thanks for breaking it"—through this loss, she found her ability to sing (173–4). As this turn of events underscores, the young woman is more than the mere object of his sexual curiosity. Rather like Anodos—and like Cosmo in the interpolated narrative—she moves away from a fetishistic obsession with an idealized object (her globe) and toward an integrated realization of this ideal. If, as Gaarden suggests, this young woman is a goddess, then she is a divinity in process, one who illuminates the spiritual and artistic maturation to which Anodos himself aspires.

As Anodos beholds "the face of the child, glorified in the countenance of the woman," this transfiguration makes him feel "ashamed and humbled." But his epiphany is at once discomforting and liberating. No sooner does he admit to himself, "I have failed … I have lost myself—would it had been my shadow," than his wish is granted: "I looked round … the shadow was nowhere to be seen. Ere long, I learned that it was not myself, but only my shadow, that I had lost." Reflecting on his experiences, he realizes that his former preoccupation with heroism had been tainted by an underlying narcissism: "my life had consisted in a vain attempt to behold, if not my ideal in myself, at least myself in my ideal" (176). He overcomes this solipsism not as an honored knight but, rather, as a lowly squire. When Anodos reaches the end of his journey, he concludes that his ultimate triumph resulted from a surprising reversal: "Thus I, who set out to find my Ideal, came back rejoicing that I had lost my Shadow" (195). Read in the context of MacDonald's expansive Christianity, this inversion of finding and losing recalls the words attributed to Jesus in the gospel of Matthew: "He that findeth his life shall lose it: and he that loseth his life for my sake shall find it" (Mt. 10:39). In the absence of a single Christ figure, *Phantastes* presents its protagonist as experiencing such a dynamic crossing as a result of meeting many incarnations of wisdom. This transformation occurs as Anodos learns to bring himself into accord with an indwelling divine music.

"Divine Harmonies Within": Tuning the Music of the Heart

Throughout *Phantastes*, the protagonist's emotional and spiritual maturation becomes measured through his songs. Anodos is first and foremost an aspiring poet—and when Mary Elizabeth Coleridge, the great grand-niece of Samuel Taylor Coleridge, published the volumes of poetry *Fancy's Following* (1896) and *Fancy's Guerdon* (1897) she took his name as her pseudonym. At the start of his adventures, Anodos has much to learn both as a man and as an artist. He yields to the temptation of the disguised Alder maid, though even then he vaguely notes that, despite her pleasing appearance, something in the sound of her voice "did not vibrate harmoniously with the beat of [his] inward music" (45). As he develops both his ethical sensibilities and his artistic talent, MacDonald explores in fairy-tale form the ideas that he later spelled out in his essay on "The Imagination": that the purpose of the imagination is to become in tune with "divine harmonies within" (35–6).

MacDonald uses the language of music and poetry to develop what he regarded as a fundamental contrast between persuasion and enchantment. A writer must "spare no logical pains" if his aim is "logical conviction," but the writer who aims to stir the "music" in his reader must instead "move by suggestion" ("The Fantastic" 321). The poetic interludes woven throughout *Phantastes* exemplify such suggestive power, introducing recurring motifs while also calling attention to that which exceeds translation into language. MacDonald's use of poetic language accords with Ricoeur's concept of a metaphor as "more than a figure of style" but as a semantic innovation capable of redescribing and even redefining reality.[56] For MacDonald, artistic expressions have the capacity to awaken new modes of perception.

Anodos describes the first of the story's love poems as a "strange sweet song" that he can neither fully understand nor put into words (30). In this episode, Anodos finds sanctuary from the Ash and the Alder in the shelter of a Beech, partly a woman and partly a tree. As she shelters him during a storm, she sings to Anodos, who renders her lyrics as follows:

> I saw thee ne'er before;
> I see thee never more;
> But love, and help, and pain, beautiful one,
> Have made thee mine, till all my years are done. (30)

He reflects that he "cannot put more of it into words," yet these enigmatic lines foreshadow the intense desire that later infuses his own poetry. As Anodos himself learns, a momentary meeting can produce a lasting longing, and his own experiences with "love, and help, and pain" prompt him to reconsider what it means to call his beloved his own.

Not long after leaving the Beech, Anodos discovers the marble statue, and his efforts to sing her into being show both his intensifying passion and its changing tenor. As if attempting to penetrate the dreams of this "vainly sleeping" woman, he progresses from the gentle charm, "Hear my voice come through the golden / Mist of memory and hope" to the desperate, even threatening, imperative, "Awake! or I shall perish here; / And thou be never more alone, / My form and I for ages near" (37–9). When he discovers her statue once more in the fairy palace, his lyrics reach new heights of sensual imagery, yet still he remains fixated on his own satisfaction. His rapturous catalogue of the woman's beauty from feet to forehead finally expires in the frustrated, almost inarticulate, exclamation: "Woman, ah! thou art victorious / And I perish, overfond" (122). Infused with the language of conquest and dying from unrequited desire, his orgasmic crescendo remains decidedly one-sided.

His tune changes, however, following his expulsion from the fairy palace. Repenting of his relentless gaze and forcible seizure of the lady's hand, he sings to himself, "In thy lady's gracious eyes / Look not thou too long" and "Come not thou too near the maid, / Clasp her not too wild"—a warning against intemperance that recalls not only what happened in the palace hall but also his encounter with the maiden and the globe (130). He repositions his experience of desire, apostrophizing his ideal lady, "If a nobler waits for thee, / I will weep aside." Turning back to his own heart, he reassures himself that the very decision to relinquish his dream has in itself at least some potency: "to yield it lovingly / Is a something still" (129). Unwilling to let go of love, he resolves to try letting go through love—but, as the conditional syntax ("If") underscores, this idea has not yet been tested. It is not until his later travels, and his encounter with another manifestation of wisdom, figured as a wise old woman, that he confronts this hypothesis as a reality. Here again, his experiences can be rendered only through poetry, sung not by Anodos but by the woman herself.

Through its blend of ecstasy, grief, and resolution, the old woman's song integrates conflicting elements into a harmonious, if paradoxical, whole:

> O light of dead and of dying days!
> O Love! in thy glory go,
> In a rosy mist and a moony maze,
> O'er the pathless peaks of snow.
> But what is left for the cold grey soul,
> That moans like a wounded dove?
> One wine is left in the broken bowl—
> 'Tis—*To love, and love, and love.* (150)

While the first four lines recall the imagery of erotic expiring that had infused Anodos's earlier songs, the following lines transfigure loss and mortality into urgent generosity. Evoking the final chapter of Ecclesiastes, with its exhortation to remember the Creator "before the golden bowl be broken" (Eccl. 12:6), the declaration "One wine is left in the broken bowl" finds joy, even pleasure, within this finite experience insofar as it becomes the site of active love. Subsequent lines similarly echo the pictures and patterns of biblical wisdom literature:

> Better to sit at the waters' birth,
> Than a sea of waves to win;
> To live in the love that floweth forth
> Than the love that cometh in. (150)

The "better ... than" structure recalls the inverted parallelism frequently used throughout Proverbs to establish memorable contrasts, as in dictums such as "Better *it is* to *be* of an humble spirit with the lowly, than to divide the spoil with the proud" and "Better *is* a little with righteousness than great revenues without right" (Prov. 16:8, 19). Furthermore, the metaphor of love as an uncontainable sea recalls Song of Songs 8:7 ("Many waters cannot quench love, neither can the floods drown it: if a man would give all the substance of his house for love, it would be utterly contemned"). As this allusion to the Bible's most forcefully erotic poetry emphasizes, MacDonald's sense of divine love is both soulful and sensual.

As these poems underscore, *Phantastes* anticipates the artistic strategies developed throughout MacDonald's later writings for children. The many incarnations of Wisdom throughout this story have archetypal similarities to the figures who populate his other fairy tales. And, though the love poems of *Phantastes* are both more erotically charged and more stylistically developed than the nonsense verse embedded in stories such as *At the Back of the North Wind* and *The Princess and the Goblin*, they serve similar functions. The third edition of *Phantastes*, a commemorative edition published by Arthur C. Fairfield the year MacDonald died (1905) and overseen by MacDonald's son Greville, underscores the continuities among MacDonald's fairy tales for child and grown-up audiences by featuring illustrations by Arthur Hughes, who had previously worked with MacDonald on *At the Back of the North Wind* (1869–70) *and The Princess and the Goblin* (1870–1).[57] As Katharine Bubel suggests, MacDonald's "relational and multi-dimensional wisdom," figured through his many wise old woman figures, offers an alternative to "the Cartesian way of knowing."[58] MacDonald emphasizes that divine things exceed human knowledge, a theological point underscored throughout his first series of *Unspoken Sermons* (1867), including his address on "The Higher Faith" that praised "the faith of ignorant but hoping children, who know that they do not know."[59] As MacDonald's eclectic recourse to Romantic philosophy and literature underscores, cultivating such wise ignorance requires a setting aside of worldly wisdom in pursuit of the divine foolishness epitomized in the incarnation.

MacDonald's use of a seemingly simple form such as the fairy tale to address complex theological issues puts him in the company of many Romantic and post-Romantic writers who sought to dissolve conventional oppositions between innocence and experience. *Phantastes* opens with the protagonist celebrating his twenty-first birthday, eager to step into his full legal rights in the world of men; to reach full maturation, however, he must first return to a state of childlike wonder in fairy land. Troubling the distinction between childhood and adulthood was an important part of the Victorian fairy tale's cultural work, and many such texts, from William Makepeace Thackeray's *The Rose and the Ring* (1854) to Oscar Wilde's *A House of Pomegranates* (1891), addressed themselves to multiple audiences. As MacDonald himself put it, "I do not write for children, but for the childlike, whether of five, or fifty, or seventy-five" ("The Fantastic Imagination" 317). MacDonald's esteem for this childlike state might appear to uphold a conventional dichotomy between faith and doubt, privileging the child's naïve belief as a form of religious propaganda. And yet, as Aubrey Plourde has shown, what seems at first to be a tidy narrative progression—one that reverses a secularizing trajectory from faith to doubt—becomes in MacDonald's fiction something much more complicated. Plourde's analysis of *The Princess and the Goblin* demonstrates that his narrative strategies suspend linear teleology, offering "a retheorization of doubt as an active and ongoing component in the fluid process of faith."[60] The earlier *Phantastes* similarly mobilizes a kind of productive doubt, foregrounding the search for wisdom not despite but through the experience of unknowing.

Even as Anodos achieves significant insight as a result of his travels in fairyland, his return to life in his own world finds him uncertain about next steps. He ponders, "Could I translate the experience of my travels there, into common life? This was the question. Or must I live it all over again, and learn it all over again, in the other forms that belong to the world of men? These questions I cannot yet answer" (194). His very readiness to question himself demonstrates his maturation beyond the cavalier overconfidence in his own abilities that led him into trouble in the first place. MacDonald's story of spiritual development thus aligns with Coleridge's affirmation in *Aids to Reflection* that "Christianity is not Theory, or a Speculation; but a *Life*. Not a *Philosophy* of Life, but a Life and a living Process."[61] For Coleridge, as for MacDonald, the soul's growth cannot be reduced to a formula. Against the stagnation of certitude, whether dogmatism or rationalism, MacDonald sees Christianity in terms of a mystery that, though fully revealed, remains incompletely understood. With its reader-oriented didacticism, *Phantastes* pursues what MacDonald later described in his essay on "The Imagination" as "the end of education." Challenging those "in whose notion education would seem to consist in the production of a certain repose," he insists, "repose is not the end of education; its end is a noble unrest, an ever-renewed awaking from the dead, a ceaseless questioning of the past for the interpretation of the future, an urging on of the motions of life, which had better far be accelerated into fever, than retarded into lethargy" (1). MacDonald reclaims embodied expressions of desire and even doubt as integral to wisdom, experienced an endless search.

MacDonald's resistance to dogmatic expressions of religious precepts did not always sit well with his Christian contemporaries. In "A Word to George Eliot and George MacDonald" (1875), the Presbyterian critic George McCrie denounced both writers for the portrayals of Calvinism in each of their fictional works, claiming that these representations demonstrate "an insidious strain of heresy" that attempts "to undermine evangelical religion." While today's literary critics are unlikely to agree with McCrie's conclusions, his identification of MacDonald and Eliot as "belonging to the same school" indicates that habitual classifications of the period's writers as alternatively religious or secular risk obscuring important commonalities among those who held different belief positions.[62] The theological differences between these two writers coexist with their shared recovery of biblical wisdom literature as a means of challenging unthinking religious platitudes. As the next chapter will show, even as Eliot concurred with the higher critical studies that called attention to issues of historical accuracy within the gospel accounts, she adapted the narrative strategies of parables in ways that display her ongoing appreciation for wisdom literature's questioning forms.

Notes

1   C. S. Lewis, *Surprised by Joy: The Shape of My Early Life* (New York: Barnes and Noble, [1955] 2002), 174–5. In his allegorical work *The Great Divorce* (1945), which adapts elements of the *Divine Comedy* in its dream vision of a journey from hell to heaven, Lewis portrays MacDonald as a guiding figure, the Virgil to his Dante.
2   On F. D. Maurice's influence on MacDonald, see Martin Dubois, "Sermon and Story in George MacDonald," *Victorian Literature and Culture* 34, no. 3 (2015): 580–1. For a discussion of MacDonald's work for *Good Words* as well as this periodical's broadly evangelical contributors and readership, see Mark Knight, *Good Words: Evangelicalism and the Victorian Novel* (Athens: Ohio State University Press, 2019), 95–103.

3   Stephen Prickett, "The Idea of Tradition in George MacDonald," in *Rethinking George MacDonald: Contexts and Contemporaries*, ed. Christopher MacLachlan, John Patrick Pazdziora, and Ginter Stelle (Glasgow: Scottish Literature International, 2013), 10.
4   George MacDonald, "The Voice of Job," in *Unspoken Sermons: Second Series* (London: Longmans, Green, and Company, 1885), 235.
5   See, for example, John Docherty, "The Sources of *Phantastes*," *North Wind* 9 (1990): 38–53; Stephen Prickett, "Fictions and Metafictions: *Phantastes*, Wilhelm Meister, and the Idea of the Bildungsroman," in *The Gold Thread: Essays on George MacDonald*, ed. William Raeper (Edinburgh: Edinburgh University Press, 1990). The annotated edition of *Phantastes*, ed. John Pennington and Roderick McGillis (Hamden: Winged Lion Press, 2017), highlights the story's literary genealogy, giving relevant excerpts from influential texts in appendices. All quotations from *Phantastes* come from this edition and are cited parenthetically in text.
6   "The Imagination: Its Functions and Its Culture" originally appeared in the *British Quarterly Review* (July 1867). "The Fantastic Imagination" was first published as the preface to the American edition of *The Light Princess and Other Fairy Tales* (New York: G. P. Putnam's Sons, 1893). Both essays were later collected in MacDonald's volume *A Dish of Orts* (London: Sampson Low, Martson & Co., 1893). References to these essays come from a later edition of *Orts* (London: Edwin Dalton, 1908) and are cited parenthetically in text.
7   Dubois, "Sermon and Story," 577–87; Knight, *Good Words*, 90–103; Aubrey Plourde, "George MacDonald's Doors: Suspended Telos and the Child Believer," *Victorian Literature and Culture* 49, no. 2 (2021): 231–58.
8   Lewis, *Surprised by Joy*, 174.
9   Paul Ricoeur, "Biblical Hermeneutics," *Semeia* 4 (1975): 89.
10 On the centrality of the pathways metaphor in Proverbs, see William P. Brown, *Wisdom's Wonder: Character, Creation, and Crisis in the Bible's Wisdom Literature* (Grand Rapids: William B. Eerdmans, 2014), 47–8.
11 Greville MacDonald, *George MacDonald and His Wife* (London: George Allen and Unwin, 1924), 297–8.
12 G. K. Chesterton, Introduction to *George MacDonald and His Wife*, by Greville MacDonald (London: George Allen and Unwin, 1924), 12.
13 Robert Alter, *The Art of Biblical Poetry* (New York: Basil Books, 1985), 163.
14 George P. Landow, *Elegant Jeremiahs: The Sage from Carlyle to Mailer* (Ithaca: Cornell University Press, 1986), 1–24.
15 MacDonald's quotations in this essay come from Prov. 25:2 and Eccl. 3:11. See MacDonald, "The Imagination," 41–2.
16 See, for instance, Morton Bloomfield, "The Tradition and Style of Biblical Wisdom Literature," in *Biblical Patterns in Modern Literature*, ed. David H. Hirsch and

Nehama Aschkensay (Atlanta: Scholars Press, 1972), 19–20; see also James L. Crenshaw, *Old Testament Wisdom: An Introduction* (Louisville: John Knox Press, 2010), 5–6.
17 William Blake, *The Marriage of Heaven and Hell* (Oxford: Bodleian Library, 2011), 11–12, 4.
18 Peter Hatton, *Contradiction in the Book of Proverbs* (Farham: Ashgate Press, 2008), 3.
19 Timothy Larsen, *George MacDonald in the Age of Miracles* (Downers Grove: Inter Varsity Press Academic 2018), 71.
20 George MacDonald, *An Expression of Character: The Letters of George MacDonald*, ed. Glenn Edward Sadler (Grand Rapids: William B. Eerdmans, 1994), 153–4.
21 Samuel Taylor Coleridge, *Collected Works of Samuel Taylor Coleridge*, vol. 11. no. 2, ed. H. J. Jackson and J. R. de J. Jackson (Princeton: Princeton University Press, 1995), 1142.
22 Ibid., 1151.
23 See 2 Cor. 3:6.
24 Gisela Kreglinger, *Storied Revelations: Parables, Imagination, and George MacDonald's Christian Fiction* (Cambridge: Lutterworth Press, 2014), 117.
25 Coleridge, *The Collected Works of Samuel Taylor Coleridge*, vol. 7. no. 1, ed. James Engell and Walter Jackson Bate (Princeton: Princeton University Press, 1983), 304.
26 Erich Auerbach, "Figura," in *Scenes from the Drama of European Literature* (Manchester: Manchester University Press), 12–15, 36.
27 David Friedrich Strauss, *Life of Jesus, Critically Examined*, trans. George Eliot (London: Swan Sonneschein & Co, 1898), 65.
28 Coleridge, *The Collected Works of Samuel Taylor Coleridge*, vol. 6, ed. R. J. White (Princeton: Princeton University Press, 1972), 30.
29 Deborah L. Madsen, *Rereading Allegory: A Narrative Approach to Genre* (New York: Palgrave Macmillan, 1994), 104.
30 Docherty, "The Sources," 38.
31 Edmund Spenser, *The Faerie Queene* (Oxford: Clarendon Press), II.XIX.49.1, 48.8, 51.7–9.
32 Review of *Phantastes. The Athenaeum* (November 6, 1858): 560. Reprinted in *Phantastes*, ed. John Pennington and Roderick McGillis (Hamden: Winged Lion Press, 2017), 201.
33 Review of *Phantastes. The Spectator* (December 4, 1858): 1286. Reprinted in *Phantastes*, ed. John Pennington and Roderick McGillis (Hamden: Winged Lion Press, 2017), 204.
34 Review of *Phantastes. The British Quarterly Review* vol. 29 (January 1859): 296–7. Reprinted in *Phantastes*, ed. John Pennington and Roderick McGillis (Hamden: Winged Lion Press, 2017), 209.

35 Coleridge, *Collected Works*, 11.2.1154–5.
36 Friedrich Schleiermacher, *Hermeneutics and Criticism and Other Writings*, trans. Andrew Bowie (Cambridge: Cambridge University Press, 1998), 24.
37 Francis Bacon, *The Advancement of Learning*, ed. Joseph Devy (New York: P. F. Collier and Son, 1905), 265.
38 Ricoeur, *The Symbolism of Evil*, trans. Emerson Buchanan (New York: Harper and Row, 1967), 349.
39 Schleiermacher, *Hermeneutics and Criticism*, 24.
40 Daniel Gabelman, *George MacDonald: Divine Carelessness and Fairytale Levity* (Waco: Baylor University Press, 2013), 199.
41 Jean Louis Chrétien, *Under the Gaze of the Bible*, trans. John Marson Dunaway (New York: Fordham University Press, 2015), 23.
42 Coleridge, *Collected Works*, 11.2.1123.
43 Prickett, "The Idea of Tradition," 15.
44 *The Bible: Authorized King James Version with Apocrypha* (Oxford: Oxford University Press, 2008). All biblical quotations are cited parenthetically in text. Rights in the Authorized (King James) Version in the UK are vested in the Crown. Reproduced by Permission of the Crown's patentee, Cambridge University Press.
45 Søren Kierkegaard, "For Self-Examination," in *The Essential Kierkegaard*, ed. and trans. Howard V. Hong and Edna H. Hong (Princeton: Princeton University Press, 2000), 396–7.
46 Chrétien, *Under the Gaze of the Bible*, 33.
47 Kierkegaard, "For Self-Examination," 401. See also. 2 Sam 12:5, 7.
48 Docherty, "The Sources," 45.
49 Coleridge, *Collected Works*, 11.2.1116.
50 Larsen, *George MacDonald*, 21.
51 Robert Browning, *Christmas-Eve* in *Robert Browning: The Poems*, ed. John Pettigrew, vol. 1 (New Haven: Yale University Press, 1981), ll. 233–4, 813.4.
52 MacDonald, "Browning's 'Christmas Eve,'" *The Monthly Christian Spectator* 3, no. 5 (May 1853): 267.
53 MacDonald, *An Expression of Character*, 60. His remark refers to Dr. William Ellery Channing (1780–1842), an American Unitarian preacher and abolitionist.
54 MacDonald, *An Expression of Character*, 124.
55 Bonnie Gaarden, "George MacDonald's Phantastes: The Spiral Journey to the Goddess," *The Victorian Newsletter* 96 (1999): 13.
56 Ricoeur, "Biblical Hermeneutics," 75.
57 Appendix E of John Pennington and Roderick McGillis's annotated edition of *Phantastes* reprints these illustrations in full (Hamden: Winged Lion Press, 2017), 332–48.

58 Katharine Bubel, "Knowing God 'Other-Wise': The Wise Old Woman Archetype in George MacDonald's *The Princess and the Goblin, The Princess and Curdie*, and *The Golden Key*," *North Wind* 25 (2006): 8.
59 MacDonald, "The Higher Faith," in *Unspoken Sermons: First Series* (London: Longmans, Green, & Co. 1887), 65.
60 Plourde, "George MacDonald's Doors," 243.
61 Coleridge, *The Collected Works of Samuel Taylor Coleridge*, vol. 9: *Aids to Reflection*, ed. John Beer (Princeton: Princeton University Press, 1995), 202.
62 George McCrie, *The Religion of Our Literature: Essays upon Thomas Carlyle, Robert Browning, Alfred Tennyson, etc.* (London: Hodder and Stoughton, 1875), 294–95, 308.

3

Wisdom's Turn: Historical Recovery, Narrative Possibility, and the Direction of Biblical Parables in George Eliot's *Romola*

George Eliot's profound investment in biblical higher criticism is well known from her English translations of David Friedrich Strauss's *Das Leben Jesu* (*The Life of Jesus*) in 1846 and Ludwig Feuerbach's *Das Wesen Des Christentums* (*The Essence of Christianity*) in 1854, which brought these controversial works of German scholarship into wider circulation in Victorian Britain. What is less clear, at least to today's literary critics, is Eliot's complex and evolving position with respect to Christianity. On first glance, her gradual distancing of herself from the evangelical fervor of her early years seems easy enough to trace, from her refusal to attend church to her editorial work for the *Westminster Review* to her unconventional relationship with George Henry Lewes. For some time, the majority view among scholars has been to regard the tale by which the pious Mary Anne Evans became the unbelieving George Eliot as "one of the paradigmatic Victorian loss-of-faith stories."[1] And yet, recent work has also called attention to her subtle reworkings of biblical texts and theological traditions. As studies by Peter C. Hodgson, Marilyn Orr, John H. Mazaheri, and Ilana Blumberg have highlighted, Eliot's novels do not align with tidy models of secularization.[2] Her creative responses to nineteenth-century debates in biblical interpretation are a vital aspect of this narrative complexity.

Even as Eliot critiques religious ideologies, her literary imagination remains productively imbued with biblical elements, from verbal echoes to ethical insights. In a letter to her father dated shortly after she announced her refusal to attend church in early 1842, Eliot at once renounced Christianity's "system of doctrines" and expressed her ongoing admiration for "the moral teaching of Jesus himself."[3] As both Eliot and several of the higher critics she read and translated clearly recognized, this "moral teaching" often took the form of parables—simple yet enigmatic stories that invite the reader's reflection. Strauss himself, whose incendiary biography of Jesus is considered likely to have "induced more crises of faith" than any other book in Victorian Britain, highlighted these qualities.[4] According to Strauss, a parable is "a kind of problem to be solved on the reflection of the hearer."[5] Such a mode of moral teaching surely appealed to Eliot, who claimed in an 1855 essay for the *Leader* that "the most effective educator" is not someone "who announces a particular discovery" but rather someone "who rouses in others the activities that must issue in discovery."[6] This idea of awakening others into action finds expression throughout her later novels, which teach by engaging readers in their intellectual and ethical dilemmas.

Of all Eliot's novels, arguably the one that presents readers with the most puzzling problem is her historical novel *Romola* (1862–3), a densely detailed portrait of fifteenth-century Florence that critics have long regarded as challenging. Felicia Bonaparte, for instance, opened her book-length study of 1979 by quoting George Henry Lewes's statement that *Romola* was received with "a universal howl of discontent" and declaring that, in the century since its publication, it "has escaped our censure only when it secured our neglect."[7] Although subsequent years have seen renewed attention to this novel, including more nuanced accounts of its reception history, Nancy Henry's observation in her *Cambridge Introduction to George Eliot* (2008) that *Romola* remains "Eliot's least read novel" holds true.[8] In their introduction to the essay collection *From Author to Text: Re-Reading George Eliot's Romola* (1998), Caroline Levine and Mark W. Turner position the novel as a "problem text" that vexes those who try to understand it "in the unitary context of George Eliot's *oeuvre*," making the case for a "pluralist criticism" that reaches "beyond the author function."[9] My approach, in turn, situates *Romola* in relation to changing developments in nineteenth-century hermeneutics.

Romola mediates its engagement with these interpretive issues through its fictional re-creation of Renaissance Florence. Published in monthly installments in the *Cornhill Magazine* (July 1862 to August 1863) alongside vivid illustrations by Frederic Leighton, this novel is itself a work of historical and mythological recovery. It takes place from 1492 to 1498, the years that span the death of Lorenzo de' Medici, ruler of Florence and enthusiastic patron of the arts, and the execution of Girolamo Savonarola, the Dominican friar, self-proclaimed prophet, and religious reformer who governed Florence as a puritanical republic for three years before church and civil authorities turned against him. This backdrop brings into sharp relief the combination of classical and Christian ideas embodied in the eponymous heroine, "the daughter of a classical scholar, married to a pagan god, instructed by a prophet, and mythologized as the Madonna Antigone," as

David Carroll aptly puts it.[10] Readers meet Romola in the library of her aging father, the blind Bardo de' Bardi, whom she serves as amanuensis; she later marries Tito Melema, a dashing yet deceitful young man, frequently likened to the Greek god Bacchus (Dionysius), who is shipwrecked in Florence. After she learns that Tito has betrayed her father's dying wishes by selling his library, which Bardo had intended to bestow as a gift to the city, Romola attempts to flee and begin a new life in Venice, hoping to put her scholarly training to good use. On the road, she is interrupted by Savonarola himself, who claims to have been given a divine mandate to recall her to Florence. She heeds his message and takes up a life of charitable work, hailed as "the Visible Madonna" by those who witness her, but her obedience to Savonarola coexists with growing reservations about his authority. These tensions culminate in a heated argument, after which Romola once again leaves Florence, this time by sea, setting herself adrift in a boat until she arrives at an unknown shore and finds an unnamed village that has been stricken by the plague. She aids the surviving villagers until she experiences an epiphany about her own limitations, prompting her to reassess her disenchantment with Savonarola and return to Florence. Rather than a story about turning from or to religious belief, *Romola* traces the gradual formation of a wisdom that resides in both self-reflection (a turn inward) and practical application (a turn outward).

As a brief plot summary underscores, Romola's journey is complicated if not downright convoluted, so perhaps it is not surprising that this novel has long frustrated readers. Publisher George Smith had hoped that Eliot's writing, along with Leighton's impressive illustrations, would boost his magazine's declining sales; ironically, however, the *Cornhill* readership largely objected to this erudite novel's remote setting, so unlike Eliot's previous portraits of British life. Even the novel's representation of Christianity takes a form less familiar to Eliot's predominantly Protestant readership, as its scenes of Florentine life are embedded in Roman Catholicism—a marked departure from Eliot's memorable depictions of evangelicalism in earlier novels such as *Adam Bede* (1859), which her initial readers deemed so compelling as to speculate that this work must surely have been written by a clergyman himself.[11] Even so, astute readers have long observed connections between Eliot's portrait of Renaissance Florence and the ideological conflicts of Victorian Britain. In an unsigned review for the *Spectator* in July 1863, R. H. Hutton remarked that "the conflict between liberal culture and the more passionate form of the Christian faith in that strange era ... has so many points of resemblance with the present."[12] Along similar lines, Christopher Herbert's recent study emphasizes that Eliot's readers would have recognized her representation of Savonarola as an allegory of "puritanical Protestantism" in their own time. Indeed, the "bonfire of vanities" by which Savonarola attempts to purge Florence of the corrupting influences of Ovid, Boccaccio, and other classical writers has some uncanny parallels to later expressions of religious fundamentalism. As Herbert sees it, Eliot's attempt at a sympathetic portrayal of Savonarola fails because his anti-intellectualism is so out of keeping with her own ethical sensibilities. He locates this cognitive dissonance not only in Romola's "extreme and entirely impulsive changes of mind," but also in the book's "breakdown of novelistic structure"—a breakdown most clearly evident during the episode in which Romola sets herself adrift, a sequence that differs markedly in mimetic mode from Eliot's otherwise densely detailed historical novel.[13]

Without discounting the Gothic sensationalism that Herbert identifies, I propose that these structural limitations might be counterbalanced with another narrative possibility: the novel incorporates a dialogism that complicates its more fundamentalist tendencies. Read with an eye to Eliot's nuanced appreciation for "the moral teaching of Jesus himself" (*GEL* 1:128), *Romola* can be seen as invested in the themes and forms of the biblical parables. Unlike some other Victorian models such as John Ruskin's recourse to the parable of the workers in the vineyard in *Unto This Last* (serialized in the *Cornhill Magazine* between August and December 1860, less than two years before *Romola*), Eliot does not retell the story of any single parable but, rather, adapts this literary form's overarching patterns. Such adaptation becomes evident not only in the novel's statements about "the kingdom of God"—the referent of the gospel parables—but also in its startling narrative trajectory.

To unfold Eliot's use of this form in *Romola*, I situate her creative work in relation to insights offered by the higher critics that she read and translated, as well as Paul Ricoeur's theoretical discussion of parables as metaphorical narratives that have a fundamentally "interrogative structure."[14] This approach builds on Susan E. Colón's discussion of extra-biblical parables in Victorian fiction, which likewise owes to Ricoeur yet does not consider Eliot's work or the higher criticism. Colón argues that parables stage "a gap between everyday human experience and a gesture of extravagance that points to human limit-experience," concluding that this narrative strategy requires "the embodied response of the reader."[15] *Romola*, the novel that Eliot described as "written with her best blood" (*GEL* 6: 335), similarly employs surprising redirections and culminates in an expression of radical compassion designed to provoke and challenge readers. While the novel's conclusion has been critiqued for its seeming re-inscription of patriarchal authority, the final scenes might rather be understood as a radical reframing of religious and social community—a newly imagined "kingdom of God" with subtle feminist potentialities.[16] Approaching this novel in light of its kinship with biblical parables, I aim to reconsider what is achieved through the provocative gap between the novel that readers expect and the novel that readers find.

Although critics have often read *Romola* as an allegory of Auguste Comte's positivism and an experiment in prophetic discourse, the novel calls into question the very interpretive frameworks it seems to invite. These challenges, in turn, demonstrate Eliot's subtle work as a hermeneutic thinker. Even as she championed the historical criticism that questioned the doctrine of inspiration and the divinity of Jesus, she retains an underlying fascination with the ethical imperatives advanced in the gospels. Romola's character development unfolds over a series of dramatic encounters with a prophetic figure, but she neither becomes Savonarola's disciple nor rejects his Christianity altogether. On the eve of her second departure from Florence, she distances herself from Savonarola's beliefs, declaring that "God's kingdom is something wider" than what the prophet conceives.[17] But when she returns to Florence, she attempts to revivify Savonarola's Christianity, albeit in a broadened sense. In keeping with the interrogative and invitational patterns of the biblical parables, Eliot advances an expansive redefinition of "God's kingdom." She thereby reimagines revelation as a participatory experience, a narrative transformation that is congruent with the effort to redeem a religious imagination traceable throughout Eliot's creative output, though it takes an unusual guise in this "problem" novel.

Eliot's Parables: Wisdom Writing in the Age of the Higher Criticism

Eliot's biblical rewritings can be most clearly appreciated against the backdrop of the higher critical studies that she read and translated. Importantly, the translator of *Das Leben Jesu* found this work not only laborious but, at times, even distressing. As she reported to her friend Caroline Bray, "dissecting the beautiful story of the crucifixion" made her "Strauss-sick" (*GEL* 1: 206). This visceral language underscores the complexity of Eliot's stance regarding both the higher criticism and the Bible itself. Her remarks about her ongoing appreciation for "the moral teaching of Jesus himself," expressed in the early letter to her father cited previously (*GEL* 1: 128), put her in the company of several of the scholars she read and translated. These include the Unitarian

Charles Hennell, whose *Inquiry Concerning the Origin of Christianity* (1838) significantly influenced Eliot when she read it in the early 1840s—and, years later, her translation of *Das Leben Jesu* took over a project originally begun by Hennell's wife, Elizabeth (or "Rufa"). Hennell's preface outlined his doubts about the literal inspiration of scripture and skepticism regarding miracles; at the same time, he proposed that to question these ideas is not necessarily "equivalent to an entire renunciation of the Christian religion."[18] Later in his study, he concluded, "the moral teaching of Jesus forms the strength of Christianity," calling attention to "the weight, the beauty, and the apparent originality of his discourses and parables."[19] Hennell's reservations about the accuracy of the biblical accounts, then, coexisted with an appreciation for their artistic and ethical qualities.

Even as the higher critics focused primarily on the historical contexts of the synoptic gospels, several of them also drew attention to these text's literary features, parables included. Schleiermacher, for example, observed in his *Über die Schriften des Lukas* (*A Critical Essay on the Gospel of St. Luke*) (1817) that the parable is a form that "imprints itself ... readily on the imagination and the memory."[20] In *Das Leben Jesu*, Strauss similarly combined an emphasis on historical context with a nascent recognition for literary form: his remarks about how the parables would have been delivered in their original setting highlight their didactic design. Arguing that the seven parables recounted in Matthew 13 would not have been spoken in the rapid succession in which they appear in the text, Strauss commented that a parable "is a kind of problem to be solved by the reflection of the hearer; hence after every parable a pause is requisite, if it be the object of the teacher to convey real instruction, and not to distract by a multiplicity of ill-understood images."[21] Subsequent developments in biblical scholarship have more fully explicated this emphasis on reflection and situated it in relation to wisdom literature. Rudolf Bultmann, among others, notes that the sayings and parables of Jesus in the synoptic gospels reflect "the basic forms of the Old Testament and Jewish *mashal*."[22] The *mashal*, as David Stern explains it, is "an allusive narrative with an unspoken message": unlike some other modes of moral teaching, it does not make its lessons explicit but rather "leaves them to its audience to figure them out."[23] As the higher critics began to recognize and subsequent scholars have more fully explicated, these parables participate in a biblical wisdom tradition that advances an invitational, even provocative, mode of didacticism.

Eliot's sensitivity to these narrative forms becomes apparent in an article she wrote for the *Westminster Review* on James Heywood's *Introduction to the Book of Genesis* (1855), an abridged translation of *Die Genesis, historischkritisch erläutert* (1835) by Peter Von Bohlen. This article reflects her budding interest in Jewish scriptural and midrashic traditions, which later found expression in her poems "The Legend of Jubal" (1869) and "The Death of Moses" (1875), as well as her novel *Daniel Deronda* (1867). Despite the disturbingly anti-Semitic sentiments expressed in some of her early letters, several literary critics have argued convincingly that Eliot developed both appreciation for and sensitivity to Jewish traditions.[24] Praising Heywood's book as a concise introduction to new developments in biblical criticism, Eliot's review closes with a memorable anecdote. She quotes Von Bohlen's account of an "an admirable Hebrew myth which has arisen since the Christian era"—a myth that appears rather like a parable in both its brevity and its surprising turns.[25] In this story, Abraham offers hospitality to an elderly stranger. When the man refuses to worship Abraham's God, the patriarch becomes wrathful and drives him out into the wilderness; however, God rebukes Abraham: "Have I borne with the man these hundred and ninety-eight years, and given him food and raiment although he has rebelled against me, and canst thou not bear with him for one night?"[26] This challenge prompts Abraham to repent, search for the old man, and treat him with kindness. In her commentary on this story, Eliot highlighted "the tolerance it breathes," which she regarded as "unknown to the Books of the Law."[27] Even so, the myth in question bears an uncanny resemblance to the final scene in the book of Jonah, where God reproaches the prophet for his self-righteous desire to see the sinful city of Nineveh destroyed.[28] These stories unsettle tidy assumptions about rewards and punishments, envisioning a new order characterized by grace.

As recent scholarship on Victorian literature and religion has demonstrated, many of the period's novelists, including Charles Dickens and Elizabeth Gaskell, looked to biblical parables as rich creative resources.[29] While *Romola* has not yet been considered in this line of inquiry, it is clear that Eliot's contemporaries recognized her as a wisdom writer for their own time. Consider, for instance, Alexander Main's collection of *Wise, Witty, and Tender Sayings* (1871), which went into eleven editions by the end of the nineteenth century. Occasionally, this collection distorts Eliot's narrative voice and didactic mode, misattributing to the narrator, identified as *George Eliot (in propria persona)*, statements that are located within the perspectives of individual characters.[30] However, many of these excerpts highlight the metanarrative digressions and thought-provoking commentary that are indeed characteristic of Eliot as narrator—and as such these fragments retain their aphoristic power even when extracted from their original contexts.

Tellingly, the very first excerpt in the *Romola* section within Main's collection is a statement that invokes the sayings and stories of the synoptic gospels. This excerpt features the closing words of chapter 67, as the treacherous Tito finally meets his death. By this point, readers are well aware of Tito's villainy—his betrayal not only of Bardo's dying wishes but also of his own adoptive father, Baldassare Calvo, in addition to his unfaithfulness to Romola. That Tito dies at Baldassare's hand would seem to satisfy a legitimate desire for revenge, and Eliot herself exclaimed in a journal entry composed shortly after writing this installment, "Killed Tito with great excitement!" (*GEL* 4: 84). And yet, the narrator calls into question this idea of retribution: "Who shall put his finger on the work of justice, and say, 'It is there?' Justice is like the Kingdom of God—it is not without us as a fact, it is within us as a great yearning" (549). These words echo a passage from the gospel of Luke in which Jesus responds to questions about this kingdom's arrival: "the kingdom of God cometh not with observation: neither shall they say, Lo here! or, lo there! for, behold, the kingdom of God is within you" (Lk. 17:20–1).[31] Effectively, Eliot locates justice not in the tidy dictum of an eye for an eye and a tooth for a tooth but within a passionate, indefinable longing. Her narrator's remarks about the complexity of justice open the way for the emphasis on mercy that prevails at the novel's conclusion.

Elsewhere in *Romola*, Eliot underscores that clear moral distinctions are difficult to draw. Her reservations with certain judgment are nowhere more apparent than in her portrayal of Savonarola. Drawn in the early 1860s, Eliot's portrait of this celebrated yet controversial figure appeared against the backdrop of the Italian *Risorgimento*, the movement for unification that culminated with the crowning of King Victor Emmanuel II. These events sparked renewed interest in a *Risorgimento* mythology that reconsidered historical individuals such as Savonarola, ranging from the enthusiastic portrayal offered by Pasquale Villari's *La Storia di Girolamo Savonarola* (1859–60) to the more critical representation in Jacob Burckhardt's *The Civilization of the Renaissance in Italy* (1860), two important sources for Eliot's historical novel.[32] *Romola* combines elements of both perspectives, as exemplified in its commentary on Savonarola's advent sermon. Even as the narrator questions his "need of personal predominance, his labyrinthine allegorical interpretations of the Scriptures, his enigmatic visions, and his false certitude about divine intentions," she affirms his "fervid pity," "passionate sense of the infinite," and "active sympathy" (234). These complexities are distilled with aphoristic concision:

> It was the fashion of old, when an ox was led out for sacrifice to Jupiter, to chalk the dark spots, and give the offering a false show of unblemished whiteness. Let us fling away the chalk, and boldly say,—the victim is spotted, but it is not therefore in vain that his mighty heart is laid on the altar of men's highest hopes.
> (235)

Whereas Savonarola admonishes the Florentines and calls them to repentance, Eliot reimagines the practices involved in seeking salvation, whether belonging to classical Rome or to the biblical prophets. Her metaphor of sacrifice at once undermines this ritual's fascination with purity and preserves its hope for restitution. She thereby adapts the basic patterns of inversion and extension that characterize the proverbial sayings of Jesus, such as those about the fulfillment of the Law throughout the Sermon on the Mount.[33] These sayings share much in common with the parables, as Ricoeur's analysis highlights: just as the proverbs "undergo a kind of *intensification*, based on hyperbole and paradox," the parables employ a "gesture of extravagance" that challenges conventional order.[34] Eliot's novel follows a similar pattern. Challenging Savonarola's claim to prophetic authority, *Romola* inaugurates an alternative vision of "the kingdom of God," one that depends less on apocalyptic warnings than on enigmatic parables.

"The Tangled Web": *Romola* and the Conflict of Interpretations

As a novel of ideas, *Romola* is also story about interpretive possibilities. Attempts at making meaning figure prominently, from the signs and portents proclaimed in Savonarola's advent sermon to the explication of a dream vision by Romola's estranged brother Dino, a member of Savonarola's Dominican brotherhood who summons his sister on his deathbed. Eliot's narrative commentary foregrounds the search for meaning, often in ways that underscore the fallibility of the novel's many interpreters. Take, for example, the meditation that closes chapter 32 ("A Revelation"). Here, Romola reflects on her disquieting meeting with Dino, which is also her first encounter with Savonarola. She does not heed her brother's deathbed warning against her upcoming marriage, and, even after subsequent events expose Tito's deceitfulness, she concludes that she was right to disregard this vision. Still, she cannot get the incident with Dino out of her mind. Her weary thoughts seem a "tangled web" that cannot be unraveled. In contrast to Dino's unwavering confidence in divine revelation, Romola's only certainty is that she has no certainty. As the narrator sees it, such is the human condition:

> In those times, as now, there were human beings who never saw angels or heard perfectly clear messages. Such truth as came to them was brought confusedly in the voices and deeds of men not at all like the seraphs of unfailing wing and piercing vision—men who believed falsities as well as truths, and did the wrong as well as the right. The helping hands stretched out to them were the hands of

men who stumbled and often saw dimly, so that these beings unvisited by angels had no other choice than to grasp that stumbling guidance along the path of reliance and action which is the path of life, or else to pause in loneliness and disbelief, which is no path, but the arrest of inaction and death.

(324)

The narrator invokes the pathways metaphor typical of proverbial wisdom literature, as discussed in my previous chapter on George MacDonald. In this case, however, the metaphor stands in tension with a marked hesitation as to where—or even whether—wisdom can be found. Whereas MacDonald's perambulatory journey in *Phantastes* (1858) explores a productive doubt that culminates in the protagonist's growing awareness of an indwelling divine wisdom, Eliot sustains a heightened degree of skepticism regarding all potential sources of light.

The narrator's insistence that there is no single and stable reference point by which to arbitrate among potentially conflicting interpretations once again militates against tying this novel too closely to any definitive interpretive framework. Much twentieth- and twenty-first-century criticism on *Romola* discusses it as an illustration of Comtean positivism, which offers a systematic account of humankind's social and moral progress trumpeted as "the Religion of Humanity." This approach has many attractions, both as a lens through which to approach this novel and as a means for understanding Eliot's revisionary engagement with Christianity more broadly. However, to identify *Romola* as a positivist allegory is to risk reducing its symbolic texture in ways that the narrative itself resists. Eliot's knowledge of and appreciation for Comte's work can hardly be denied: she wrote an appreciative essay on Comte for the *Leader* in 1854, and her poem "O May I Join the Choir Invisible" (1874) was adapted by Comte's disciple Richard Congreve in positivist services later in the century.[35] But even as *Romola* draws on positivist images and themes, the novel conveys an overriding dissatisfaction with schematic accounts of history—whether parsed in religious or secular terms. Readings that see *Romola* as a positivist book have made much of its suggestive combination of classical and Christian images, particularly as presented in a scene describing a sketch by the artist Piero di Cosimo, one of several historical figures who serves as a minor character in Eliot's fictional account. Shortly after Tito, the "shipwrecked stranger," arrives in Florence, he visits the shop of the barber Nello, where he encounters this drawing. Bonaparte calls this sketch a "pictorial prophecy," arguing that its various figures anticipate the characters who influence Romola's ethical development, which she then outlines according to Comte's three stages of moral evolution: the theological, the metaphysical, and the positive.[36] Similarly, Mary Wilson Carpenter regards this piece as emblematic of "the four-part division of Romola's spiritual progress," which she too parses as a function of "the Comtean structure of history."[37] While these accounts suggest useful structural devices, they neglect to consider the uncomfortable possibility that to focus on the sketch in this way is to approximate the remarks made by the villainous Tito himself.

Although the drawing's four figures invite philosophical speculation, the narrator ironizes Tito's attempts to decipher Piero's images:

> The sketch Nello pointed to represented three masks—one a drunken, laughing Satyr, another a sorrowing Magdalen, and the third, which lay between them, the rigid, cold face of a Stoic: the masks rested obliquely on the lap of a little child, whose cherub features rose above them with something of the supernal promise in the gaze which painters had by that time learned to give to the Divine Infant.
>
> "A symbolical picture, I see," said the young Greek, touching the lute while he spoke, so as to bring out a slight musical murmur. "The child, perhaps, is the Golden Age, wanting neither worship nor philosophy. And the Golden Age can always come back as long as men are born in the form of babies, and don't come into the world in a cassock or furred mantle. Or, the child may mean the wise philosophy of Epicurus, removed alike from the gross, the sad, and the severe."
>
> "Ah! Everybody has his own interpretation for that picture," said Nello.
>
> (34)

The extent of Tito's selfishness has yet to be revealed, but his calculated posturing with the musical instrument hints at his untrustworthy charm. This scene occurs only a few moments after he has coldly dismissed the Gothic beauty of the Florentine Duomo, the cathedral designed by Giotto di Bondone in the fourteenth century. Whereas the narrator appreciates the cathedral's "harmonious variety of colour and form," Tito responds to the architecture with "a slight touch of scorn on his lip" and a "scanning coolness from his eyes" (32). As an artistic critic, Tito is unreliable at best. The critical challenge offered by this scene in the barber shop may be not to better Tito's interpretation but to resist the lure of pinpointing the novel's symbolism. After all, as Nello's remark underscores, one reader's best efforts to decode this symbolism will surely be less than satisfying to every other reader.

Related to the critical trend of reading *Romola* as a positivist allegory is the habit of seeing it as an experimentation with prophetic discourse. This scholarship usefully highlights the discursive intersections between positivism and prophecy while also illuminating broader trends within nineteenth-century patterns of thought, including the recourse to apocalyptic frameworks to give meaning to history. Bonaparte's discussion of this novel's positivism underscores its prophetic qualities, and Carpenter likewise situates *Romola* within the "rekindling excitement about prophecy" resulting from the "continuous historical" school of biblical scholarship.[38] This scholarship has its roots in the eighteenth century, though it did not reach a wide audience in Britain until many decades later—the very years when *Romola* was composed and published. At the time that *Romola* made its appearance, Victorian readers were still reeling from the aftermath of Strauss's work and its more recent translation. In October of 1862, just a few months after this novel began its serial run, Bishop John William Colenso published *The Pentateuch and the Book of Joshua Critically Examined*, a rigorous mathematical critique of the genealogies, dimensions, and other figures in these accounts that roiled the Victorian reading public by putting pressure on literalist exegesis.[39] Colenso's work followed *Essays and Reviews* (1860), which featured work by a variety of Anglican clerics and scholars (Frederick Temple, Rowland Williams, Baden Powell, Henry Bristow Wilson, Mark Pattison, Charles Wycliffe Goodwin, and Benjamin Jowett) and expounded the principles of German higher criticism. The first article within this collection, Temple's "The Education of the Human Race" borrowed rhetorically from prophetic discourse, much as Thomas Carlyle did in polemics such as "The Signs of the Times" (published in 1829 in the *Edinburgh Review*) and "Characteristics" (published in the same periodical in 1831)—the very strategies that literary scholars have seen as typifying the cultural formation of Victorian sage writing.[40] For Temple, the prophetic mode offered a platform for advancing a Eurocentric belief in progress derived not only from Comtean positivism but also from Gotthold Ephraim Lessing's *Die Erziehung des Menschengeschlechts* (*The Education of the Human Race*) (1780), which appropriates and recasts the biblical narrative of the fall and redemption as *universalgeschichte*—that is, an account of humankind's development toward perfection. Whether parsed in religious or secular terms, prophetic discourse assigns meaning to events by putting them in a teleological context.

Romola, however, expresses distinct reservations with such teleology. Even as narrative devices such as dramatic irony and prolepsis invite readers to think in terms of an overarching design, the fact that so many characters are frustrated in their interpretive efforts suggests that readers, too, should think twice before claiming to have cracked this novel's hermeneutic code. Eliot, who greatly admired Carlyle, has by several critics been associated with Carlyle's mode of prophetic sage writing; even so, to appreciate the subtleties of her narrative art, critics would do well to consider genres and interpretive modes beyond prophecy.[41] By both entertaining and critiquing prophetic discourse, Eliot departs from the prevailing patterns of her contemporaries and anticipates something that more closely resembles the "conflict of interpretations" that Ricoeur later identified as characterizing the field of hermeneutics in the post-Marxist, post-Nietzschean, and post-Freudian era. As Ricoeur summarizes it, these theoretical developments have underscored that there is "no universal canon for exegesis, but only disparate and opposed theories concerning the rules of interpretation." He identifies a central tension between the basic understanding of hermeneutics either as *kerygma* ("the manifestation of a message") or as demystification ("the reduction of illusion"), which in turn gives rise to a "double motivation of willingness to suspect, willingness to listen; vow of rigor, vow of obedience."[42] In strikingly similar terms, Eliot describes Romola's inner dilemmas regarding Savonarola as a matter of discerning "where the sacredness of obedience ended, and where the sacredness of rebellion began" (468). Like Ricoeur, Eliot upholds elements of a hermeneutics of suspicion or resistance, while also holding out for the possibility of a revelatory *kerygma*. Her heroine's journey unfolds as an attempt to hold these two modes in productive tension. Unlike Savonarola's oracular pronouncements, Romola's reflections on her experiences in the unnamed village, in the novel's final epiphanic moment, consist primarily of unanswered questions. What Romola learns exceeds Savonarola's command to cultivate "the wisdom that has hitherto been as foolishness to [her]" (335)—a statement that echoes the Pauline contrast between the wisdom of God and the wisdom of the world.[43] More profoundly, Romola discovers the wisdom of interrogating her own wisdom.

This questioning energy issues from the dialectical model of revelation in concealment and concealment in revelation that is characteristic of the parables and more broadly of biblical wisdom literature as a genre. As Ricoeur emphasizes, much of this wisdom literature underscores the ineffability of divine things.[44] Eliot's fictionalized Renaissance Florence combines classical and Christian elements, but the novelist herself leans more toward the style of Genesis than that of Homer, to evoke Erich Auerbach's memorable distinction between these two methods of representation—that is, she favors "obscurity," leaving important ideas "unexpressed" and "mysterious."[45] The sequence of meetings between Romola and the novel's prophetic figures further aligns with the "strategic variation in the pattern of repetitions" that Robert Alter finds characteristic of biblical narratives, with their subtle manipulation of predetermined motifs.[46] Biblical narrative, as Alter explains, presents meaning "as a *process*, requiring continual revision ... continual suspension of judgement, weighing of multiple possibilities, brooding over gaps in the information provided."[47] Much the same might be said of what happens in *Romola*. Lacking intervention from "the seraphs of unfailing wing and piercing vision," Eliot's protagonist has only the "stumbling guidance" provided by her fellow human beings (324–5). Her portrayal of these humans as flawed yet insightful reveals her dialogue with thinkers such as Feuerbach, pondering the underlying questions that this scholarship raised about divinity and humanity.

Stumbling Guidance on the Way to the Kingdom of God

In keeping with the numerical patterns of biblical narratives, Romola's journey includes a threefold series of dramatic encounters with a figure of religious authority—encounters that seem, at first glance, to be either a potential conversion scene or a potential moment of apostasy. What results, however, is something far more ambiguous. Taken together, these episodes shift the locus of religious revelation from heavenly messages to earthly sympathies. Cultivating sympathy (which, as discussed in the nineteenth century, is closer to what we would today define as empathy) emerges as a paramount concern across Eliot's writings, as critics have long recognized.[48] Suzy Anger locates this concern in relation to Eliot's reading of Schleiermacher, arguing that she advances a "hermeneutics of sympathy" that highlights the ethical imperative to understand another's intent, even as Eliot, like Schleiermacher himself, recognizes as well the difficulty of doing so.[49] Whereas Anger regards this hermeneutics as secular in the sense of a departure from religion, Eliot's concept of sympathy, expressed in distinctly embodied terms, might also be seen in terms of her enduring interest in incarnation theology.

The first event in this series of dramatic encounters occurs when Romola travels to the convent of San Marco, the dwelling place of Savonarola's Dominican brotherhood. She goes in response to a message from her estranged brother, Dino, known to his fellow monks as Fra Luca, saying that he is ill and requesting that Romola visit him. On his deathbed, Dino issues a prophetic warning against his sister's upcoming marriage. He insists that his dream was divinely inspired, pronouncing it "a message from heaven," and describes it in allegorical terms similar to those that characterize Savonarola's sermons: a priest with "the face of death" marries Romola to a man with "the face of the Great Tempter," and these nuptials mark the beginning of great tribulation (153). Although Dino commands Romola "to renounce the vain philosophy and corrupt thoughts of the heathens," she does not heed this call to repentance (158). Then again, nor can she dismiss Dino's dream as a mere "monkish vision, bread of fasting and fanatical ideas," as Tito advises her when the pair converse afterwards (176). Her brother's words have a lingering and disquieting effect on her. As the narrative unfolds, Tito proves false, much as Dino had warned; however, accurate foretelling is not what Romola finds most compelling about her experiences in San Marco. On the contrary, she regards this predictive accuracy as a mere accident. Appalled at the prospect that she might become "a creature led by phantoms and disjoined whispers," Romola assures herself that she was right to have disregarded her brother's warning. Nevertheless, she remains "conscious of something deeper than that coincidence of words," speculating that "there seemed to be something more than madness in that supreme fellowship with suffering" (323–4). For Romola, what is most attractive about her brother's religious framework is its capacity to invest human experiences with sacred significance and thus to generate an expansive idea of community. The narrator's remark that, when Dino dies, "the revelation that might have come from the simple questions of filial and brotherly affection had been carried into irrevocable silence" upholds the intriguing prospect that guidance resides not in foresight but in fellowship. As the narrator sees it, Dino's vision arises from the "shadowy region" that lies apart from "the human sympathies which are the very life and substance of our wisdom" (160). Savonarola, in turn, offers a more substantial, yet still markedly imperfect, manifestation of this corporeal wisdom. When Romola first hears Savonarola speak, in the company of her dying brother, she describes his manner of speaking in contrast to Dino's and calls attention to his physical presence. This incident foreshadows Romola's subsequent encounter with Savonarola in chapter 40, aptly entitled "An Arresting Voice."

This second encounter with Savonarola causes Romola to reverse her intended course of action, though she does not become Savonarola's unquestioning disciple. Following her musings about Dino's vision, Romola resolves to leave Tito and depart from the city of Florence. Though disguised in "the grey serge dress of a sister belonging to the third order of St. Francis," she plans not to take refuge in the cloister but "to go to the most learned woman in the world, Cassandra Fedele, at Venice, and ask her how an instructed woman could support herself in a lonely life there" (322). On the road, however, she meets Savonarola, who recognizes Romola and tells her that he has been given "a command from God" to recall her to Florence (355). Upon hearing this voice, Romola feels "shaken, as if that destiny which men thought of as a sceptred deity had come to her and grasped her with fingers of flesh" (355). As underscored by this simile's conditional syntax ("as if"), she heeds Savonarola not because she believes in any literal "sceptred deity" but because his words resonate with her previous wonderings about religion's capacity to generate sympathy, described in embodied terms. Even as this incident evokes the conversion of the apostle Paul on the road to Damascus, Romola's meeting with Savonarola is but one of many steps in a process of reorientation. This process continues as she confronts both her frustrations with Savonarola's Catholicism and her yearning for the sacred sympathy adumbrated by his religious vision.

These struggles surface throughout chapter 44, "The Visible Madonna," which focuses on Romola's newfound charitable work in Florence and depicts her as a manifestation of "The Unseen Madonna," the Virgin Mary. Here again, Romola's free indirect discourse underscores the complexity of her inner dilemmas:

> if she came away from her confessor, Fra Silvestro, or from some contact with the disciples of Savonarola amongst whom she worshipped, with a sickening sense that these people were miserably narrow, and with an almost impetuous reaction towards her old contempt for their superstition—she found herself recovering a firm footing in her works of womanly sympathy.
>
> (387–8)

Her consciousness that Savonarola's disciples are "narrow" anticipates her later declaration that God's kingdom must be "wider" than Savonarola's party (492), even as her metaphor of "firm footing" develops the imagery of "the path of life" introduced previously (324). Eliot's kinaesthetic language goes beyond the predominantly visual language in the model advanced by Adam Smith's influential *The Theory of Moral Sentiments* (1759), which figures sympathy as an imaginative process in which the "spectator" envisions himself in the position of the sufferer.[50] By contrast, *Romola* uses more fully corporeal and proprioceptive terms that combine seeing, hearing, touching, and walking.

Eliot's concept of embodied compassion is informed by but not reducible to Feuerbach's theories in *The Essence of Christianity*, including his claim that "the essence of Christianity is the essence of human feeling."[51] Feuerbach, too, describes charity as grounded in the physical senses: "No abstract beings—no! only sensuous, living beings are merciful. Mercy is the justice of sensuous life .... The blood of Christ cleanses us from our sins in the eyes of God; it is only his human blood that makes God merciful."[52] Yet where Feuerbach remarks that "all religions rest on abstraction," Eliot's narrative art shows a stronger investment in reconceiving religion reconceived in terms of embodied sympathy.[53] In a letter to her friend Sara Hennell, the sister of Charles Hennell and a freethinking author and translator in her own right, Eliot summed up her combination of esteem for and distance from *The Essence of Christianity* in the following terms: "With the ideas of Feuerbach I everywhere agree, but of course I should, of myself, alter the phraseology considerably" (*GEL* 2: 153). As translator, Eliot had limited artistic license in adjusting matters of "phraseology"; her work as a novelist, by contrast, allowed for greater creative play.

At the same time that Eliot rejected inherited religious doctrines, she appreciated the artistic qualities of religious texts, a point underscored throughout her correspondence. During the Christmas season of 1862, when she was in the midst of composing *Romola*, Eliot wrote again to Sara Hennell, "What pitiable people those are who feel no poetry in Christianity! Surely the acme of poetry hitherto is the conception of the suffering Messiah—and the final triumph, 'He shall reign for ever and ever'" (*GEL* 4: 71). Eliot was not alone among Victorian freethinkers in seeking to reimagine the figure of Jesus while also questioning Christianity's historical accuracy, as Gareth Atkins observes in his discussion of readers of the higher criticism from Eliot to Matthew Arnold.[54] Sebastian Lecourt further highlights the ways in which both Eliot and Arnold used historical biblical scholarship as a resource for developing a "religion of many-sidedness," beyond the confines and preoccupations of evangelical Protestantism.[55] Other critics emphasize the extent to which Eliot's own vision of Jesus differed from that conveyed by the works she translated: Hodgson, for instance, goes so far as to claim that "the Jesus of Strauss's *Life of Jesus* is far removed from the Jesus to whom George Eliot was attracted, namely the Man of Sorrows who proclaimed the friendship of God."[56] While it would be reductive to elide the distinctions between, on the one hand, Eliot's sense of Jesus as human, and, on the other, the Christocentric visions of such heterodox believers as Elizabeth Barrett Browning and George MacDonald, it would also be problematic for scholars to turn a blind eye to Eliot's impassioned declaration of "the conception of the suffering Messiah" as "the acme of poetry" (*GEL* 4: 71). As studies by both Charles LaPorte and Wendy Williams have demonstrated, Eliot's sense of poetry as a vital means of both apprehending and shaping religion's cultural legacies, including its capacity to elicit the human sympathy that she regarded as truly sacred, undergirds her own all-too-often overlooked experiments in verse.[57]

Within *Romola*, Eliot's interest in rethinking the incarnation appears not simply in her representation of Savonarola as a martyr, which Carroll has contextualized in relation to the many "lives of Christ" of the Victorian age, but,

I would suggest, in her portrayal of Romola.[58] Eliot figures Romola in terms that combine biblical symbolism with imagery associated with classical goddesses including Minerva, Aurora, and Ariadne.[59] This multiplicity reflects a conceptual plurality that productively nuances the novel's religion of feeling. Even as she entertains doubts regarding Savonarola's Christianity, Romola determines that the "pressing problem" is not "to settle questions of controversy" but "to keep alive that flame of unselfish emotion by which a life of sadness might still be a life of active love" (389). Although this turn away from debate might risk embedding a kind of anti-intellectualism, Romola's recognition of the limits of knowledge entails not a rejection of her scholarly training, but, rather, an awareness that preoccupation with intellectual debate can be an impediment to compassionate action.

As a result of the third incident in the novel's threefold pattern—the final confrontation between the heroine and Savonarola—what Romola eventually concedes is not a specific doctrinal position but the broader point that wisdom cannot be found in winning an argument. Following Savonarola's excommunication by the pope and his falling out of favor with the Florentine people in the August of 1497, Romola returns to San Marco for a private audience with Savonarola. When she implores him to intervene on behalf of her godfather, who has been imprisoned and accused of conspiracy, he dismisses her supplications with a cold calculation: "the death of five men" is a "light matter" when "weighed against the furthering of God's kingdom upon earth" (492). As the debate escalates, Savonarola equates this latter goal with his own aims in Florence, declaring, "the cause of my party *is* the cause of God's kingdom" (492). Indignant, Romola responds, "God's kingdom is something wider—else, let me stand outside it with the beings that I love" (492). What would at first seem to be a clear rejection of both Savonarola's politics and his religion becomes complicated when she returns from this second departure from Florence.

Disillusioned not only with Savonarola but also with Tito, whose unfaithfulness has now been made known to her, Romola travels to the village of Viareggio, near the Mediterranean, and purchases a small boat from a local fisherman. Unfurling and fastening the sail to catch the breeze, she puts out to sea, reposes in the vessel, and wishes for death, patterning her actions after the story of Gostanza from Boccaccio's *Decameron*. As Carroll sees it, this episode signifies "the breakdown of the attempt to create and live out a coherent world-view in Renaissance Florence."[60] Yet this breakdown is also a breakthrough, resulting in Romola's achieving a widened understanding of "God's kingdom." As the novel moves through a dream-like, almost fantastical, sequence and then once again returns to the realistic and quotidian scene of domestic Florence, Eliot reclaims the realm of the ordinary. This plot twist aligns not only with the narrative strategy of parables but also with broader turns within Eliot's Romantic and religious imagination. As Colón explains them, parables juxtapose "an ordinary situation" with "an extraordinary turn of action," thereby offering an "extravagant reversal" that redefines reality.[61] This redefinition does not merely redescribe reality but, according to Ricoeur's analysis, prompts the reader to recreate it.[62] So, too, the closing chapters of Eliot's novel attempt to usher in a new concept of religious and political community—and, if readers find themselves shocked or provoked by these narrative turns, that may well be part of the point.

The Extraordinary Turn to the Ordinary

The sequence that comprises Romola's second departure from Florence, described by Eliot as a "symbolical" moment belonging to her "earliest vision" of her book (*GEL* 4:104), reads like a story within a story, a mythic interlude within the realist novel. No longer are people and places described in careful detail; instead, the chapter in which Romola awakens from her slumber in the boat and arrives on an unknown shore at an unnamed village lacks any clear geographical markers, unfolding with a sparseness that seems almost allegorical. Romola awakens "on the shores of that loveliest sea" and then moves from this idyllic scene to a nightmarish "village of unburied dead" (550, 552). Amid the dead bodies bearing the signs of the bubonic plague are cries of distress from those still living, whom Romola aids by bearing them water in an act of deliverance that prompts the villagers to regard her as "the Blessed Lady," also described as "the Holy Mother, come to take care of the people" (562, 554). In Herbert's view, the novel's swerve into "strangely lyrical phraseology," which also intrudes into Romola's praise for Savonarola, "ought to make a reader cringe." He argues that the "inflationary jargon" that presents Savonarola as the image of "something deeper" or "something unspeakably great" obscures practical realities, regarding the novel's recourse to the "register of gothic sensationalism" as reflecting an ideology of religious fundamentalism.[63] However, this hyperbolic language takes a productively self-reflexive turn. Even though Eliot's superlatives risk abstraction, her heroine's concern rests ultimately with practical application.

Romola asks herself a series of increasingly probing questions: "What if Fra Girolamo had been wrong? What if the life of Florence was a web of inconsistencies? Was she, then, something higher, that she should shake the dust from off her feet and say, 'This world is not good enough for me?'" (562). Her inner dialogue indicates a growing recognition that, even if she had been in the right in her dispute with Savonarola, her abrupt departure might not have been the wisest course of action. As she rejects the idea that she should "shake the dust from off her feet," she recalls and revises the command that Jesus gives the twelve disciples when they leave a house or city that does not receive them—much as many of his aphoristic sayings, as in the Sermon on the Mount and the Sermon on the Plain, have the effect of challenging and intensifying received wisdom.[64] Romola, who returns to the city, repositions these words to articulate a still more radical vision of the kingdom of God.

This widened vision is described in sacramental terms, reflecting Eliot's broader engagement with religious and Romantic philosophy. The narrator characterizes this event as being "like a new baptism to Romola," and the story follows this symbolic baptism with something akin to the ritual of confirmation—though, in this instance, rather than receive the spirit through being anointed by others' hands, Romola stretches out her own hands to those in need (560). Eliot's revitalization of these rituals echoes Feuerbach's reframing of the Eucharist in the resonant closing statement of *The Essence of Christianity*: "It needs only that the ordinary course of things be interrupted in order to vindicate to common things an uncommon significance, *to life, as such, a religious import*. Therefore let bread be sacred for us, let wine be sacred, and also let water be sacred! Amen."[65] For Feuerbach, who regarded God as a fictitious creation of the human mind, holiness results from seeing immanent realities with the eyes of love, so that ordinary existence takes on an extraordinary value. This affirmation of ordinary life constitutes what Charles Taylor sees as a signature legacy of Romanticism, which emerged in dialogue with ideas deeply rooted in Christian traditions.[66] Feuerbach's statements here are remarkably akin to Samuel Taylor Coleridge's discussion in his *Biographia Literaria* of "the prime merit of genius" as the capacity to inculcate a childlike wonder for everyday occurrences: "to represent familiar objects, as to awaken in the minds of others a kindred feeling concerning them."[67] Both texts are good examples of what Louis Dupré discusses as "the religious language of Romanticism," which sought new ways of understanding both transcendence and immanence.[68] The commonalities between Feuerbach, on the one hand, and more theologically committed thinkers such as Coleridge, on the other, help to illuminate the vital religious elements informing Romantic thought.

Another important aspect of this religious Romanticism appears in Feuerbach's understanding of "the mystery of the incarnation," which he explains as "the consciousness of divine love" and regards as present in all religious traditions.[69] Identifying an overarching tension within Christianity between divine omnipotence and divine love, he declares, "As God has renounced himself out of love, so we, out of love, should renounce God; for if we do not sacrifice God to love, we sacrifice love to God, and in spite of the predicate of love, we have the God—the evil being—of religious fanaticism."[70] This thought-provoking chiasmus ultimately rejects divinity, though it does so by way of a willing acceptance of limitation not utterly unlike that found in kenotic theology. Later thinkers who engage with Christian and Jewish traditions in both critical and mystical ways, such as Simone Weil, have further illuminated this paradox and its ethical implications: "He emptied himself of his divinity. We should empty ourselves of the false divinity with which we were born."[71] In the final chapters of *Romola*, Eliot at first seems to do almost the opposite of what Feuerbach advises, reclaiming if not literally resurrecting the fanatic Savonarola. Ultimately, however, Romola's renunciation of her own claim to righteousness might also be read as the triumph of love.

More than conversion or unconversion, more than education by disillusionment, Romola's character formation consists of a series of reorientations that hold together skepticism and sympathy. Such is the creed that Romola voices after her "new baptism":

> If everything else is doubtful, this suffering I can help is certain; if the glory of the cross is an illusion, the sorrow is only the truer. While the strength is in my arm, I will stretch it out to the fainting; while the light visits my eyes they shall seek the forsaken.
>
> (560)

These statements underscore her capacity to hold together seemingly antithetical ideas, as well as her commitment to charitable action over argumentative debate. More broadly, Eliot's recovery of application as an interpretive principle constitutes an important departure from prevailing nineteenth-century trends. Schleiermacher and his contemporaries privileged authorial intent and historical context, departing from the concern with applying scripture to the present day and one's own life that had characterized older exegetical models. By contrast, Eliot's emphasis on application accords not only with patristic exegesis but also with Aristotelian ethics, as Hans-Georg Gadamer highlights in his discussion of application as a hermeneutic principle.[72] The fusion of classical and Christian ideals within *Romola* conceptualizes wisdom not only in the transcendental terms of *sophia* but also in the practical terms of *phronesis*. Furthermore,

Eliot's focus on application accords with her narrative recourse to parable, a form "generically tuned to provoke a response," as Colón puts it.[73] As Romola relinquishes her role as the "Blessed Lady"—the role that her previous work as "The Visible Madonna" would seem to have foreshadowed—and places herself within a much humbler sphere, Eliot creates an "extravagant reversal" of the kind that Colón, following Ricoeur, identifies as integral to the narrative strategy of the parables.[74] Such esteem for ordinary life constitutes a pattern within Eliot's novels at large, from the realist manifesto in her well-known metanarrative digression in the seventeenth chapter of *Adam Bede* to the memorable closing sentences of *Middlemarch* (1871–2), which locate the "growing good" of the world in "unhistoric acts."[75] *Romola* ends on a similarly understated note. Eliot's heroine concludes that "God's kingdom" is not abstracted and idealized but, as Hodgson puts it, "a matter of bringing the utopian into the real, of realizing the wider kingdom under specific, always difficult circumstances."[76] Her readiness to work through difficult circumstances finds its most radical expression in her responses to Tito's infidelity.

Following her return to Florence, the widowed Romola welcomes into her household Tessa—the peasant maid whom Tito had deceived into thinking that a carnival ruse meant that they were legally married—and her two illegitimate children, along with Romola's widowed cousin, Monna Brigida. While Romola's assumption of a place within the domestic sphere might seem to uphold the traditional structures of patriarchy, the sisterhood that develops between Romola (the "wife") and Tessa (the "mistress") problematizes the reductive polarization of "the angel in the house" versus the "fallen woman" that characterized Victorian gender ideologies. Rather, Romola's extravagant hospitality recalls the counterintuitive order of the biblical parables, as in the welcoming of the wayward young man in the parable of the prodigal son and the inversion of hierarchies of wealth in the parable of the wedding banquet.[77] These stories depend on what Robert Funk identifies as a "central irony," one that "contravenes the traditional way of representing God as a royal monarch" and advances instead "the unkingdom of the unGod," where "outsiders become insiders and insiders are left out."[78] *Romola* ends with a similar turn. Revising the heroine's earlier assertion that, if Savonarola's view is correct, she will "stand outside" God's kingdom (492), the novel's closing pages suggest, in a more provocative and compassionate gesture, that there is no "outside" God's kingdom.

The final scene, which moves forward in time to the year 1509 and depicts Romola as teacher to Tessa's growing children, underscores this expanded moral framework. Her role as storyteller—as one who speaks in parables—consolidates her standing as a wisdom figure, while also providing an analogue to Eliot's own novelistic method. The novel concludes with a dialogue between Romola and Tessa's son Lillo about ambition and happiness—*eudaimonia*, to put it in Aristotelian terms. Guiding Lillo beyond his initial impulse to associate happiness with his own pleasure, Romola tells him that the "highest happiness" results from "having wide thoughts" and "much feeling for the rest of the world as well as ourselves." She then cites two examples of the type of "great man" that Lillo might himself become: her father Bardo, the scholar who achieved "the greatness that belongs to integrity" and Savonarola, who modeled "the greatness of a life spent struggling against powerful wrong" (582). Coexisting with Romola's reverence for Savonarola is her ongoing esteem for the classical scholarship that Savonarola himself opposed.

More noteworthy still is the undertone of compassion within Romola's memory of Tito, a veiled yet important part of this conversation. She closes her philosophical discussion with a short narrative that begins "There was a man to whom I was very near." She speaks not only about the selfishness of one who "cared for nothing else so much as his own safety" but also about this man's initial good intentions, expressing a clear belief that, at least in the early days of their acquaintance, "he never thought of doing anything cruel or base." This story serves, in part, as a cautionary tale, but it is not a tidy didactic fable: it ends obliquely, leaving Lillo "looking up at her with awed wonder" as Romola assures him that she will tell him more "another time" (583). While the narrator's cryptic comment that "her voice was unsteady" makes it difficult to discern Romola's emotions, the few words readers are given underscore her depth of feeling. The narrative itself extends a form of kindness to Tito insofar as his legacy survives through his children: not only his son Lillo but also his daughter Ninna, depicted here as a thirteen-year-old girl, delicate but skilled in the craft of weaving—an activity that recalls the symbolism of Ariadne as weaver and interpreter elsewhere associated with Romola. Far from visiting the sins of the past generation on its children, Eliot's novel concludes with an understated yet significant gesture of forgiveness for its many imperfect father figures—Bardo, Savonarola, and even Tito.

Taken together, Eliot's novelistic engagement with higher critical ideas and her interest in parable as a literary form underscore her sense of both the limitations and the possibilities of religious discourse. She herself articulated this compound stance in a letter dated July 30, 1863, just before *Romola* completed its serial run. Commenting on her recent reading of Ernest Renan's *Vie de Jésus* (*Life of Jesus*), she reflected, "We can never have a satisfactory basis for the history of the man Jesus, but that negation does not affect the Idea of Christ either in its historical influence or in its great symbolic meanings" (*GEL* 4: 95). While skeptical of the Bible's literal truth, she nevertheless affirms its creative potentiality. In its combination of classical and Christian wisdom traditions, *Romola* has important elements in common with John Ruskin's *The Queen of the Air* (1869), which presents the goddess Athena in terms that owe to both Greek mythology and biblical poetry. Ruskin goes even further than Eliot in his challenge to the higher criticism's historicizing methods. Much as Eliot models an interpretive approach based not on deciphering a code but on proliferating questions, so also Ruskin approaches the stories about Athena in an imaginative mode: not as claims to be proved but as mysteries to be pondered.

Notes

1 J. Russell Perkin, *Theology and the Victorian Novel* (Montreal: McGill-Queen's University Press, 2009), 142. Eliot's translation of Feuerbach was the only one of her publications to be released under the name "Marian Evans." Born Mary Anne Evans, she began spelling her name "Mary Ann Evans" following her mother's death in 1836; after she became assistant editor of the *Westminster Review* in 1851, she started using "Marian Evans." The pseudonym "George Eliot" first appeared with *Scenes from Clerical Life* (1857), published by John Blackwood.

2 Peter C. Hodgson, *The Mystery beneath the Real: Theology in the Fiction of George Eliot* (Philadelphia: Fortress Press, 2000; Marilyn Orr, *George Eliot's Religious Imagination: A Theopoetics of Evolution* (Evanston: Northwestern University Press, 2018); John H. Mazaheri, *Essays on Religion in George Eliot's Early Fiction* (Cambridge: Cambridge Scholars Publishing, 2018); Ilana Blumberg, "Sympathy or Religion? George Eliot and Christian Conversion," *Nineteenth-Century Literature* 74, no. 3 (2019): 380–7.

3 George Eliot, letter to Robert Evans, January 2, 1842. In *The George Eliot Letters*, ed. Gordon S. Haight, vol. 1 (New Haven: Yale University Press, 1974), 128. All subsequent references to Eliot's correspondence come from Haight's edited collection and are cited parenthetically in text, abbreviated as *GEL*.

4 Timothy Larsen, *Contested Christianity: The Political and Social Contexts of Victorian Theology* (Waco: Baylor University Press, 2004), 43.

5 David Friedrich Strauss, *Life of Jesus, Critically Examined*, trans. George Eliot (London: Swan Sonnenschein & Co., 1898), 345.

6 George Eliot, "Thomas Carlyle." In *Essays of George Eliot*, ed. Thomas Pinney (London: Routledge and Kegan Paul, 1963), 212.

7   Felicia Bonaparte, *The Triptych and the Cross: The Central Myths of George Eliot's Poetic Imagination* (New York: New York University Press, 1979), 1.
8   Nancy Henry, *The Cambridge Introduction to George Eliot* (Cambridge: Cambridge University Press, 2008), 73–4. On *Romola*'s reception history, see Carol A. Martin, *George Eliot's Serial Fiction* (Columbus: Ohio State University Press, 1994).
9   Caroline Levine and Mark W. Turner, Introduction to *From Author to Text: Re-reading George Eliot's* Romola, ed. Caroline Levine and Mark W. Turner (Aldershot: Ashgate, 1998), 2.
10 David Carroll, *George Eliot and the Conflict of Interpretations* (Cambridge: Cambridge University Press, 1992), 197.
11 See, for instance, the discussion of the periodical response to *Adam Bede* in letters exchanged between George Eliot and Jane Welsh Carlyle, wife of Thomas Carlyle (*GEL* 3:17–19). Critical commentary on Eliot's engagement with Catholicism in this novel has drawn connections to the discourses of medievalism as advanced by Victorians such as Carlyle and John Ruskin; other critics have underscored the links between Catholicism's veneration of the Virgin Mary and the "Religion of Humanity" formulated by Auguste Comte, whose positivism has often been seen as one of this novel's chief philosophical underpinnings. See Bonaparte, *The Triptych and the Cross*, 179–80; see also T. R. Wright, *The Religion of Humanity: The Impact of Comtean Positivism on Victorian Britain* (Cambridge: Cambridge University Press, 1986), 25–8.
12 R. H. Hutton. Review of *Romola* in *The Spectator* (July 18, 1863, xxxvi, 2265–7), in *George Eliot: The Critical Heritage*, ed. David Carroll (London: Routledge and Kegan Paul, 1971), 200.
13 Christopher Herbert, *Evangelical Gothic: The English Novel and the Religious War on Virtue from Wesley to Dracula* (Charlottesville: University of Virginia Press, 2019), 196, 202.
14 Paul Ricoeur, "Biblical Hermeneutics," *Semeia* 4 (1975): 33.
15 Susan E. Colón, *Victorian Parables* (London: Continuum, 2012), 16.
16 See, for instance, Kelly E. Battles, "George Eliot's *Romola*: A Historical Novel 'Rather Different in Character,'" *Philological Quarterly* 88, no. 3 (2009): 232–3; see also Mary Wilson Carpenter, "The Trouble with *Romola*," in *Victorian Sages and Cultural Discourse: Renegotiating Gender and Power*, ed. Thaïs E. Morgan (New Brunswick: Rutgers University Press), 116–19.
17 George Eliot, *Romola* (London: Penguin Books, 2005), 492. All subsequent quotations from the novel come from this edition and are cited parenthetically in text.
18 Charles Hennell, *Inquiry Concerning the Origin of Christianity*, second edition (London: Trübner and Company, 1870), vi.
19 Ibid., 435.

20 Friedrich Schleiermacher, *A Critical Essay on the Gospel of St. Luke*, trans. Connop Thirlwall (London: John Taylor, 1825), 396.
21 Strauss, *Life of Jesus, Critically Examined*, 345.
22 Rudolf Bultmann, *The History of the Synoptic Tradition*, trans. John Marsh (New York: Harper and Row, 1963), 81. See also Ben Witherington, *Jesus the Sage: The Pilgrimage of Wisdom* (Philadelphia: Fortress Press, 1994), 115; and Charles W. Hedrick, *The Wisdom of Jesus: Between the Sages of Israel and the Apostles of the Church* (Eugene: Cascade Books, 2014), 118–19.
23 David Stern, *Midrash and Theory: Ancient Jewish Exegesis and Contemporary Literary Studies* (Evanston: Northwestern University Press, 1996), 40, 44.
24 For relevant examples from Eliot's correspondence, see *GEL* 1: 246–7. For scholarship that highlights Eliot's development of a more generous and thoughtful engagement with Judaism, see William Baker, *George Eliot and Judaism* (Salzburg: Institut für Englische Sprache und Literatur, Universität Salzburg, 1975), 9–55; Saleel Nurbhai and K. M. Newton, *George Eliot, Judaism, and the Novels* (New York: Palgrave, 2002), 25–45; and Richa Dwor, *Jewish Feeling: Difference and Affect in Nineteenth-Century Jewish Women's Writing* (London: Bloomsbury Academic, 2015), 85–114.
25 George Eliot, "Introduction to Genesis," in *Essays of George Eliot*, ed. Thomas Pinney (London: Routledge and Keagan Paul, 1963), 259.
26 Qtd. in Eliot, "Introduction to Genesis," 260.
27 Eliot, "Introduction to Genesis," 259.
28 See Jonah 4:1-10.
29 In addition to Colón's *Victorian Parables*, as cited previously, see also Linda M. Lewis, *Dickens, His Parables, and His Reader* (Columbia: University of Missouri Press, 2011); and Amy Coté, "Parables and Unitarianism in Elizabeth Gaskell's *Mary Barton*," *Victorian Review* 40, no. 1 (2014): 59–76.
30 Leah Price, "George Eliot and the Production of Consumers," *NOVEL: A Forum on Fiction* 30, no. 2 (1997): 147.
31 *The Bible: Authorized King James Version with Apocrypha* (Oxford: Oxford University Press, 2008). All biblical quotations are cited parenthetically in text. Rights in the Authorized (King James) Version in the UK are vested in the Crown. Reproduced by Permission of the Crown's patentee, Cambridge University Press.
32 Andrew Thompson, *George Eliot and Italy* (New York: Macmillan, 1998), 7.
33 See Mt. 5:21-48.
34 Ricoeur, "Biblical Hermeneutics," *Semeia* 4 (1975): 32.
35 Wright, *The Religion of Humanity*, 173–6.
36 Bonaparte, *The Triptych and the Cross*, 34–6.
37 Mary Wilson Carpenter, *George Eliot and the Landscape of Time: Narrative Form and Protestant Apocalyptic History* (Chapel Hill: University of North Carolina Press, 1986), 64.

38 Bonaparte, *The Triptych*, 27; Carpenter, *George Eliot*, 29.
39 See the discussion of Colenso's reception offered by Timothy Larsen, *Contested Christianity: The Political and Social Contexts of Victorian Theology* (Waco: Baylor University Press, 2004), 72–5.
40 See, for instance, George P. Landow, *Elegant Jeremiahs: The Sage from Carlyle to Mailer* (Ithaca: Cornell University Press, 1986), 41–71. See also John Holloway, *The Victorian Sage: Studies in Argument* (New York: Norton, 1953), which informs Landow's study.
41 See Holloway, *The Victorian Sage*, 111–57; see also Carpenter, "The Trouble with *Romola*," 105–28.
42 Paul Ricoeur, *Freud and Philosophy: An Essay on Interpretation*, translated by Dennis Savage (New Haven: Yale University Press, 1970), 26–7.
43 See 1 Cor. 1:18–28.
44 Ricoeur, "Toward a Hermeneutic of the Idea of Revelation," in *Essays on Biblical Interpretation*, ed. Lewis S. Mudge, trans. David Pellauer (Philadelphia: Fortress Press, 1980), 75–81.
45 Erich Auerbach, *Mimesis: The Representation of Reality in Western Literature*, trans. Willard R. Trask (Princeton: Princeton University Press, 1953), 11–12.
46 Robert Alter, *The Art of Biblical Narrative* (New York: Basil Books, 1981), 97.
47 Ibid., 12.
48 See Audrey Jaffe, *Scenes of Sympathy: Identity and Representation in Victorian Fiction* (Ithaca: Cornell University Press, 2000), 127–57; Suzy Anger, *Victorian Interpretation* (Ithaca: Cornell University Press, 2005); Rae Greiner, "Sympathy Time: Adam Smith, George Eliot, and the Realist Novel," *Narrative* 17, no. 3 (2009): 291–311; and Rebecca N. Mitchell, *Victorian Lessons in Empathy and Difference* (Athens: Ohio State University Press, 2011), 49–69.
49 Anger, *Victorian Interpretation*, 96.
50 Adam Smith, *The Theory of Moral Sentiments* (Amherst: Prometheus Books, 2000), 22.
51 Ludwig Feuerbach, *The Essence of Christianity*, trans. George Eliot (New York: Harper and Row, 1957), 140.
52 Feuerbach, *The Essence of Christianity*, 53.
53 Ibid., 97.
54 Gareth Atkins, "'Strauss-Sick?' Jesus and the Saints of the Church of the Future," in *The Figure of Christ in the Long Nineteenth Century*, ed. Elizabeth Ludlow (London: Palgrave Macmillan, 2020), 227–8.
55 Sebastian Lecourt, *Cultivating Belief: Victorian Anthropology, Liberal Aesthetics, and the Secular Imagination* (Oxford: Oxford University Press, 2018), 109.
56 Hodgson, *The Mystery Beneath the Real*, 7.

57 Charles LaPorte, *Victorian Poets and the Changing Bible* (Charlottesville: University of Virginia Press, 2011), 189–230; Wendy Williams, *George Eliot, Poetess* (Burlington: Ashgate, 2014), 39–66.
58 Carroll, *George Eliot*, 196–7.
59 See the discussion of this symbolism by Gail Turley Houston, *Victorian Women Writers, Radical Grandmothers, and the Gendering of God* (Athens: Ohio State University Press, 2013), 121.
60 Carroll, *George Eliot*, 192.
61 Colón, *Victorian Parables*, 13.
62 Ricoeur, "Biblical Hermeneutics," 75.
63 Herbert, *Evangelical Gothic*, 203–5.
64 See Mt. 10:14; Mt. 5–7; Lk. 6.
65 Feuerbach, *The Essence of Christianity*, 278.
66 Charles Taylor, *Sources of the Self: The Making of a Modern Identity* (Cambridge: Harvard University Press, 1989), 232–3.
67 Coleridge, *The Collected Works of Samuel Taylor Coleridge*, vol. 7. no. 1, ed. James Engell and Walter Jackson Bate (Princeton: Princeton University Press, 1983), 81.
68 Louis Dupré, *The Quest of the Absolute: Birth and Decline of European Romanticism* (Notre Dame: University of Notre Dame Press, 2013), 336, 309–35.
69 Ibid., 49.
70 Ibid., 43.
71 Simone Weil, *Gravity and Grace*, trans. Arthur Wills (Lincoln: University of Nebraska Press, 1997), 80.
72 Hans-Georg Gadamer, *Truth and Method*, 2nd edn., trans. Joel Weinsheimer and Donald G. Marshall (New York: Continuum, 1975), 307–10.
73 Colón, *Victorian Parables*, 122.
74 Ibid., 13.
75 Eliot, *Middlemarch: A Study of Provincial Life* (Peterborough: Broadview Press, 2004), 640.
76 Hodgson, *The Mystery beneath the Real*, 92.
77 See Mt. 22:1-14; Lk. 15:11-32.
78 Robert Funk, *A Credible Jesus: Fragments of a Vision* (Salem: Polebridge Press, 2002), 18, 135.

4

Wisdom's Reach: Mythmaking, Incarnational Poetics, and Interpretive Limits in John Ruskin's *The Queen of the Air*

Among the many works published by the polymath John Ruskin, from his five-volume *Modern Painters* to his incomplete autobiography *Praeterita*, Ruskin himself singled out *The Queen of the Air* as a personal best—a seemingly odd choice.[1] *The Queen of the Air* presents itself as a collection of lectures about the Greek goddess Athena, an academic discussion addressed primarily to students of classical mythology. Yet it also offers a wide-ranging meditation on wisdom that stretches this scholarly form to its limits. Subtitled "A Study of the Greek Myths of Cloud and Storm" and based on a series of talks given at University College in March of 1869, the volume opens with a preface recommending its contents to "persons who are beginning to take an interest in the aspects of mythology which only recent investigation has moved from the realm of conjecture to the realm of rational inquiry" (*WJR* XIX: 292). Ruskin alludes to the non-doctrinal and textually rigorous approach championed by philologists such as Friedrich Max Müller. Müller, who moved from Germany to England in 1846 and was subsequently appointed professor at Oxford, emphasized the historical contexts informing religious texts, studying them without theological motivation.[2] Aside from this prefatory gesture, however, Ruskin departs from the dispassionate analysis prized by Müller, instead presenting Athena in terms that embody his own aesthetic and ethical vision.

The Queen of the Air offers an innovative act of mythmaking that took shape against a defining moment within nineteenth-century intellectual history: the advent of comparative religious study, a field with close ties to the work of biblical higher critics. Ruskin's imaginative synthesis draws from a variety of wisdom traditions, both classical and biblical, as Paul L. Sawyer highlights.[3] According to Ruskin, Athena is the "forming power" that has "by all nations" been "understood as a creative wisdom, proceeding from the Supreme Deity; but entering into and inspiring all intelligences that work in Harmony with Him" (*WJR* XIX: 378). This description recalls the eighth chapter in the book of Proverbs, which portrays Wisdom as present from the laying of the earth's foundations and imploring all people to hearken to her call.[4] As his lectures unfold, Ruskin develops this imagery not only by making recourse to descriptions of God the Son and God the Holy Spirit throughout the Christian New Testament—a standard typological move—but also by invoking the apocryphal books of Ecclesiasticus (also known as Ben Sira [Hebrew] or Sirach [Greek]) and the Wisdom of Solomon, which likewise hypostasize Wisdom. These texts reflect the efforts of Jewish sages to harmonize and amplify their cultural traditions within a Hellenistic context.[5] Ruskin, in turn, appropriates this wisdom writing in ways that not only reflect his participation in the imperialist and gendered discourses of Victorian Britain but also unsettle prevailing ideologies. By the time that Ruskin delivered these lectures in the late 1860s, he had distanced himself from the Evangelical Protestantism that informed his early years. Nevertheless, as scholars have long noted, his published writings make frequent and creative use of Christian texts and theology. Perhaps the most striking quality of *The Queen of the Air* is the extent to which it takes up biblical wisdom literature's characteristic literary forms, incorporating what amounts to Ruskin's own hymn to personified Wisdom. Questioning prevailing ideas about historical and scientific objectivity, *The Queen of the Air* probes the affective potentialities of poetic metaphor. This creative approach invites a broader critical reassessment of Ruskin's authorial voice and didactic strategies.

When Ruskin first edited his lectures for publication, he hoped that they would become the first installment of a revised and corrected series of his collected writings—"a kind of 'prequel' to *Modern Painters*, *The Stones of Venice*, and the other early works," to quote John Batchelor's apt description.[6] Cast in this light, *The Queen of the Air* would provide a reader's first point of entry into the artistic criticism and social commentary that came to influence both the Pre-Raphaelite Brotherhood (the painterly and poetic initiative spearheaded by Dante Gabriel Rossetti, John Everett Millais, and William Holman Hunt) and William Morris's Arts and Crafts Movement, which championed the beauty and everyday use of artisanal work in protest against industrial progress. But though *The Queen of the Air* was published in volume form by Smith, Elder, and Company only a few months after the lectures were delivered, this revised and corrected series never saw the light of day, partly due to Ruskin's declining health. Still, traces of his bold ambitions can be found throughout his published text. His three lectures outline Athena's activity in expansive terms. First, "Athena Chalinitis" (which Ruskin initially translates as "Athena the Restrainer" and later restates as "Athena in the Heavens") attempts to interweave classical myth and modern science in its account of atmospheric phenomena and reflections on humankind's attempts to discern the ordering of the cosmos. Next, "Athena Keramitis" (which Ruskin renders as both "Athena, fit for being made into pottery" and "Athena in the Earth") traces the goddess's presence within plant and animal life, while also identifying her as a force that inspires creative activity among humankind. Athena's role in shaping human art takes center stage in the final lecture "Athena Ergane" (translated as both "Athena the Worker" and "Athena in the Heart"), where Ruskin forges extravagant connections to ideas discussed in his earlier works, including his forceful critique of political economy in *Unto This Last* (1862). These echoes and ambitions indicate that *The Queen of the Air* merits attention in relation to a broader framework than critics tend to pursue. Several studies have situated it in relation to developments in nineteenth-century studies of mythology, including work by Müller as well as Edward Burnett Tylor.[7] To further illuminate Ruskin's revisionary portrait of Athena, my analysis puts *The Queen of the Air* within related yet wider contexts: not only Ruskin's reading of biblical higher criticism but also the interpretive and didactic frameworks that he developed in response. Seen in this light, *The Queen of the Air* offers a self-reflexive meditation on questions about right reading and good teaching.

Ruskin's concerns with these crucial questions take center stage in the opening of his first lecture. Appealing to his audience for permission to consider Greek mythology "in a temper differing from that in which it is frequently treated," he insists, "we cannot justly interpret the religion of any people unless we are prepared to admit that we ourselves, as well as they, are liable to error in matters of faith" (*WJR* XIX: 295). His emphasis on this shared propensity to error is in keeping with the discoveries of an increasing number of British biblical scholars who, by the 1860s, were not only translating and reviewing continental higher criticism but also publishing their own studies, including such controversial works as the collectively authored *Essays and Reviews* (1860) and Bishop John William Colenso's *The Pentateuch and the Book of Joshua Critically Examined* (hereafter, *The Pentateuch*, 1862). Both Ruskin's direct statements about this scholarship in his letters and his indirect responses to it throughout *The Queen of the Air* demonstrate that he shared with these scholars an interest in recontextualizing biblical texts and challenging literalist interpretation. At the same time, his poetic approach to wisdom literature runs counter to the higher criticism's methodological impulses.

Even as *The Queen of the Air* criticizes both the "masters of history" and the "masters of modern science" (*WJR* XIX: 299, 294), Ruskin self-consciously acknowledges his own fallibility. His remarks about the limits of his own knowledge, in turn, invite a reconsideration of his authorial voice. Literary critics have long called attention to the heavy-handed, even patronizing, temper of Ruskin's works: Dinah Birch identifies an "assumption of secure authority" as a characteristic feature of his public persona, and George P. Landow classifies him as a textbook example of the Victorian sage, a self-appointed prophet and one who speaks as a "master of experience."[8] My approach complements and complicates this portrait of Ruskin by reconsidering moments when he speaks as a sage in dialogue—with himself, as well as with his audiences or readers. From time to time, Ruskin's statements about interpretive practice reflect the emphasis on recovering authorial intent that dominated nineteenth-century hermeneutics. For the most part, however, his creative rewritings reflect a much greater appreciation for the reader's active work.

This chapter situates Ruskin's mythmaking in relation to specific nineteenth-century controversies, while also showing how his emphasis on the world-building capacity of metaphor might be brought into productive alignment with Paul Ricoeur's theoretical writings. Ruskin's expansive discussion of mythology participates in the higher criticism's work of situating biblical texts in broader cultural contexts, even as his poetic approach offers a useful critique of narrowly historicizing modes of inquiry. Ranging across religious traditions, Ruskin engages with both the problems and the possibilities raised by emergent ideas of universalism. Similarly, his portrayal of Wisdom as a female goddess at once reflects the patriarchal gender ideologies of Victorian Britain and destabilizes its prevailing rhetoric of separate spheres for men and women. His personified Wisdom, envisioned in the wake of the many "lives of Jesus" that circulated in Victorian Britain following Eliot's landmark translation of Strauss's *Das Leben Jesu*, reflects his development of an incarnation theology that esteems embodied, earthly existence. What results is an imperfect yet powerful reframing of both imperfection and aspiration. As Ruskin himself admits, his lectures reach after ideas beyond his grasp. Nevertheless, his ambitious efforts suggest that writing about wisdom in forms that cannot easily accommodate the subject may be as productive as it is challenging.

Storms of Controversy: Ruskin and the Higher Critical Debates of the 1860s

Ruskin's "Study of the Greek Myths of Cloud and Storm" reconsiders ancient stories about atmospheric phenomena, while also responding to a still more figurative variety of "storm": the interpretive controversies galvanized by the spread of biblical higher criticism in mid-Victorian Britain. *Essays and Reviews* featured contributions from seven British scholars (Frederick Temple, Rowland Williams, Baden Powell, Henry Bristow Wilson, Mark Pattison, Charles Wycliffe Goodwin, and Benjamin Jowett) who explained and defended the findings and principles of the German higher criticism—much to the shock of many Victorian readers, given that six of the seven contributors (all except the geologist Goodwin) were also ordained Anglican ministers. By 1869, the year of Ruskin's lectures, *Essays and Reviews* had entered its thirteenth edition and sold over 24,250 copies.[9] First issued in October 1862, Colenso's *The Pentateuch* sold 8,000 copies in three weeks and eventually went into four editions. A skilled mathematician as well as the first Bishop of Natal, Colenso was tried for and convicted of heresy, though acquitted on appeal in 1865. His work caused an uproar not merely for questioning Mosaic authorship but, rather, for offering a rigorous mathematical critique of these biblical accounts, showing that their dates, dimensions, and figures could not be literally correct. In his own approach to comparative mythology, Ruskin similarly calls attention to the problems with putting too much stock in the exact language of sacred texts, whether classical or biblical. However, he takes a different tactic than either Colenso or the contributors to *Essays and Reviews*, calling into question both literalism and historicism.

At the time that Ruskin formulated *The Queen of the Air*, he had read these controversial works of biblical scholarship and even entered the social circles of these scholars themselves, mainly through his acquaintance with Margaret Alexis Bell, a personal friend of Colenso as well as several contributors to *Essays and Reviews*. Bell founded Winnington Hall, an innovative school for girls at which Ruskin lectured throughout the 1860s.[10] Ruskin's range across Greek, Egyptian, Jewish, and Christian traditions aligns with one of the basic claims advanced in *Essays and Reviews*: that biblical texts should be seen as equivalent to other religious writings and, indeed, emerged in dialogue with other religions. Earlier scholarly forays into mythology, such as the work of Richard Payne Knight, similarly called attention to the correspondences between Christian traditions and other cultural rites based in fertility worship.[11] For his part, Ruskin invites his audience to put themselves in the place of the ancient Greeks, reminding them, "this literal belief was, in the mind of the general people, as deeply rooted as ours in the legends of our own sacred book; and that a basis of unmiraculous event was as little suspected ... by them, as by us" (*WJR* XIX: 289). This statement does not directly address the question of whether he regarded the "legends" of the Bible as equally fallible, though private letters to his father indicate his agreement with the authors of *Essays and Reviews*.[12] Even so, his reliance on the first-person pronoun highlights the enduring legacy of his own Evangelical heritage. As underscored throughout *The Queen of the Air*, his quest for Wisdom was not merely academic but also deeply personal.

Ruskin's own belief position was both dynamic and nuanced. Although he claims in *Praeterita* to have experienced a "final apostasy from Christian doctrine" during the spring of 1858, his autobiography suggests something more complicated than a definitive loss of faith (*WJR* XXXV: 492). Once upon a Sunday morning in Turin, Ruskin recalls, he disregarded a sermon on the world's wickedness and ventured into an art gallery to look at Paolo Veronese's *Solomon and the Queen of Sheba* (c.1555). Viewing this painting prompted an epiphanic moment, with Ruskin concluding that all "things done delightfully and rightly" are "done by the help and in the Spirit of God" (*WJR* XXXV: 496). As Stephen Cheeke emphasizes in his study of the "religion of art" in Victorian culture from the Pre-Raphaelites to the Arts and Crafts Movement, Ruskin's realization would be best understood not as a loss of faith but rather as "an expansion of the horizon of divinity in the world, an increase in the possibility of what and where to worship rightly."[13] Indeed, Ruskin is difficult to pinpoint within clearly defined religious communities. His family belonged to the Church of England, but he was influenced as much by Scotch dissent as by Anglicanism during his early years.[14] By 1864, he entertained a budding if cautious fascination with spiritualism and participated in his first seance—hardly a conventional interest for a Victorian Christian, though one that he shared with Elizabeth Barrett Browning (EBB), as noted in Chapter 1. In a letter dated that same year to George MacDonald, the former Congregationalist minister with whom Ruskin shared a close personal friendship, he playfully identified as "a pagan."[15] But if by "pagan" Ruskin meant someone enchanted with a variety of religious and literary traditions, then MacDonald might not have been so far from paganism himself, as suggested in Chapter 2. Ruskin's turn to Egyptian and Greek mythology throughout the 1860s issued from a growing conviction that no single religious tradition has a monopoly on truth. However, this conviction coexisted with an imaginative use of biblical language, not only as a means of wielding authority when addressing a predominantly Christian audience but also as a creative resource.

Ruskin turns to biblical wisdom poetry throughout *The Queen of the Air* to articulate a model of imaginative reading that is responsive to yet critical of recent scholarly developments. Invoking Job 38:38, he identifies "the nymph Taygeta" from Greek mythology as "one of those Pleiades of whom is the question to Job,—'Canst thou bind the sweet influences of Pleiades, or loose the bands of Orion?'" (*WJR* XIX: 321). Such cross-referencing seems in keeping with burgeoning developments in comparative religious study, yet Ruskin's approach to Greek mythology takes issue with what he calls "modern historical inquiry." He claims that stories of Athena possess "a veracity of vision" that "no merely historical investigator can understand," as such truths "can only be interpreted by those ... who themselves in some measure also see visions and dream dreams" (*WJR* XIX: 309). These words echo Peter's description of the outpouring of the Holy Spirit in the second chapter of Acts, itself a quotation from the prophet Joel: "your young men shall see visions, and your old men shall dream dreams" (Acts 2:17).[16] Furthermore, this emphasis on the reader's subjectivity departs from the concern with recovering a text's original situation upheld by biblical and classical scholars such as Jowett, who wrote the final piece in *Essays and Reviews*. However, Jowett too suggested that certain poetic forms, including those found within biblical wisdom traditions, possess "a depth and inwardness" that requires "a measure of the same qualities in the interpreter himself."[17] If only subtly, Jowett affirmed variety within the Bible's literary forms, which demand to be read not only within their historical contexts but also for their artistic and reflective qualities—a point expressed more emphatically and self-consciously in Ruskin's meditations on Athena as Wisdom.

Insofar as it emphasizes the poetic functions of religious language, *The Queen of the Air* shares something in common with Matthew Arnold's arguments in *Literature and Dogma*, a series of essays on biblical interpretation initially published serially in the *Cornhill Magazine* in 1871. Building on the broadly Romantic philosophies of writers such as Thomas Carlyle and challenging those who purported to prove or disprove points of doctrine on the basis of exact scriptural language, Arnold claimed that these interpreters fail to grasp the metaphorical nature of religious language, described as being "*thrown out at an object of consciousness not fully grasped.*"[18] As Arnold put it, "terms ... with which St. Paul are *literary* terms, theologians have employed as if they were *scientific* terms."[19] This injunction to read the Bible as poetry aimed to correct not only the conservative theologians who held to literalist modes of exegesis but also those opponents of Christianity who claimed that biblical texts had been discredited by science. While Arnold and Ruskin concur about the nature of religious language, Ruskin goes to unusual lengths in relying on metaphor as a means through which to articulate this very point. To put it in Ricoeurian terms, whereas *Literature and Dogma* employs argumentative *rhetoric* (that which "aims at persuading men by giving to discourse pleasing ornaments"), *The Queen of the Air* pursues something closer to Ricoeur's concept of *poetics*, with its invitation to follow "the twisting pathway of heuristic fiction."[20]

Concerns about the limitations of approaching biblical texts through a narrowly historical lens became uppermost in the debates surrounding Colenso's *The Pentateuch*. Not long before this book's publication, Ruskin predicted in a letter to Bell that Colenso's work would make "a splendid crash," going so far as to speculate that even *Essays and Reviews* would be "nothing to it."[21] These forecasts proved largely accurate. Whereas *Essays and Reviews* polarized public opinion, *The Pentateuch* found fewer defenders, even within religiously liberal contexts. To many readers, Colenso's arithmetic seemed only to exacerbate the worst, most tedious tendencies of literal reading. Arnold, for one, lamented the attention given to Colenso's work, which he saw as lacking in its critical method: "It is really the strongest possible proof of the low ebb at which, in England, the critical spirit is, that while the critical hit in the religious literature of Germany is Dr. Strauss's book, in that of France M. Renan's book, the book of Bishop Colenso is the critical hit in the religious literature of England."[22] Given Ruskin's complaints against "frigid scholarship" (*WJR* XIX: 309) throughout *The Queen of the Air*, his support for the mathematician might seem surprising. And yet, he told Bell, who provided refuge to Colenso in the aftermath of the book's publication, "*I will stand by your Bishop* .... I'll stand by him to *any* extent .... I'll say anything that I can—anywhere—to anybody—publicly—in print—in private—as he chooses."[23] In a letter to his father, Ruskin similarly sided with Colenso, claiming that he himself had ventured "far beyond the point at which [Colenso] is standing now."[24] Although there would seem to be little resemblance between Colenso's mathematics and Ruskin's mythmaking, their divergent approaches arrived at related conclusions. Colenso's work was deemed heretical, but his point was hardly to reject biblical authority—rather, his commentary indicated that to approach these texts as precise historical records is to distort them. Ruskin, in turn, went one step further, modeling an alternative approach of reading mythological texts in light of their symbolic multiplicity.

Perceiving Darkly: Mythmaking and Ruskin's Resistance to Scholarly Certitude

Rather than uncover the historical contexts that produced the myths of Athena, *The Queen of the Air* comments on the affordances of mythic expression itself: it is, as Sawyer puts it, "both an original act of myth-making and a myth *about* myth-making."[25] According to Ruskin's lectures, a *myth* is first and foremost "a story with a meaning attached to it, other than it seems to have at first" (*WJR* XIX: 296). By defining *myth* in terms of what is "other," Ruskin implies that it is a form of allegory (from the Greek "allos," meaning "other"), though a complex one: he goes on to claim that these multiple layers of meaning cannot be easily determined, continue to develop over time, and signify across cultural traditions. Landow usefully sums up Ruskin's definition of myth as "polysemous allegory," a descriptor that can be amplified to illuminate Ruskin's subtle repositioning of typological exegesis in response to biblical higher criticism.[26] As Landow highlights elsewhere, typology presupposes a belief in the literal inspiration of scripture's exact words: exegetical handbooks such as Thomas Hartwell Horne's *An Introduction to the Critical Study and Knowledge of the Holy Scriptures* (1825) distinguish a *type* from a *parable* on the basis that the former is "grounded in fact, not in a fictitious narrative."[27] Conversely, Ruskin's fusion of classical and biblical texts undoes this distinction and reclaims such "fictitious narrative" as possible grounds for truth.

Outlining "the right reading of myths," Ruskin claims that mythology requires a participatory model of interpretation, whereby the reader becomes a co-creator. This model proceeds from what Ruskin saw as four foundational principles about mythology's "true vision": first, that it is "founded on constant laws common to all human nature"; second, "that it perceives, however darkly, things which are for all ages true"; third, "that we can only understand it so far as we have some perception of the same truth"; and fourth, "that its fulness is developed and manifested more and more by the reverberation of it from minds of the same mirror-temper, in succeeding ages" (*WJR* XIX: 310). As Ruskin theorizes it, mythology is legible only to receptive individuals who, in the act of reinterpreting these primal stories, also extend them. Setting aside the scholarly preoccupation with the "interpretation of human myths," he instead prioritizes "natural myths," or "the dark sayings of nature" (*WJR* XIX: 361). His phrasing evokes the description of "dark sayings" in the opening to the book of Proverbs, positioning *The Queen of the Air* itself as a kind of wisdom writing.[28]

Ruskin advances this concept of mythmaking as part of his critique of "historical analysis," spurned for its "clumsy and vapid veracity of externals," and it serves his challenge to "modern science" as well (*WJR* XIX: 309, 294). These two discourses overlapped in the nineteenth century, as the spread of historical-critical biblical scholarship coincided and intersected with the development of evolutionary theory. Within *Essays and Reviews*, the articles by both Baden Powell and Jowett directly reference Charles Darwin's *On the Origin of the Species*, published only the previous year. As it contested accepted ideas about biblical inspiration, *Essays and Reviews* also called into question the natural theology advanced by earlier thinkers such as William Paley.[29] *The Queen of the Air* responds to these dual pressures by revitalizing what Ruskin calls "myths relating to natural phenomena" to advance a radically different approach to both word and world.

Ruskin's resistance to Darwin emerges in his second lecture, where he discusses Athena's presence in plant and animal life. Following a brief reference to "the distinctions of species," Ruskin appends a footnote stating that his ideas "are in nowise antagonistic to the theories which Mr. Darwin's unwearied and unerring investigations are every day rendering more probable." However, he goes on to remark, "it has always seemed to me, in what little work I have done upon organic forms, as if the species mocked us by their deliberate imitation of each other when they met; yet did not pass into one another" (*WJR* XIX: 358). Analyzing the frequent and often deriding references to Darwin throughout Ruskin's writings, George Levine argues that these two thinkers "practiced two conflicting kinds of science" that, in turn, reflect conflicting uses of language.[30] Whereas "Darwin's thought" shows "the impulse to substantiate metaphor and particularly to find a real place in the material order for older mythological expression," Ruskin progresses in the opposite direction: "to transform the material into metaphor."[31] Ruskin's disagreement with Darwin, then, issues from his commitment to metaphor as a dynamic mode of perceiving darkly.

This basic contrast finds a useful parallel within Ricoeur's concept of *poetics*. For Ricoeur, this category signifies not a particular kind of writing but a particular linguistic use, one that exercises "a referential function that differs from the descriptive referential function of ordinary language and above all of scientific discourse." Unlike science, which conceptualizes truth according to "the criteria of verification or falsification," the "poetic function" conceives of truth as a revelatory "manifestation" resistant to empirical verification.[32] Ruskin valorizes such a "poetic function" when he insists that "the Myth of Athena as a Formative and Decisive Power" continues to signify even "after science has done its worst" (*WJR* XIX: 354). He further celebrates the vitality of metaphors by claiming that the poetry of John Keats and William Morris offers "a more truthful idea of the nature of Greek religion and legend" than does "frigid scholarship" (*WJR* XIX: 309).

Ruskin closes the preface to his lecture series with an apostrophe to men of learning, calling on them to return to the simple wisdom of mythmaking:

> Ah, masters of modern science, give me back my Athena out of your vials. You have divided the elements, and united them; enslaved them upon the earth, and discerned them in the stars. Teach us, now, but this of them, which is all that man need know,—that the Air is given to him for his life; and the Rain to his thirst, and for his baptism; and the Fire for warmth; and the Sun for sight; and the Earth for his meat—and Rest.
>
> (*WJR* XIX: 294)

Insisting that the project of analyzing and classifying nature has not enriched human understanding in a meaningful way, Ruskin urges his readers to focus not on the increase of knowledge but on the ethics of knowledge. His phrasing invokes that of Percy Bysshe Shelley's *A Defence of Poetry* (written in 1821 but published only posthumously, in 1841), which likewise claims that want of the "poetical faculty" means that "man, having enslaved the elements, remains himself a slave."[33] These statements accord with Ruskin's broader critique of science and technology for their abuse of the earth: to have enslaved the elements is, for Ruskin, a moral fault, as several recent studies of him as an ecocritical thinker have emphasized.[34] Despite the anthropocentrism underlying this passage, which describes the natural world as designed for human uses, his elemental, even sacramental, language initiates a primal reorientation to both word and world.

To find an ecological interconnectivity within Ruskin's poetics is not to discount the many hierarchical constructions that inform this work. Published the same year as Arnold's *Culture and Anarchy* (1869), *The Queen of the Air* emerged against the backdrop of Victorian constructs of "Hellenism" and "Hebraism," along with other orientalist and racialized frameworks. Positioning himself as a redactor who has curated the more palatable aspects of his subject and discarded others, Ruskin tells his audience that he has assembled "only instances of what is beautiful in Greek religion," warning that "even in its best time" this religion contained "deep corruptions" and "degraded forms" (*WJR* XIX: 365). While these reservations distinguish Ruskin's view of Greek culture from the "sweetness and light" that characterize the Arnoldian version of

Hellenism, he nevertheless advances his own reductive categories. He follows this remark about the "degraded forms" of Greek religion with the more disturbingly paternalistic statement that "in the religions of the lower races, little else than these corrupted forms of devotion can be found" (*WJR* XIX: 365). Such a claim reflects the hierarchical constructs informing nineteenth-century approaches to comparative religion, which regarded the so-called "high" religions of Hinduism and Buddhism as exotic objects of fascination yet discounted the beliefs of allegedly "primitive" societies such as tribal groups in Africa and the Caribbean as not worthy of serious study.[35] Even as Ruskin presented Athena as "the Desire of all nations," he joined his contemporaries in regarding some nations as more discerning than others.

These tensions reflect larger conflicts within emergent concepts of universalism, concepts that played a substantial role in shaping critical discourse as new disciplines developed. At large, the work of nineteenth-century anthropologists and philologists reveals what Sebastian Lecourt summarizes as "at least two different roads to universalism that intersect in frequently vexing ways": on the one hand, there is "a universalism that attempts to impose a single set of values on the entire world," and, on the other, "a universalism that would try to sum up a world of contending values within one framework."[36] These paths cross throughout Ruskin's writings as well as the scholarship informing it, including Colenso's biblical criticism, which emerged within the context of his missionary activity in South Africa. Colenso, who was criticized for his tolerance of Zulu practices of polygamy, objected to the doctrine of eternal punishment, much as did other liberal theologians such as F. D. Maurice and MacDonald, who likewise came under fire for their ideas about universal salvation. Colenso's theology was informed by his experiences in Natal, and his preface to *The Pentateuch* memorably presents his scholarly inquiry as prompted by a conversation with the Zulu man who helped him to translate the Bible. He recounts that this man's question "is all this true?" gave him pause: "'Shall a man speak lies in the name of the Lord?' ... I dared not do so."[37] This anecdote prompted some of Colenso's more resistant readers to mock him as "the missionary who was converted by the natives."[38] Caricatures aside, however, Colenso's case shows that the exchange of ideas resulting from missionary activity was not necessarily a one-way street. Recent work on nineteenth-century religion within global frameworks has demonstrated that nineteenth-century missionaries played a more complicated role in the development of cosmopolitan thought than critical narratives about religion and empire tend to credit. Scholarship in this vein has further highlighted that, insofar as Victorian studies has inherited the "comparativist" models of nineteenth-century discourse, these models have restricted critical understanding of global religion, proposing that scholarship adopting a "connective" method might be brought forward as a resource for "undisciplining" and expanding the field.[39] These proposals indicate that there is a critical imperative to reconsider Ruskin's conflicted concepts of universalism, both for their Eurocentric assumptions and for their more complex distinctions.

Tellingly, one passage within *The Queen of the Air* that approaches a more hospitable variety of universalism, one that opens toward plurality and even interconnectivity, draws on the account of the apostle Paul's missionary activity at the Athenian Areopagus. Recalling Acts chapter 17, Ruskin states that "opposite to the temple of this Spirit of the breath"—that is, to Athena—stood "an altar to a God unknown;—proclaimed at last to them, as one who, indeed, gave all men life, and breath, and all things" (*WJR* XIX: 386). The sermon to which Ruskin alludes dismisses these Greek rituals, calling for repentance and conversion, though it does so by appealing to the putatively "pagan" poets.[40] Whereas the Pauline sermon purports to proclaim a hitherto "unknown" God, Ruskin expresses far less confidence in his speech's revelatory power. He supplements his allusion to the speech in the Areopagus with a distinctly cautionary note: "we ourselves, fretted here in our narrow days, know less, perhaps, in very deed, than they, what manner of spirit we are of, or what manner of spirit we ignorantly worship" (*WJR* XIX: 387). His suggestion that these religious mysteries remain unknown develops the points about epistemic limitation emphasized from his first lecture's beginning. Warning against dismissing the myths of Athena as superficial and mistaken, Ruskin implores, "remember that, whatever charge of folly may justly attach to the saying, 'There is no God,' the folly is prouder, deeper, and less pardonable, in saying, 'There is no God but for me'" (*WJR* XIX: 296).[41] His addition "but for me" cautions against definitive proclamations, especially those of one claiming to speak as a divine mouthpiece.

This emphasis on epistemic limitation conditions the primitivism that emerges throughout *The Queen of the Air*. Taking issue with the reductive terminology whereby "superstition" denotes "the creeds of the past" and "religion" signifies "the creeds of the present day," Ruskin insists that both understandings are incomplete (*WJR* XIX: 295). His seemingly dismissive statement that the Greek storyteller may be "a reserved philosopher, who is veiling a theory of the universe under the grotesque of the fairy tale" warrants consideration in relation to his larger theory of the grotesque as an aesthetic category (*WJR* XIX: 297). As indicated by his discussion of grotesque symbolism in the third volume of *Modern Painters* (1856), his use of the term "grotesque" is far from pejorative: rather, he praises "the noble nature and power of grotesque conception." In particular, Ruskin valorizes the "fine grotesque," a form that he explains as "a series of symbols thrown together in a bold and fearless connection, of truths which it would have taken a long time to express in any verbal way, and of which the connection is left for the beholder to work out for himself," citing Edmund Spenser's presentation of "malicious Envy" in the first book of *The Faerie Queene* as an example (*WJR* V:132). For Ruskin, the "fine grotesque" requires the imagination of the beholder or reader to supplement that which exceeds the artist or author's capacity to render in words or pictures.

This emphasis on both the writer and the reader's emotion, in turn, underscores the complexity of the "pathetic fallacy," one of Ruskin's most often-cited—if also commonly misunderstood—terms. In the same volume of *Modern Painters*, he introduces this concept in broad terms, as "a fallacy caused by an excited state of the feelings, making us, for the time, more or less irrational," though his subsequent discussion focuses more specifically on personifications of nature (*WJR* V:210). Even though Ruskin claims that the best poets avoid this tendency, the contrast he draws between Samuel Taylor Coleridge (whom he favors) and Alexander Pope (whom he criticizes) shows that the pathetic fallacy may be moving and pleasurable, if it reflects genuine passion rather than artifice. While Ruskin's attitude toward the pathetic fallacy tends to be misremembered as wholly condemning, it emerges within a sophisticated commentary on the relationship between beauty and feeling. His own reliance on the pathetic fallacy in *The Queen of the Air* is fitting given that he saw Athena as embodying a wisdom that is not "intellectual" but "of the heart" (*WJR* XIX: 305).

His discussion of Athena's presence in the natural world swerves away from detached observations, reasoned conclusions, and scholarly certitude, reclaiming instead both the pathos and the ambiguity of the pathetic fallacy:

> If you ask an ordinary botanist the reason of the form of a leaf, he will tell you it is a "developed tubercle," and that its ultimate form "is owing to the directions of its vascular threads." But what directs its vascular threads? "They are seeking for something they want," he will probably answer. What made them want that? What made them seek for it thus? Seek for it, in five fibres or in three? Seek for it, in serration, or in sweeping curves? Seek for it, in servile tendrils, or impetuous spray? Seek for it, in woollen wrinkles rough with stings, or in glossy surfaces, green with pure strength, and winterless delight?
>
> There is no answer. But … over the entire surface of the earth and its waters … there is engraved a series of myths, or words of the forming power, which,

according to the true passion and energy of the human race, they have been enabled to read into religion.

(*WJR* XIX: 378)

Ruskin incorporates this creative force's passionate energy into the rhythms of his own prose. Layering interrogative on interrogative, his anaphoric patterns underscore that nature's design and purpose remain indiscernible. In its implicit universalism, this passage attempts to combine singularity and plurality: Ruskin speaks of a single "human race" while also recognizing various attempts ("a series of myths") to articulate this "forming power." This variety complicates the patriarchal ideologies informing his personification of Wisdom as a female goddess.

Shapeshifting Goddess and Dynamic Logos: Ruskin's Incarnational Wisdom

Ruskin's writings about and relationships with women have been the subject of much speculation, if not fascination, from his short-lived marriage to Effie Gray, who had their union annulled on the grounds of non-consummation before taking up with the Pre-Raphaelite artist John Everett Millais (whom Ruskin had mentored), to his adoration of Rose la Touche, nearly thirty years his junior. Feminist critics have long called attention to the limited roles assigned to women throughout his published writings, as in Kate Millett's influential contrast between Ruskin and John Stuart Mill, which criticizes Ruskin's attempt "to ennoble a system of subordination through hopeful rhetoric." Subsequent decades have witnessed continued debate on the subject, often concentrating, as Millett did, on the separate spheres for men and women delineated in Ruskin's "Of Queen's Gardens" (1865).[42] As suggested by the similarities in their titles, this text bears close connections to *The Queen of the Air*. Ruskin's imaginary Athena effectively reverses the power relationships sustained between men and women in the Victorian social world—an inversion that seems designed primarily to perpetuate these hierarchies. Contrary to Ruskin's intent, however, Athena's function is bivalent: "confirming patriarchal hegemony but also making new roles for women thinkable," as Sawyer puts it.[43] Throughout the nineteenth century, women writers constructed powerful proto-feminist platforms by recovering imagery drawn from ancient goddesses: the millenarian socialist Eliza Sharples celebrated Isis as a model of female power and agency,

EBB named the eponymous poet of her verse novel *Aurora Leigh* after the Greek goddess of the dawn, and George Eliot offered a symbolic combination of the Virgin Mary and a variety of classical goddesses in the heroine of *Romola*, to cite but a few examples.[44] These patterns lend credence to the latter, more hopeful, possibility. As Ruskin personifies her, Wisdom embodies a dynamic combination of masculine and feminine attributes. This combination destabilizes Victorian gender roles in ways that have both theological and ecological implications.

Ruskin describes Athena as having a composite morphology: she is at once serpent and bird, a combination notable both for its sexual suggestiveness and for its play with biblical symbolism. His vision of personified Wisdom takes substantial artistic license with Jewish, Christian, and classical wisdom traditions: as several studies have noted, his portrayal of Athena as a "Formative and Decisive Power" (*WJR* XIX: 354) departs from the Greek tradition wherein such power is specifically gendered masculine.[45] The cumulative effect of these combinations is not simply to feminize Christ or to masculinize Athena but to display the irreducibility of Ruskin's personified Wisdom to a single type. Even as Ruskin explicitly likens Athena to the Holy Spirit of Christian scriptures, he extends his metaphors beyond their biblical contexts, suggesting that the Greek image of Athena as an "unconsuming fire" influenced "the symbol of direct inspiration, in the rushing wind and divided flames of Pentecost" (*WJR* XIX: 341). He later ventures this comparison in more daring terms: "You would, perhaps, hardly bear with me if I endeavoured farther to show you ... the analogy between the spiritual power of Athena in her gentle ministry, yet irresistible anger, with the ministry of another Spirit whom we also ... are forbidden, at our worst peril, to quench or grieve" (*WJR* XIX: 346)—an allusion to the statement attributed to Jesus in the gospel of Matthew that blasphemy against the Holy Spirit will not be forgiven.[46] Beyond simply suggesting that all wisdom finds its fulfillment in Christ, this analogy serves, more radically, to push beyond the boundaries of any single religious tradition.

In his emphasis on the non-Christian precedents for Christian symbolism, Ruskin fractures and reverses typology's unifying, progressive force. From the early church fathers onward, many Christian exegetes used typology to obscure Jewish culture, transforming its scared scriptures "from a book of laws and a history of the people of Israel into a series of figures of Christ and the Redemption," as Erich Auerbach observes.[47] Ruskin participates in this cultural formation, but rather than progress neatly from "old covenant" to "new covenant," he departs from this ordering and opens canonical boundaries. While his discussion of Athena's place among the clouds draws direct connections to

Greek and Egyptian mythology (*WJR* XIX: 319–23), his descriptions also recall the book of Ecclesiasticus, which portrays Wisdom as dwelling among the clouds and reigning over all nations and peoples.[48] The title for his third lecture, "Athena Ergane" (translated as "Athena the Worker"), echoes the Wisdom of Solomon, which calls Wisdom as "the worker of all things" (Wis. 7:22). Such allusions are part of a larger pattern of evoking apocryphal wisdom literature, evident throughout Ruskin's oeuvre. He tentatively entitled a projected chapter of *Praeterita* "The Laws of the Sons of Sirarch," and his *Mornings in Florence* again evokes the seventh chapter from the Wisdom of Solomon: "I prayed, and the Spirit of Wisdom came upon me" (*WJR*; Wis. 7:7).[49] As these references underscore, his creative engagement with wisdom literature resists classification along canonical lines.

Ruskin's play with typology reflects the nuanced Christology he articulated in response to the higher criticism. While *The Queen of the Air* does not directly discuss the many "lives of Jesus" that circulated in Victorian Britain following Eliot's 1846 translation of Strauss's *Das Leben Jesu* (1835), this meditation on Wisdom reflects, albeit in more subtle ways, Ruskin's response to the nineteenth century's renewed interest in the historical person of Jesus. The publication and translation of Strauss's *Das Leben Jesu* and Ernest Renan's *Vie de Jésus* (1863) prompted several subsequent studies in Victorian Britain. John Seeley's *Ecce Homo* (1865) attempted to navigate a middle path between historical and devotional study; meanwhile, F. W. Farrar's *The Life of Christ* (1874) adopted a primarily devotional perspective but made some notable concessions to the higher criticism. Farrar, in turn, influenced a range of later devotional studies, including Henry James Coleridge's *The Public Life of Our Lord* (1874), G. S. Drew's *The Son of Man* (1875), and John Cunningham Geikie's *The Life and Words of Christ* (1877).[50] In *St. Mark's Rest* (1877), Ruskin briefly references such "various 'lives of Christ,'" which he classifies as ranging from the "critical" to the "sentimental" but concludes "there is only one light by which you can read the life of Christ—the light of the life you now lead in the flesh" (*WJR* XXIV:304). Setting aside both "historical" and "sentimental" approaches, Ruskin swerves from textual study to embodied practice. Rather than simply replace letter with spirit, his emphasis on "the life of the flesh" suggests his broader investment in reclaiming materiality. A similar emphasis on embodiment informs his portrayal of Wisdom in *The Queen of the Air*. Taken together, Ruskin's supplementary glosses on his lecture titles ("Athena in the Heavens," "Athena in the Earth," and "Athena in the Heart") trace a trajectory of descent and internalization that figures Wisdom as an immanent divine presence.

In much the same way that EBB's *A Drama of Exile* makes kenotic Christology part of a broader cosmological project, as discussed in Chapter 1, so too Ruskin calls for a reorientation toward all life, not just human life. The range of activities associated with Ruskin's Athena militates against the very concept of separate spheres, whether for men and women or for vegetable, animal, and human beings. As Ruskin portrays her, Athena possesses both a "physical power" and a "spiritual power" that intersect in important ways: she is "the Spirit of Life in material organism," the "formative energy in the clay" (*WJR* XIX: 346). His explanation of this spiritual power highlights its expansive domain: it includes "the power that catches out of chaos charcoal, water, lime, or what not," and Ruskin insists that "we shall not diminish but strengthen our conception of this creative energy by recognizing its presence in lower states of matter than our own" (*WJR* XIX: 356–7). Even as his words about the "lower states of matter" embed an anthropocentric hierarchy, he underscores the common creative energy that imbues them.

Departing once again from Müller, who identified the worship of the sun as the origin of all mythologies, Ruskin locates Athena within the air and wind.[51] This understanding of Athena's presence likely owes to the image of the creative breeze prominent in Romantic poetry, and it also recalls the theological concept of inspiration that rose to the forefront of British debates about the higher criticism, from Samuel Taylor Coleridge's *Confessions of an Inquiring Spirit* (originally entitled "Letters on the Inspiration of the Scriptures") to Jowett's contribution to *Essays and Reviews*. Midway through his first lecture, Ruskin outlines Athena's activity as an interanimating and sustaining of all things:

i. She is the air giving life and health to all animals.
ii. She is the air giving vegetative power to the earth.
iii. She is the air giving motion to the sea, and rendering navigation possible.
iv. She is the air nourishing artificial light, torch or lamplight; as opposed to that of the sun, on one hand, and of *consuming* fire, on the other.
v. She is the air conveying vibration of sound. (*Works* XIX: 328)

At first glance, this catalogue reads like a schematic outline of subsequent points, a typical feature of the academic lecture. On closer examination, this passage offers what Sawyer calls "a Universal Prayer to a kind of *natura naturans*."[52] More particularly, Ruskin's portrait of Athena as the Wisdom that shapes and enlivens all things, from vegetable and animal activity to human artifice, recalls the praise for God the Son as Creator who remains immanently present in all things in the epistle to the Colossians ("by him were all things created, that are in heaven, and that are in earth, visible and invisible, whether they be thrones, or dominions, or principalities, or powers: all things were created by him, and for him: And he is before all things, and in him all things consist").[53] Just as EBB portrays Christ as *"gradually transfigured"* into *"humanity and suffering"* by evoking the hymn on Jesus's humility in Philippians, so too Ruskin advances a wisdom Christology that reimagines the Word made flesh.

Ruskin's reverence for God as manifest in the natural world is hardly unique to *The Queen of the Air*, but this text's engagement with the biblical wisdom tradition inflects Ruskin's voice in unusual ways. Perhaps Ruskin's most memorable statements as an ecological thinker are those that appear in *The Storm-Cloud of the Nineteenth Century* (1884), a jeremiad denouncing both the environmental devastation and the moral degradation of Victorian Britain. This later work reflects an apocalyptic imagination expressed primarily through the tropes of biblical prophecy, a typical rhetorical move for Ruskin and for the Victorian sage at large.[54] Prophetic and wisdom literatures overlap and intersect throughout many biblical texts, and yet prophecy's emphasis on an overarching narrative of salvific history—and, specifically, the covenant made with Israel—is seldom so explicitly stated within the wisdom books, as Ricoeur observes.[55] Leo G. Perdue goes so far as to claim that "the theological grounding of wisdom literature is creation and not redemptive history" and to define this conceptual center both in terms of the ordering of the cosmos (divine creation) and in terms of imaginative art (human creation).[56] Building on Ricoeur's writings on metaphor, Perdue calls attention to the poetic innovations of the wisdom writers, who sought "to engage the attention and move the audience out of a normal, everyday frame of rational thought and logical discourse to awaken the imagination in order to consider new possibilities of meaning and insight."[57] Such, too, is the artistic mode adopted by Ruskin in *The Queen of the Air*, which performs its ecological work not by warning of calamities to come but by inviting readers to see the natural world anew. Positioning his work as part of a long-standing attempt to unfold truths buried within ancient stories, he emphasizes the riddling qualities of his subject matter and the paramount importance of the reader's response. When Ruskin does call attention to his own writerly authority, it is with a consciousness of participating in a tradition of dialogic wisdom that exceeds his individual efforts.

A Sage in Dialogue: Reaching toward the Reader

Throughout *The Queen of the Air*, Ruskin's moments of direct address reflect a larger conceptual shift away from an understanding of the reader's mind as a passive object on which the writer or teacher might make an impression. This shift marks a departure from the priority assigned to authorial intent in several of his earlier writings, including *Sesame and Lilies* (1865), which encompasses both the discussion of femininity in "Of Queen's Gardens" and the corresponding account of masculinity in "Of King's Treasuries," as well as *The Ethics of the Dust* (1865). A series of ten Socratic dialogues between a group of young girls and an ancient Lecturer who instructs them in a variety of subjects, *The Ethics of the Dust* clearly recalls Ruskin's own situation at Winnington Hall. The self-assured paternalism of the Lecturer, an obvious stand-in for Ruskin himself, is admittedly clunky. By contrast, *The Queen of the Air* expresses a greater appreciation for the reader's active interpretive work. His second lecture, "Athena Keramitis," closes with the recognition that he himself would require several more days to fully "disentangle" his subject matter; however, Ruskin refrains from doing so in the hope that the reader may nonetheless be able not merely to "follow" but even to "reanimate" the "vestiges of the Myth of Athena" that he has presented (*WJR* XIX: 385). In effect, it is the reader who breathes new life into old stories. Ruskin further suggests that such revitalization has less to do with intellectual mastery than with character formation.

Right reading, as Ruskin's lecture series would have it, depends in large part on the reader's inner state. Whereas the school of interpretation that followed Friedrich Schleiermacher emphasized authorial intent, Ruskin focuses instead on cultivating a receptive disposition: art can convey its message "just so far as we are of the temper in which it must be received" (*WJR* XIX: 395). For Ruskin, developing this temper requires a full-bodied ethical commitment that is experienced both aesthetically and affectively: "all lovely art" is "rooted in virtue" and "full of myths that can be read only with the heart" (*WJR* XIX: 394). Although Ruskin does not go as far as MacDonald, whose essay on "The Fantastic Imagination" (1893) discounts intentionality altogether, as discussed in Chapter 2, both writers depart from the prevailing nineteenth-century emphasis on historical recovery, instead attending to subjective reading experiences. Whereas MacDonald envisions this reading practice in plainly devotional terms that recall the tradition of *lectio divina*, Ruskin pursues a more subtle, self-reflexive model of ethical engagement.

At the beginning of his first lecture, he takes pains to differentiate his approach to Greek mythology from both church tradition and academic authority, distinguishing them in the following terms:

> It is the task of the Divine to condemn the errors of antiquity, and of the Philologist to account for them: I will only pray you to read, with patience, and human sympathy, the thoughts of men who lived without blame in a darkness they could not dispel.
>
> (*WJR* XIX: 296)

By distancing himself from "the Divine," Ruskin underscores that he is not in the business of proclaiming hidden truths or correcting those who have gone astray. Similarly, his remarks about "the Philologist" hint at his rejection of Müller's theory that mythology reflects the decay or disease of language; rather, Ruskin finds value in such indirect and seemingly primitive modes of expression.[58] What is at stake, for Ruskin, is a fundamental reorientation toward the experience of being wrong, something that he takes pains to explain as pertaining equally to past and present readers. Lest the Greek stories appear simple or foolish, Ruskin reminds his audiences that those who study such mythology face their own limitations: "absolutely right no one can be in such matters; nor does a day pass without convincing every honest student of antiquity of some partial error, and showing him better how to think, and where to look" (*WJR* XIX: 291–2). His efforts to explicate the myths of Athena are frequently paired with emphatic statements about the limits of all knowledge on this subject.

In keeping with broad trends in Aristotelian thought, Ruskin draws a crucial distinction between objective knowledge and moral knowledge, aligning Wisdom with the latter. As he describes her, Athena "does not make men learned, but prudent and subtle" (*WJR* XIX: 388). This distinction results in a further distinction between *being wrong* and *doing wrong*. His third and final lecture ("Athena Ergane") emphatically protests the perils of wrongful action, challenging Mill's utilitarian argument in "On Liberty" (1859). Intellectual mistakes, by contrast, Ruskin regards not just as unavoidable but as potential teachable moments—more, as integral aspects of experiencing wonder, art, and mystery, rather as Elaine Scarry has proposed about perceiving beauty.[59] For Ruskin, the task of wisdom writing is by its very nature inexhaustible, but that is precisely what makes it so hermeneutically generative.

Ruskin's critique of Mill in this lecture series revisits and reframes the arguments he had advanced in *Unto This Last*, a series of four essays serialized in the *Cornhill Magazine* in the fall of 1860 and published as a volume in 1862. Arguing against Mill's *Principles of Political Economy* (1848), Ruskin challenges the idea that the wages of domestic labor should be set at the lowest feasible rate. As his title indicates, Ruskin makes inventive use of the parable of the workers in the vineyard—another borrowing from wisdom literature—to articulate an alternative model of economy.[60] Calling for "wise consumption," Ruskin argues that the terms *money* and *wealth* are not synonymous, emphatically concluding, "THERE IS NO WEALTH BUT LIFE" (*Works* XVII: 98–105). In "Athena Ergane," Ruskin revisits this distinction, not only in his brief remarks about material prosperity but also in his commentary on the value of wisdom writing. For Ruskin, mythmaking possesses "a vague poetical influence of the highest value in its own imaginative way" (*WJR* XIX: 367). Ruskin writes much in the spirit of Thomas Carlyle, who likewise challenged political economy and contrasted the "mechanical" approach of the economist and scientist, on the one hand, with the "dynamical" energy of the artist and poet, on the other. Organic metaphors infuse *Unto This Last*, as becomes apparent from the very titles of his first two essays ("The Roots of Honour" and "The Veins of Wealth"), which evoke trees and circulatory systems as examples of how life cannot be contained by an utilitarian calculus. As Ruskin develops his alternative concept of poetic value throughout *The Queen of the Air*, he shifts his rhetorical positioning, away from the authoritarian stance modeled by Carlyle and toward a more lateral concept of the relationship between speaker and addressees. He generates a complex ethos that pushes against the limits of what Landow identifies as the "appeal to credibility" that "subsumes the sage's other rhetorical devices." For Landow, the Victorian sage's claim to authority might be reduced to his implicit statement, "I deserve your attention and credence, for I can be trusted."[61] By contrast, *The Queen of the Air* shifts the center of gravity from ethos to pathos and, as a result, prioritizes readerly affect above writerly mastery.

Ruskin's self-reflexive acknowledgment of his own limitations is nowhere more apparent than in the preface added for the volume's publication in May 1869. He begins on a confessional note that underscores both his personal difficulties and his commitment to working with his unrefined material:

> My days and strength have lately been much broken; and I never more felt the insufficiency of both than in preparing for the press the following desultory memorabilia on a most noble subject. But I leave them now as they stand, for no time nor labour would be enough to complete them to my contentment.
>
> (*WJR* XIX: 291)

His frank declaration of weakness is striking. To be sure, admissions of weakness or error can themselves serve as part of an appeal to ethos, as Landow argues is the case in the apologetic opening to Ruskin's "Traffic," a lecture on architectural design delivered at the Bradford town hall on April 21, 1864.[62] However, reducing this statement to a rhetorical pose would be both ungenerous and inaccurate, given that Ruskin had indeed suffered from intense periods of depression throughout 1868 and 1869 that significantly inhibited his writing and thinking. Furthermore, this candid acknowledgment of his own partial knowledge brings his lectures into accordance with the concept of poetic truth that this discussion unfolds.

Insofar as Ruskin acknowledges epistemic limitation yet refuses to become complacent with error, his pursuit of wisdom aligns with the aesthetic of the imperfect previously advanced in "The Nature of Gothic," the central chapter of *The Stones of Venice* and an important inspiration for the Arts and Crafts Movement. Reprinted in 1854 as a pamphlet for distribution at the Working Men's College, where Ruskin taught drawing, and again in 1892 by Morris's Kelmscott Press, "The Nature of Gothic" champions the medieval, or Gothic, style of architecture for both aesthetic and ethical reasons. Ruskin proposes that the nineteenth-century British preference for the Grecian style of architecture, as well as his culture's growing tendency toward mechanized industrial labor, indicates not only a limited sense of beauty but also a moral failure. He argues that the seemingly crude or rugged qualities of Gothic architecture are vital because they allow for greater individual liberty and creativity on the part of the worker. As Ruskin puts it, the flawed majesty of such artwork indicates that "*the demand for perfection is always a sign of a misunderstanding of the ends of art*" (*WJR* X: 202). His arresting phrase signals purposefulness rather than termination. For Ruskin, "*the ends of art*" find expression in the laws of "Effort" and "Mercy" that govern human life and judgment (*WJR* X: 203–4). These laws are less prescriptive than invitational: effort and mercy are values to strive for, not quotas to meet.

This alignment between "The Nature of Gothic" and *The Queen of the Air* would seem to be an odd one, given that the earlier text draws such an emphatic antithesis between Grecian and Gothic art and architecture. As he attempts to integrate and find connections among various wisdom traditions, Ruskin's discussion of Greek mythology incorporates some of his former ideas about Gothic architecture's grotesque irregularities. His self-conscious effort to reconcile his several arguments on the subject becomes evident in his explanation of why he attempts to trace Athena "in the Greek mind" rather than in "Greek art." He claims that the "triumphs" of Greek art obscure "the religious passion," which "can be traced only through the efforts of trembling hands, and the strange pleasures of untaught eyes"; by contrast, the dark perception of Greek mythology admits more poetic vitality (*WJR* XIX: 384). Such fine distinctions might seem to be a kind of hair-splitting, and Ruskin himself readily acknowledged his own inconsistencies. As he memorably stated in his inaugural address at the Cambridge School of Art (delivered on October 29, 1858), "For myself, I am never satisfied that I have handled a subject properly till I have contradicted myself at least three times." In addition to its endearingly self-deprecatory humor, this statement reveals Ruskin's belief in a pluralistic concept of truth, expressed in geometric terms: "Mostly, matters of any consequence are three-sided, or four-sided, or polygonal; and the trotting round a polygon is severe work for people of any way stiff in their opinions" (*WJR* XVI: 187). Efforts to apprehend such multi-sided shapes produce not only contradictions but, more powerfully, the kind of creative synthesis that enables one to perceive interconnections among seemingly incongruous things—a mode of perception that Francis O'Gorman sees as traceable throughout Ruskin's output.[63] What is needed is not just consistency in logic but also flexibility of mind.

For all the gaps, flaws, and failings of Ruskin's mythmaking, there might still be lessons to learn from *The Queen of the Air*, especially insofar as this extravagant, impassioned lecture series does exactly what narrowly academic modes of reading and teaching have often shied away from: Ruskin frequently puts himself in front of the text, self-consciously reflecting on his own activity within the stories he unfolds. Such a personal approach is lacking in critical distance, and yet the scholarly preoccupation with analytical detachment comes with its own blind spots, as recent forays into postsecular and postcritical reading have suggested.[64] Searching for meaning within moments of contradiction or paradox, as Ruskin does, can be surprisingly productive, if only insofar as this orientation goes against the grain of received assumptions. The imaginatively imperfect approach exemplified in *The Queen of the Air*, then, might prove instructive in our current moment, as we, like Ruskin, seek to calibrate an effective and ethical balance between proximity to and distance from what we read.

Another potentially eye-opening model, and one that is likewise rooted in the images, metaphors, and dialogic forms of wisdom literature, emerges in Olive Schreiner's *The Story of an African Farm* (1883), the subject of Chapter 5. Published more than a decade after Ruskin's *The Queen of the Air*, this semi-autobiographical and highly metafictional novel engages retrospectively and intensively with the debates about biblical interpretation that shaped the 1860s.

An outspoken freethinker, Schreiner nevertheless advances an imaginative approach to biblical wisdom literature—in particular, the book of Ecclesiastes—that shares much in common not only with Ruskin and Eliot but also with MacDonald and EBB. The most subversive but by no means the least religiously engaged of the Victorian writers discussed in this book, Schreiner probes the depths of both skepticism and hope.

Notes

1 See Ruskin's letter to J. P. Faunthorpe on December 6, 1888, collected in *The Works of John Ruskin*, ed. E. T. Cook and Alexander Wedderburn, 39 vols. (London: George Allen, 1903–12), XXXVII: 380. All references to Ruskin's published works are taken from this edition. Hereafter, this collection is abbreviated as *WJR* and cited parenthetically by volume number and page number.

2 On Müller's approach to comparative mythology and the influence of his work in Victorian Britain, see J. Jeffrey Franklin, *Spirit Matters: Occult Beliefs, Alternative Religions, and the Crisis of Faith in Victorian Britain* (Ithaca: Cornell University Press, 2018), 68–72.

3 Paul L. Sawyer, "Ruskin and the Matriarchal Logos," in *Victorian Sages and Cultural Discourse: Renegotiating Gender and Power*, ed. Thaïs E. Morgan (New Brunswick: Rutgers University Press, 1991), 139.

4 See Prov. 8:23-32.

5 On the historical context informing Ecclesiasticus (*c*. second century BCE) and the Wisdom of Solomon (first century BCE), see Leo G. Perdue, *Wisdom and Creation: The Theology of Wisdom Literature* (Nashville: Abingdon Press, 1994), 243–6, 291–4.

6 John Batchelor, *John Ruskin: A Life* (New York: Carroll and Graf, 2000), 139.

7 See, for example, Dinah Birch, *Ruskin's Myths* (Oxford: Clarendon Press, 1988), 116–21; Sawyer, "Ruskin and the Matriarchal Logos," 132–4; and Kevin A. Morrison, "Myth, Remembrance, and Modernity: From Ruskin to Benjamin via Proust," *Comparative Literature* 60, no. 2 (2008): 125–41.

8 Dinah Birch, "Lecturing and Public Voice," in *The Cambridge Companion to John Ruskin*, ed. Francis O'Gorman, (Cambridge: Cambridge University Press, 2015), 203; George P. Landow, *Elegant Jeremiahs: The Sage from Carlyle to Mailer* (Ithaca: Cornell University Press, 1986), 132.

9 See the editorial material provided by Victor Shea and William Whitla, *Essays and Reviews: The 1860 Text and Its Reading* (Charlottesville: University of Virginia Press, 2000), 848.

10 Van Akin Burd, Introduction to *The Winnington Letters: John Ruskin's Correspondence with Margaret Alexis Bell and the Children and Winnington Hall*

(Cambridge: Harvard University Press, 1969), 72–3; see also Batchelor, *John Ruskin*, 199–201.
11 Birch, "Ruskin, Myth, and Modernism," in *Ruskin and Modernism*, ed. Giovanni Cianni and Peter Nicholls (New York: Palgrave, 2001), 34.
12 See Ruskin's letters collected in Burd, *The Winnington Letters*, 457.
13 Stephen Cheeke, *Transfiguration: The Religion of Art in Nineteenth-Century Literature before Aestheticism* (Oxford: Oxford University Press, 2016), 135.
14 See Dinah Birch, "'Who Wants Authority?': Ruskin as a Dissenter," *The Yearbook of English Studies* 36, no. 2 (2006): 68.
15 Ruskin, *The Winnington Letters*, 486.
16 *The Bible: Authorized King James Version with Apocrypha* (Oxford: Oxford University Press, 2008). All biblical quotations are cited parenthetically in text. Rights in the Authorized (King James) Version in the UK are vested in the Crown. Reproduced by permission of the Crown's patentee, Cambridge University Press.
17 Benjamin Jowett, "On the Interpretation of Scripture," in *Essays and Reviews: The 1860 Text and Its Reading*, ed. Victor Shea and William Whitla (Charlottesville: University Press of Virginia, 2000), 503.
18 Matthew Arnold, *Literature and Dogma: An Essay towards a Better Apprehension of the Bible* (London: Macmillan and Co., 1895), 36.
19 Ibid., 21.
20 Paul Ricoeur, "Biblical Hermeneutics," *Semeia* 4 (1975): 88–9.
21 Ruskin, *The Winnington Letters*, 376, 379.
22 Matthew Arnold, "The Function of Criticism at the Present Time," in *Essays in Criticism: First Series* (London: Macmillan and Co., 1903), 33. This essay identifies Renan's scholarship as a superior example of the higher criticism. In "The Bishop and the Philosopher" (1863), Arnold criticized both *The Pentateuch* and *Essays and Reviews* for employing what he saw as insufficient critical methods. For discussion of Arnold's response to Colenso as well as Colenso's reception in Britain more broadly, see Timothy Larsen, *Contested Christianity: The Social and Political Contexts of Victorian Theology* (Waco: Baylor University Press, 2004), 72–7.
23 Ruskin, *The Winnington Letters*, 384.
24 Ibid., 457.
25 Paul L. Sawyer, *Ruskin's Poetic Argument: The Design of the Major Works* (Ithaca: Cornell University Press, 1985), 253.
26 George P. Landow, *The Aesthetic and Critical Theories of John Ruskin* (Princeton: Princeton University Press, 1971), 407.
27 Thomas Hartwell Horne, qtd. in Landow, *Victorian Types, Victorian Shadows: Biblical Typology in Victorian Literature, Art and Thought* (New York: Routledge, 1980), 51.
28 See Prov. 1:16.

29 On Ruskin's engagement with natural theology, see Robert Hewison, "'Paradise Lost': Ruskin and Science," in *Time and Tide: Ruskin and Science*, ed. Michael Wheeler (Yelvertoft: Pilkington Press, 1996), 38.
30 George Levine, "Ruskin, Darwin, and the Matter of Matter," *Nineteenth-Century Prose* 35, no. 1 (2008): 224.
31 Ibid., 245.
32 Paul Ricoeur, "Toward a Hermeneutic of the Idea of Revelation," in *Essays on Biblical Interpretation*, ed. Lewis S. Mudge, trans. David Pellauer (Philadelphia: Fortress Press, 1980), 100–102.
33 Percy Bysshe Shelley, *A Defence of Poetry* (Indianapolis: Bobbs-Merrill Company, 1904), 75.
34 See, for example, Allen MacDuffie, *Victorian Literature, Energy, and the Ecological Imagination* (Cambridge: Cambridge University Press, 2014) and Vicky Albritton and Frederick Albritton Jonsson, *Green Victorians: The Simple Life in Ruskin's Lake District* (Chicago: University of Chicago Press, 2016).
35 Terence Thomas, "The Impact of Other Religions," in *Religion in Victorian Britain. Volume II. Controversies*, ed. Gerald Parsons (Manchester: Manchester University Press, 1980), 283.
36 Sebastian Lecourt, *Cultivating Belief: Victorian Anthropology, Liberal Aesthetics, and the Secular Imagination* (Oxford: Oxford University Press, 2018), 71.
37 Colenso, *The Pentateuch*, 7.
38 Larsen, *Contested Christianity*, 75.
39 See Winter Jade Werner, *Missionary Cosmopolitanism in Nineteenth-Century British* (Athens: Ohio State University Press, 2020); see also Winter Jade Werner and Mimi Winick, "How to See Global Religion: Comparativism, Connectivity, and the Undisciplining of Victorian Literary Studies," *Modern Language Quarterly* 83, no. 4 (December 2022): 409–502.
40 See Acts 17:22-31.
41 See Ps. 14:1.
42 Kate Millett, "The Debate over Women: Ruskin versus Mill," *Victorian Studies* 14, no. 1 (1970): 72. Other notable contributions to this debate include Jennifer M. Lloyd, "Raising Lilies: Ruskin and Women," *Journal of British Studies* 34, no. 3 (1995): 325–50; and Sharon Aronofsky Weltmann, "Mythic Language and Gender Subversion: The Case of Ruskin's Athena," *Nineteenth-Century Literature* 52, no. 3 (1997): 350–71.
43 Sawyer, "Ruskin and the Matriarchal Logos," 141.
44 For further discussion of these and a range of other examples, including those drawn from works by Charlotte Brontë, Florence Nightingale, and Anna Jameson, see Gail Turley Houston, *Victorian Women Writers, Radical Grandmothers, and the Gendering of God* (Athens: Ohio State University Press, 2013).

45 Sawyer, "Ruskin and the Matriarchal Logos," 140; Weltman, "Mythic Language," 358.
46 See Mt. 12:31-2.
47 Erich Auerbach, "Figura," in *Scenes from the Drama of European Literature* (Manchester: Manchester University Press, 1984), 30.
48 See Ecclus. 24:3-6.
49 Burd, Introduction to *The Winnington Letters*, 19–20.
50 Daniel L. Pals, *The Victorian "Lives" of Jesus* (San Antonio: Trinity University Press), 80–94.
51 Birch, "Ruskin, Myth, and Modernism," 36–7.
52 Sawyer, "Ruskin and the Matriarchal Logos," 139.
53 See Col. 1:15-17.
54 See Landow, *Elegant Jeremiahs*, 41–71.
55 Ricoeur, "Toward a Hermeneutic," 85.
56 Perdue, *Wisdom and Creation*, 19.
57 Ibid., 62.
58 See Birch, "Ruskin, Myth, and Modernism," 37.
59 Elaine Scarry, *On Beauty and Being Just* (Princeton: Princeton University Press, 1999), 27–8.
60 See Mt. 20:41.
61 Landow, *Elegant Jeremiahs*, 155.
62 Ibid., 170.
63 Francis O'Gorman, "Ruskin, Science, and the Miracles of Life," *The Review of English Studies New Series* 61, no. 249 (2010): 277.
64 See, for instance, Mark Knight, "Natural Theology and the Revelation of *Little Dorrit*," *LIT: Literature Interpretation Theory* 31, no. 1 (2021): 13.

5

Wisdom's Breath: Revelation, Concealment, and the Energy of Ecclesiastes in Olive Schreiner's *The Story of an African Farm*

The daughter of Methodist missionaries to South Africa, Olive Schreiner rejected her religious upbringing as early as 1864, or so the story goes. Retrospectively, Schreiner reported that the death of her baby sister Ellie led her, as a nine-year-old child, to question the tenets of Christianity. By the early 1880s, when she traveled from the Cape Colony to Britain, she publicly identified as a "freethinker," a term widely adopted by those critical of organized religion.[1] Even so, her discarding of accepted teachings about suffering and salvation coexisted with an intensive rereading of biblical texts. This coexistence appears tellingly in a letter to her friend Havelock Ellis, well-known for his pioneering studies of human sexuality, whom she met in England and with whom she corresponded almost daily throughout the 1880s:

> ^Please buy & send me a bible, as like my old one in size & print as you can. It was one of those cheap bibles published by the ^British &^ Foreign Bible Society. Not with the very fine print.^
>
> I am always quoting from the bible sometimes for the devil's own purposes & I find as the years pass my memory sometimes wavers with regard to an exact ^wording of a^ passage.[2]

On the one hand, Schreiner's statement that she no longer has a Bible in her possession, as well as her endorsement of "the devil's own purposes," distances her from Christianity. On the other hand, her nostalgic desire to recover this book, particularly in a familiar form that would aid her rereading, suggests an ongoing investment in its stories.

This twofold energy of rebellion and recovery informs Schreiner's engagement with biblical texts throughout her writings, especially her semi-autobiographical novel *The Story of an African Farm*. Published in two volumes by Chapman and Hall in 1883, this best-selling first book is an experimental *bildungsroman* that follows two characters, Lyndall and Waldo, from their childhood to their untimely deaths in early adulthood. As a novel of ideas, its many topics span women's suffrage, British imperialism, and religious doubt. From an early review in the *Spectator* praising *The Story of an African Farm* as a novel that "looks Agnosticism fairly in the face" to more contemporary assessments of Schreiner's philosophical leanings, critics have long focused on her intellectual debt to Herbert Spencer, whose *First Principles* (1862) made a significant impression on Schreiner when she first encountered it, at sixteen years of age.[3] My analysis recovers the advent of modern biblical scholarship as a crucial context for understanding Schreiner's critique of organized religion. Her creative participation in nineteenth-century interpretive debates can be seen not only in the reading practices modeled by this novel's various characters but also in her own provocative rewritings of biblical texts. Taken together, both the biblical exegesis *depicted in* the novel and the biblical exegesis *performed by* the novel challenge dogmatic claims to certainty and invite the reader's participation in an ongoing search for meaning. Much as the higher criticism interrogated accepted ideas about the Bible's inspiration, authority, and theological unity, so also *The Story of an African Farm* poses searching questions about the experience of revelation.

Schreiner's religious revisionism draws heavily from biblical wisdom literature, the book of Ecclesiastes in particular. At the heart of her novel is a metafictional sequence entitled "Times and Seasons," an extended meditation on the third chapter of Ecclesiastes, with its memorable beginning, "To everything there is a season, and a time to every purpose under heaven" (Eccl. 3:1).[4] This echo is more than a passing literary allusion or even a recurring thematic motif. Rather, the fragmentary, dialogic, and self-reflexive form of *The Story of an African Farm* might almost be seen as a novelistic adaptation of the book of Ecclesiastes. Schreiner ruminates on the very questions of mortality, meaninglessness, and meaning-making that animate her biblical source text, departing from the formal conventions of the realist novel to privilege philosophical reflection. Following the "Times and Seasons" interlude, her next chapter features an interpolated narrative that she later referred to as a parable—a literary form with strong ties to the biblical wisdom tradition.[5] Like Ecclesiastes, the composite qualities of which were brought into sharp relief as a result of higher critical scholarship, this novel interweaves many different, and, at times, conflicting, narrative strands. And, like Ecclesiastes, *The Story of an*

African Farm brings together an unruly assortment of voices that ultimately serve not to discredit biblical texts but to dialogize them, not to overturn the wisdom tradition but to intensify it.

As many biblical scholars have noted, the Hebrew word for the book's title and speaker or teacher, "Qohelet," vexes English translation. That said, its resemblance to the root for *gather* or *flock* has led many commentators to highlight the book's work of gathering or assembling. Wilhelm Martin Leberecht De Wette, a disciple of David Friedrich Strauss, whose *Das Leben Jesu* (*Life of Jesus*) sent shockwaves throughout Victorian Britain, parsed it as "*speaker in the assembly*," and, in the twenty-first century, Robert Alter has proposed "the one who assembles."[6] This book's dialogic qualities have long been recognized: Gregory the Great in the sixth century BCE, for one, regarded Solomon as "dialoguing with a fool or knave."[7] Even so, the historical criticism of the eighteenth and nineteenth centuries gave rise to new understandings of this book's contradictions and ironies. In contrast to the long-standing allegorical reading that sees Ecclesiastes as a meditation on the meaninglessness of a life without God, higher critics such as De Wette argued that this book resists easy reconciliation within a tidy theological framework.[8] By and large, the higher critics overturned the notion of Solomonic authorship, instead classifying this text as participating in an evolving genre of wisdom literature composed by multiple writers and redactors. They suggested, for instance, that the more traditional affirmation of divine judgment and the injunction to fear God in the book's closing epilogue are likely editorial additions. De Wette, for one, highlighted what he saw as the "objectionable character" of Ecclesiastes and called attention to its imbrication within Hellenistic philosophies.[9] Writing near the end of the Victorian era, the Anglican biblical scholar Thomas Kelly Cheyne accepted the higher critical findings about the book's composite authorship and likewise termed it "a work of a dark post-exilic period," albeit a less objectionable one.[10] Cheyne's commentary underscored the literary afterlife of Ecclesiastes during the Victorian era, commenting on this text's remarkable presence within the literature of his own time.[11] These observations invite further attention to how Victorian writers returned to this text for purposes alternatively skeptical or reverential—or, as in the case of *The Story of an African Farm*, both skeptical and reverential at once.

True to the spirit of Ecclesiastes, Schreiner's episodic novel uses a series of dialectical pairings and ironic contrasts to reflect on the frustrated yet enduring search for order, purpose, and meaning. Her novel brings together a motley crew: Lyndall, the beautiful and intelligent niece of Tant' Sannie, the Boer woman who has charge of their farm; Em, Lyndall's mild-mannered cousin; Waldo, the daydreaming son of the German overseer, Otto; and a series of other individuals whose comings and goings make up the story's action. Time's passage brings several strangers, including Bonaparte Blenkins, the Irish con artist who manipulates his way into privileged positions around the farm until his sham is finally exposed, and Gregory Rose, the melancholic Englishman who joins the farm as a hired hand and becomes romantically attracted to both Em and Lyndall. Interwoven within these characters' attempts to make sense of their world is Schreiner's own interpretive commentary, which appears in its most concentrated form in the "Times and Seasons" chapter. Bridging the novel's two parts, this section extrapolates from Waldo's spiritual struggles to consider broader existential questions about the human soul. As Schreiner outlines the soul's growth through apparent contradictions, encompassing both nihilistic denial ("nothing maters") and mystical affirmation ("all is meaning-full"), she explores the tensions that animate the central refrain in Ecclesiastes, rendered in the Authorized Version as "vanity of vanities" (Eccl. 1:2).[12] This translation, along with most subsequent English versions, obscures the connotations evoked by the original metaphor, as Alter observes: the Hebrew word *hevel* suggests "the flimsy vapour that is exhaled in breathing," the opposite of *ruah*, that is, "life-breath" or "the animating force in a living creature."[13] This embodied imagery gathers both the ephemerality and the vitality of human experience, much as Schreiner's own exploration of religious and existential questions ranges from emptiness to fullness. As reimagined in *The Story of an African Farm*, wisdom is a matter of artistic and interpretive craft—not something that one finds but something that one makes.

My discussion begins by situating *The Story of an African Farm* in relation to Schreiner's expression of freethought, informed as it was by developments in biblical higher criticism. This context facilitates a reassessment of the novel's religious and political work. Hailed by Schreiner's contemporaries as an important development within the women's rights movement, this book has since come under scrutiny for its seeming idealization of the self-sacrificing woman, a religiously inflected trope that subsequent feminist critics have seen as perpetuating the very patriarchal logic it seeks to challenge. However, a closer look at Schreiner's subtle biblical intertexts indicates that her rewriting of Christianity's master narratives complicates received models of both self-abnegation and self-actualization. Her engagement with questions of imperialism is similarly complex: despite her complicity in this project, her revisionary engagement with wisdom literature destabilizes key elements of

Britain's imperialist rhetoric, including its appropriation of prophetic tropes. Schreiner concentrates her satire of organized Christianity on authoritarian, exclusivist uses of religious discourse, which the novel portrays as exacerbated by reductive reading practices. As an alternative, she advances her own hermeneutics of searching, expressed most succinctly in her embedded parable. Through her twofold vision of hope and bleakness, she probes inherited religious and literary traditions not only to expose their limitations but also to explore their potentials. Her self-reflexive engagement with questions of meaning-making epitomizes the work of creative interpretation that this book has traced throughout Victorian literary responses to biblical higher criticism. This twofold model of reading for critique and reading for appreciation, in turn, facilitates a symbolic transformation whereby religious language betokens not the presence of truth but the ongoing search for it.

Forms of Freethought: Schreiner's Creative Participation in the Higher Critical Project

As its title implies, *The Story of an African Farm* draws on Schreiner's own memories of growing up on a Wesleyan mission station near Wittebergen, South Africa. This retrospective account was composed in the 1870s, during which time Schreiner worked as a governess in the Cape Colony, and finalized after her journey to England in 1881, when, following several failed attempts at starting a medical career as a nurse or midwife, she sent the manuscript to Chapman and Hall, who accepted it on the recommendation of reader George Meredith. Throughout her time in England, she actively participated in societies such as Karl Pearson's Men's and Women's Club, which engaged in open debate about marriage and sexuality, and these circles brought her into company with leading radical, socialist, and atheist intellectuals.[14] Not surprisingly, several critics have highlighted her first novel's autobiographical qualities. Ruth First and Ann Scott, for instance, claim that Schreiner uses Waldo and Lyndall to mediate a story about her own development, and Mike Kissack and Michael Titlestad claim that Schreiner's intellectual trajectory replicates the "crisis of faith" experienced by many nineteenth-century thinkers, listing George Eliot and John Ruskin among their examples.[15] As I have argued in previous chapters, however, simplistic versions of this "crisis" paradigm risk obscuring the more complex repositioning of religion evident in the lives and writings of many Victorians. So, too, Schreiner's turn away from Christianity merits careful analysis. Following in the footsteps of Romantic writers such as William Blake, she expresses her critique of organized religion in terms that rewrite some of this religion's most radical stories.

Although Schreiner joined many socialists and freethinkers in critiquing doctrines of original sin, substitutionary atonement, and eternal damnation, she upheld broadly mystical ideas about an immanent divine presence. Her insistent use of the word *God* to describe this presence not only prompted criticism from some of her more militantly anti-religious freethinking friends but also earned her some unlikely admirers, including John T. Lloyd, a Presbyterian minister based in Kimberly, South Africa, who regarded Schreiner as a "religious genius."[16] A letter exchanged between Schreiner and Lloyd on October 29, 1892, provides insight into Schreiner's heterodox mysticism, as well as her nuanced standpoint regarding biblical texts. Even as Schreiner claimed to care nothing for the gospel teachings "except the 5th & 6th chapters of Matthew," she also speculated, "if we knew really what the beautiful soul of Jesus thought & felt, we should find it loved wider & deeper than its followers left us any record of."[17] Though skeptical of canonical authority, Schreiner was nevertheless attracted to the radical ethical vision offered by the Sermon on the Mount. Other letters express her disdain for religious institutions in terms that underscore her fascination with the person of Jesus. As Schreiner put it, her chief complaint with "all Christianity" was that it is "so un-Jesus-like"; she further speculated, "if Jesus were on the earth now it is very certain he would not be a Christian; but, as he was in his own day, a freethinker."[18] Schreiner's sense of Jesus as a freethinker was further informed by the higher critical studies praised throughout her letters. In a letter to Ellis, she expressed her appreciation for both Strauss's *Das Leben Jesu* (1835) and Renan's *Vie de Jésus* (1862).[19] She even went so far as to say to Karl Pearson, "the dream of my life has been to create a life of Jesus (in verse)," a remark that plainly shows her desire to participate creatively in the higher critical project.[20]

While it is not quite the poetic "life of Jesus" of Schreiner's dreams, *The Story of an African Farm* offers an artistic portrayal of the life of the soul, managing to be both playfully irreverent and deeply mystical. Her influences and tonalities are subtly intimated in the pseudonym under which the novel first appeared: Ralph Iron. This moniker at once pays tribute to Ralph Waldo Emerson, whom Schreiner greatly admired, and evokes the biblical symbolism of the "pen of iron," as in the books of Jeremiah and Job.[21] In addition to highlighting these echoes, Gerald Monsman proposes that this pseudonym hints darkly at the novel's insistent and cosmic *irony*, at once giving the illusion of a single, stable voice behind its many narrative threads and undermining this claim to authority.²² He further proposes that *The Story of an African Farm* might be seen as a "hermeneutic autobiography" in the tradition of Thomas Carlyle's *Sartor Resartus*, one of Emerson's favorite works, for which he wrote an enthusiastic preface when the first volume edition was published in America in 1836. As Monsman emphasizes, both texts are "more directly focused on self-interpretation than on self-presentation, more concerned with understanding events than with narrating them."²³ Originally published in serial installments in *Fraser's Magazine* from August 1833 to November 1834, Carlyle's experimental prose combines a variety of genres. Drawing on both the *bildungsroman* and the review essay, *Sartor Resartus* presents itself as the fragmentary writings of the fictitious Professor Diogenes Teufelsdröckh, punctuated by the remarks of an equally fictitious editor, who provides background information about the author, translates his work into English, and frequently comments on the difficulties of this task. Much as Carlyle's Menippean satire self-reflexively calls attention to issues of interpretive limits, so also *The Story of an African Farm* suggests that the views advanced by "Ralph Iron" may be no more authoritative than those put forth by any of the novel's flawed readers.

In the preface added to her second edition, signed "R. Iron," Schreiner defined her novelistic style in terms of the absence of any teleological design or plan. Distinguishing her approach from what she calls "the stage method," where human action unfolds according to an "immutable certainty," she claims that in her writings, as in life itself, "nothing can be prophesied"—individuals simply "appear, act and re-act upon each other, and pass away" (xxxix). Far from prophetic foreknowledge, this description of human experience as unpredictable and ineffable recalls Qohelet's reflections "*One* generation passeth away and *another* generation cometh, but the earth abideth for ever" (Eccl. 1:4). This is the very passage that Cheyne's commentary remarks for its "elemental force" and its memorable adaption in Carlyle's *Sartor Resartus*.²⁴ Carlyle, an early reader of the biblical scholarship that made its way into broader circulation in Britain later in the nineteenth century, adopts a pose of philosophical yet playful reflection in this early text—a stance that differs markedly from the more militantly authoritarian model advanced throughout his later works. Carlyle's discussion of "The Hero as Man of Letters" in his subsequent lecture series *On Heroes, Hero-Worship, and the Heroic in History* (1840) offers what Carol T. Christ identifies as "the definitive statement of the Victorian conception of the writer as prophet," and Carlyle himself figures as the paradigmatic Victorian sage in studies by John Holloway and George P. Landow.²⁵ As Landow sees it, the hallmarks of Victorian sage writing are its strategic adaptation of tropes derived from biblical prophecy and its rhetorical emphasis on the sage's superior moral and intellectual vision, over and above his audience. In *Sartor Resartus*, however, Carlyle writes in a different mode, drawing as much from Job and Ecclesiastes as from the prophetic tradition and using the conceit of the editor to call attention to his philosopher's "mixture of insight, inspiration, with dullness, double-vision, and even utter blindness."[26] The very name "Diogenes Teufelsdröckh" (God-Breathed Devil's-Dung) signals this text's sprawl from the sublime to the ridiculous. Schreiner, writing as Ralph Iron, likewise underscores the vanity of all human endeavor, and she too reaches into the scatological register to do so. Her book's second part opens with an epigram taken from an earlier passage within her own novel, an episode in which Waldo, who has recently had his own handiwork cruelly destroyed by the conniving and manipulative Bonaparte, observes the thwarted efforts of a dung beetle who tries to roll away a large ball of excrement only to be eaten by a dog. Waldo reflects, "And it was all play, and no one could tell what it had lived and worked for. A striving and a striving and an ending in nothing" (74). Repeating these lines at the beginning of the "Times and Seasons" chapter, Schreiner underscores Waldo's sense of futility; however, as the novel unfolds, she continues to revisit and revise this idea. While critical of reductive claims about certainty or progress, the novel ultimately complicates its own pessimism.

The fragmentation and dialogism that characterize *The Story of an African Farm* demonstrate Schreiner's departure from the progressive narratives that tend to characterize both the *bildungsroman* and Victorian models of self-development at large—cultural formations that, as Patricia Murphy highlights, were typically gendered masculine.[27] Furthermore, these narrative features suggest Schreiner's awareness of how insights derived from the higher criticism might be used to challenge patriarchal expressions of Christianity. In one of the few studies to date to consider this novel in relation to developments in biblical hermeneutics, Galia Ofek draws connections among Schreiner's emphasis on narrative discontinuities within her own fiction, developments within biblical source criticism, and attendant debates about canonicity in New Woman fiction at large.[28] Read in this light, Schreiner can be seen as participating in a broader movement among late-nineteenth-century women writers who marshaled the higher criticism's findings to challenge misogynistic expressions of Christianity. Important initiatives included the collaborative project *The Woman's Bible*, initiated by the American suffragette Elizabeth Cady Stanton, who led an international committee in compiling a commentary that reassessed the position of women in biblical texts, including discussion of both canonical and apocryphal sources.²⁹ So too, Schreiner both repositions and revivifies the religious traditions woven throughout her novel. This work underscores her place within what Simon Lewis describes as the transnational circulation of "heterodox theism" in the aftermath of mid-century controversies about biblical interpretation. Lewis identifies the work of Bishop John William Colenso, active in South African missionary work, as the region's "most famous colonial counter-flow, theologically speaking."³⁰ Indeed, Colenso's account of the historical inaccuracies within biblical texts, expressed in his highly controversial *The Pentateuch and the Book of Joshua Critically Examined* (1862), caused him to be popularly seen as the missionary who was converted by the natives. Tried and convicted of heresy though acquitted on appeal, Colenso came under fire both for challenging the literal truth of these texts and for questioning doctrines of eternal punishment, evident in his earlier commentary on the Epistle to the Romans (published in 1861 and informed by his missionary experiences in South Africa).³¹ Colenso's universalist leanings find parallels within Schreiner's novel, which, though implicated in nineteenth-century racist discourses, nevertheless advances a forceful challenge to religious exclusivism.

"Under the Sun": Renegotiating Gender and Empire in *The Story of an African Farm*

The Story of an African Farm was widely recognized by Schreiner's contemporaries as an important intervention within the women's rights movement, though twentieth- and twenty-first-century feminist readers have called attention to the novel's complicity within late-Victorian patriarchal frameworks. The British journalist W. T. Stead hailed *The Story of an African Farm* as "the forerunner of all the Novels of the Modern Woman," positioning Schreiner as the leading figure in a cluster of writers including Mona Caird, Sarah Grand, and Ella Hepworth Dixon.³² Subsequent literary scholars, however, have been less optimistic in their assessments. Citing Elaine Showalter's disparaging remarks about Schreiner's "perverse will to fail," John Kucich highlights the critical dissatisfaction with Schreiner's uncompromising destruction of her own female characters, a narrative trajectory that he identifies as a form of masochism resulting from a glorification of maternal self-sacrifice.³³ As Ann Heilmann puts it, the trouble that feminist critics have with both Schreiner and many of her New Woman contemporaries arises from the extent to which their writings seem to perpetuate "the trope of female self-immolation," especially when these writers attempt to use religious symbolism as a political strategy.³⁴ Within *The Story of an African Farm*, this trope appears in the fate of Lyndall, who is secretly pregnant when she returns to the farm after her education abroad, at the beginning of the novel's second part. When the unnamed father of her child comes to claim her, Lyndall leaves the farm with him but refuses to marry him, and he subsequently abandons her. Her baby dies only two hours after birth, and Lyndall herself perishes some weeks later. This fate is disquieting, yet to fully appreciate Schreiner's proto-feminist interventions it is necessary to look not only at the novel's major plot points but also at its more subtle narrative strategies. As she repositions biblical language, Schreiner at once deconstructs the patriarchal ideologies that condemn Lyndall and reconstructs these source texts for new purposes.

The chapter entitled "Lyndall," the fourth in the novel's second part, makes innovative use of Ecclesiastes to express frustration with patriarchal systems—a literary move that is all the more subversive given that Ecclesiastes is not a text that speaks favorably of women. Whereas Qohelet describes in vivid terms the seductress who leads men to their downfall and claims that an upright woman is impossible to find, Lyndall takes back this book's refrains to condemn the cultural institutions that bind women's knowledge, teaching them only what will make them more attractive to men.³⁵ In this chapter, Lyndall returns to the farm after four years of schooling and talks about her learning with Waldo. Three times, she uses the expression "under the sun," a refrain that reverberates throughout Ecclesiastes, to convey both disillusionment and newfound worldly wisdom. She reflects, "of all the cursed places under the sun, where the hungriest soul can hardly pick up a few grains of knowledge, a girl's boarding school is the worst" (151). Furthermore, she suggests that even if she could manage to satisfy her desire for learning, these efforts would be futile: "Look at this little chin of mine, Waldo, with the dimple in it. It is but a small part of my person; but though I had a knowledge of all things under the sun … it would not stead me through life like this little chin" (155). In addition to highlighting the patriarchal economy that reduces women's value to their physical appearance, this statement emphasizes the paucity of all that is done "under the sun." And yet, Lyndall goes on to use this same phrase to betoken a stoic resolution to make the most of her time on earth. Criticizing Waldo's habit of retreating into daydreams, she contrasts his idealism with her own realism. Despite her frustration with societal conventions, she insists, "I like to see real men. Let them be as disagreeable as they please, they are more interesting to me than flowers, or trees, or stars, or any other thing under the sun" (164). Here, the line from Ecclesiastes serves not simply to suggest vanity but also to underscore the breadth of Lyndall's experiences. Her recognition that attempts to escape from patriarchal society are likely to fail does not utterly diminish her zest for life.

Perhaps this novel's most fascinating, if also perplexing, use of religious traditions to reframe issues of gender and power concerns not Lyndall but the man who falls in love with her: Gregory Nazianzen Rose. This naming associates him with St. Gregory Nazianzen, the fourth-century theologian known for both his defense of the Trinity and his poetry. During the Victorian era, his work received renewed attention as a result of writings by John Henry Newman, which, as Matthew Fike observes, celebrated the saint's "affection, gentleness, kindness, tenderness, warmth, and basic good nature, despite occasional irritability and imperfect control over his passions"—in other words, qualities typically regarded as "feminine." Fike proposes that Schreiner's characterization reflects her familiarity with Newman's portrait of the saint, and indeed her own Gregory Nazianzen Rose is ambiguously gendered.[36] His passionate yet capricious spirit prompts him to pursue Lyndall after she leaves the farm with the father of her unborn child; when he finds her, he cross-dresses as a nurse in order to care for his beloved in her dying hours. Several critics have recognized in Schreiner's Gregory an early iteration of the New Man of her later fiction, a counterpart to the New Woman, who likewise integrates masculine and feminine characteristics within a more androgynous identity.[37] Gregory is an imperfect type of this new man, lacking in gentleness and kindness, yet his presence disrupts Victorian gender norms in potentially productive ways. Schreiner's reference to this saint has elements of parody, as the novel sets up its own unholy trinity in the love triangle encompassing Gregory, Lyndall, and Em, whom Gregory eventually marries according to Lyndall's dying wish. And yet, her nod to a Trinitarian theologian bears traces of a longing for a mystical model by which to reimagine human relationships in terms not of rivalry or hierarchy but harmony.

Such is the concept that emerges in one of the most radical statements within Lyndall's entire feminist polemic. Her speech concludes not by drawing stark lines between patriarchal oppressors and those who fight for liberty but by gathering all humankind into a heterogeneous yet intricate whole. She reflects:

> [S]ometimes it amuses me intensely to trace out the resemblance between one man and another: to see how Tant' Sannie and I, you and Bonaparte, St. Simon on his pillar, and the emperor dining off larks' tongues, are one and the same compound, merely mixed in different proportions. What is microscopic in one is largely developed in another; what is a rudimentary in one man is an active organ in another; but all things are in all men, and one soul is the model of

all. We shall find nothing new in human nature after we have once carefully dissected and analyzed the one being we ever shall truly know—ourself.

(164)

To admit kinship with Tant' Sannie and Bonaparte is a startling recognition, given that Lyndall elsewhere perceives these characters to be deeply flawed, if not downright reprehensible. Her speech echoes the language used throughout the "Times and Seasons" chapter, which likewise closes with a meditation on the interconnectivity of all living things. Surveying a diverse catalogue that encompasses the intestines of a drowned gander, the silhouette of a tree, and the minute features of an insect, the narrator marvels, "are they not all the fine branches of one trunk, whose sap flows through us all?" (118). This vision of the natural world incorporates a post-Darwinian sense of nature's brutal indifference, as well as a reverential appreciation for non-human life that inexplicably combines individuality and collectivity ("ourself"). These mystical expressions reflect Schreiner's efforts to integrate a variety of spiritual traditions. She regarded Buddha as a great religious teacher, claiming to prefer him over Jesus because of his appreciation for "the divinity in plant and animal, as well as man."[38] Her fascination with Buddhism participates in what J. Jeffrey Franklin terms "the Victorian Jesus-versus-Buddha debate," a contest that relied on a reductive and imperialistic concept of Buddhism yet nevertheless prompted an important rethinking of religious and moral discourse.[39]

Analyzing Schreiner's relationship to imperialism is a complex task, as critics have long recognized. Her later novella *Trooper Peter Halket of Mashonaland* (1897) offers a forceful critique of Cecil Rhodes and his British South Africa Company, and she herself resigned her seat as vice-president of the Women's Enfranchisement League to protest the League's exclusion of black women from membership in 1909.[40] However, her first novel's portrayals of the Santu, Bantu, and Khoisan people, who appear only in minor roles, are reductively stereotypical. Ryan Fong's rereading of *The Story of an African Farm* in light of archival materials and work by contemporary Khoisan scholars calls attention to the stories and voices silenced in Schreiner's narrative, recovering Indigenous ways of knowing as part of the critical project of unsettling Victorian studies' colonial assumptions.[41] Jade Munslow Ong offers another approach to reconsidering Schreiner's racialized terms, observing that her lexical choices often do the work of exposing and critiquing racial discrimination—in *The Story of an African Farm*, for instance, it is the villainous Bonaparte who uses the most dehumanizing terms.[42] More broadly, Ong sees Schreiner's revision of Christian master narratives as a form of "writing back," as Schreiner refashions the very religious and literary traditions that were often used to justify colonial activity, advancing an "admittedly problematic, but nevertheless important" expression of anti-colonial politics that laid the groundwork for subsequent developments in postcolonial literature.[43]

Within *The Story of an African Farm*, Schreiner's repurposing of religious discourse evinces subtle signs of disquiet with the British imperial project. She questions the ideology of nationalist supremacism that many British imperialists advanced in terms that appropriated biblical accounts of the mission given to Israel.[44] Tellingly, her metafictional account in the "Times and Seasons" chapter presents a young believer who reads a chapter in the prophets only to be beset by the devil's question, "is it right that there should be a chosen people?" (106). The believer can give no answer. Voicing her resistance to this idea (and the nationalistic framework it implies) through the figure of the devil is clearly a subversive move. And yet, Schreiner's attention to the theological and ideological tensions within biblical texts might be seen as working less in the spirit of the devil than that of Qohelet. Qohelet himself engages in critical and creative dialogue with inherited wisdom traditions, mobilizing aphoristic patterns such as those found throughout the book of Proverbs yet taking these sayings to surprisingly skeptical conclusions—valuing death over birth, sorrow over laughter.[45] This work finds a compelling counterpart in William Blake's "Proverbs of Hell" from *The Marriage of Heaven and Hell*, which at once recall typical proverbial images and rhetorical structures and put them to subversive ends ("If the fool would persist in his folly he would become wise," and "Improvement makes straight roads, but the crooked roads without Improvement are roads of Genius").[46] Like Blake and Qohelet, Schreiner challenges the beliefs and structures of organized religion at the same time that she reworks religious metaphors.

The book of Ecclesiastes itself looks beyond the framework of the "chosen people," as biblical scholars have long recognized. Cheyne's late-nineteenth-century commentary, for one, calls attention to the fact that Qohelet's references to God are "under the name Elohim, which belonged to Him as the Creator, not under that of Yahweh, which an Israelite was privileged to use."[47] This observation about the significance of divine names extends and develops the findings of biblical source criticism developed by scholars including Jean Astruc and Alexander Geddes in the eighteenth century. Twentieth- and twenty-first-century scholars have further suggested that biblical wisdom literature's broad purview is one of its distinctive features. Leo G. Perdue contrasts the emphasis on salvific history throughout the prophetic books with the creation theology that he identifies as integral to wisdom literatures.[48] Throughout her biblical rewritings within *The Story of an African Farm*, Schreiner probes a variety of genres. While her parodic account of Bonaparte's fire-and-brimstone sermon destabilizes prophetic rhetoric and exposes how this discourse might be subject to authoritarian abuses, her recourse to wisdom literature, including both her echoes of Ecclesiastes and her adaptation of the parable as a narrative strategy, performs a sophisticated symbolic renewal.

Challenging False Prophets: Subversive Parody and Transformative Dialogue

Among this novel's most pointedly satirical passages is Schreiner's account of the sermon on lies, an apocalyptic tirade delivered by the con artist Bonaparte Blenkins. His very name has a farcical ring: "Blenkins" sounds like a "Dickensian corruption" of the words *blink* and *blench*, as Monsman remarks, while "Bonaparte" calls to mind the French military and political leader Napoleon Bonaparte, with whom Schreiner's character makes a far-fetched claim of kinship.[49] Upon arrival at the farm, Bonaparte manages not only to obtain food and shelter but also to manipulate his way into positions of privilege. His tall tales charm Tant' Sannie and deceive the all-too-trusting overseer Otto, whose position he usurps and whose son he subjects to ridicule and abuse until at last Bonaparte goes too far and is driven away. Before his manipulative tactics become evident, he manages to secure the role of occasional preacher, one of many offices that he steals from Otto. His sermon elides the narrative complexity of Christianity's sacred stories, playing fast and loose with biblical texts.

Predictably, this sermon opens with a brief reading from the Book of Revelation, "all liars shall have their part in the lake which burneth with fire and brimstone: which is the second death" (cf. Rev. 21:8). But Bonaparte goes on to illustrate the point less with examples from scripture than with his own fabrications, including anecdotes about his second-hand knowledge of hot-blooded Italians, and what begins as a warning about the evils of lying culminates in the moral, "let us not love too much" (38). Attempting to find a biblical basis for this injunction, Bonaparte exclaims, "Was Jeremiah ever in love, or Ezekiel, or Hosea, or even any of the minor prophets? No!"—emphatically dismissing the very thought (39). But given that Hosea's entire prophetic mission was enacted through his marriage to and care for the prostitute Gomer, this tidy dismissal of complicated human affairs and affections suggests a blatant ignorance of the very stories invoked. Within the narrative frame of *The Story of an African Farm*, the irony is all the sharper given that Bonaparte's own activities might be summed up in two words: lying and licentiousness. At the end of the sermon, the narrator's observation that "the Bible closed with a tremendous thud" metonymically and comically underscores Bonaparte's clumsy appropriation of prophetic authority and his ham-handed attempts to foreclose on interpretive possibilities (39).

This satirical portrait is the second episode in a chapter entitled "Sunday Services," subtitled *Service No. II*. By contrast, the preceding *Service No. I*. depicts Waldo's private attempts to wrestle with difficult questions resulting from the discrepancies among the synoptic gospels—the same questions raised by the biblical higher critics. Plagued with "adder-like thoughts," Waldo ponders, "*Why did the women in Mark see only one angel and the women in Luke two? Could a story be told in opposite ways and both ways be true?*" (33). Whereas Bonaparte simply glosses over anything in the text that does not serve his own purposes, Waldo yearns for a more capacious interpretive model. He gets something of an answer, albeit a cryptic one, through a story told by another traveling stranger— an episode modeled after Schreiner's own encounter with Willie Bertram, the freethinking son of a South African minister and the one who introduced her to the works of both Spencer and Emerson.[50] Just as Bonaparte's hypocritical public pronouncements serve as a foil to Waldo's sincere and private devotions, so also the sermon on lies finds a productive counterpoint in the parable on truth.

While Waldo and Bonaparte represent two diametrically opposed approaches to religious texts, one characterized by exploitative appropriation and the other by earnest questioning, the novel complicates this portrayal by introducing an unstable third term in its cluster of Bible readers: Otto, Bonaparte's first victim and Waldo's father. On first glance, it would seem that Otto represents a naïvely literal mode of exegesis that the novel itself ridicules. At the close of the day on which he welcomes Bonaparte into his home, he opens his "much-worn" Bible to the gospel of Matthew, where he reads, "I was a stranger, and ye took me in" (23).[51] Rereading the day's events in light of this text, Otto looks again on Bonaparte, seeing neither his "bloated body" nor his "evil face" but sensing only "that Christ was very near him" (23). It is, of course, Otto, who, in quite another sense of the phrase, gets *taken in* by the con artist. Even so, Schreiner's portrait of Otto's simple faith is not always critical but, on occasion, remarkably compassionate. His final words take the form of a farewell letter that he writes to Waldo, Em, and Lyndall, after Bonaparte robs him of his position as overseer: "My little children, serve the Saviour; give your hearts to him while you are yet young. Life is short" (60). This exhortation bears an uncanny resemblance to the statements exhorting the reader to remember the Creator "in the days of thy youth" in the final chapter of Ecclesiastes (Eccl. 12:1). These surprising echoes unsettle clear distinctions between wisdom and foolishness. Moreover, the parable on truth—an important metafictional moment within this novel—appears in the narrative as an interpretive commentary on a carving that Waldo has made to honor the memory of his father, who dies the night after his unjust dismissal. As these details suggest, Schreiner's revisionary engagement with biblical texts is more than a mere inversion or subversion of Christianity. Rather, her creative interpretations return to the roots of this religious tradition in ways that open up new possibilities for transformation and dialogue.

The interpolated narrative in *The Story of an African Farm*, which Schreiner later extracted and reprinted as a parable entitled "The Hunter" in her collection of short allegories entitled *Dreams* (1890), features a sorrowing man who is instructed by Wisdom to pursue Truth, figured as a beautiful and elusive bird. He does so with the full knowledge that, at most, he will obtain only a single feather: his hope is that subsequent seekers might weave this feather and others into a net that will one day be capable of catching Truth. The hunter spends many years facing temptations in the wilderness before he climbs a mountain, gasps out his final breaths, and dies as a single feather descends on him. This story evokes a range of biblical and classical precedents, from Deuteronomy's account of the death of Moses on Mount Nebo, with his distant glimpse of the Promised Land, to the Isis and Osiris myth as retold in John Milton's *Areopagitica* (1644). That Schreiner may have had in mind Milton's pamphlet defending the liberty of the press seems all the more likely given the book-burning scene earlier in the novel, where Bonaparte incinerates Waldo's copy of John Stuart Mill's *Principles of Political Economy* (1848), deeming it a dangerous influence even though he knows nothing about it. In the context of Milton's argument for unlicensed printing, the story of Isis's search for the dismembered body of Osiris serves to allegorize an ongoing search for Truth. Milton's remarks about this myth affirm the exercise of individual reason and concede the idea that Truth itself might take multiple forms or, at least, that "it is not impossible that she may have more shapes than one."[52] Schreiner, in turn, rewrites these mythic traditions to pursue a still more expansive pluralism.

As embedded within *The Story of an African Farm*, this parable emerges in the context of a conversation that opens with the stranger's queries about Waldo's carving and concludes with Waldo's questions about how the storyteller could have understood his meaning so well. The stranger responds that "all true art" creates "a little door that opens into an infinite hall where you may find what you please." Truth, as defined by the stranger, is inherently multiple: it "has a thousand meanings and suggests a thousand more." Rather than identify authorial intention as something that restricts or governs meaning, he declares that the act of "reading more into this or that work of genius than was ever written into it" is in fact "the highest compliment" (133–4). In this view, interpretation becomes a form of co-creation, unfolding as an interactive process between the reader and the text. Such an interpretive model of reading goes against the grain of much nineteenth-century hermeneutic theory, which, following Friedrich Schleiermacher, focused on determining a text's original historical situation.[53] And yet, the stranger's ideas also suggest Schreiner's familiarity with the more subtle points advanced by Schleiermacher's contemporaries. The higher criticism's prevailing focus on historical contexts had the effect of uncovering the Bible's variety of genres, some of which invite greater attention to readerly agency—as several higher critics themselves noted. Renan, for one, highlighted the artistic qualities of the biblical parables, which he described as "not fixed dogmas but images susceptible of infinite interpretations."[54] Schreiner, who read and admired Renan, puts very similar words into the mouth of the stranger. This definition of parable—a form rooted in the biblical wisdom tradition—aligns in notable ways with ideas advanced by later hermeneutic thinkers such as Paul Ricoeur, who characterizes the biblical parables as metaphorical narratives that have a fundamentally "interrogative structure": their dynamic symbols reach toward the reader in a gesture of extravagance that makes possible new ways of redefining reality.[55] As Schreiner's storyteller suggests, the task of the wisdom writer resides not with persuading readers to adopt a given position but with awakening a heightened capacity to question.

Schreiner's creative engagement with biblical symbolism, as well as her suggestion that truth is something called into being, emerges most powerfully at the parable's end. As the hunter gasps out his final breaths, the story reprises the biblical scene of the Pisgah Sight—that is, Moses's glimpse of the Promised Land just before his death, a scene that occupied a vital place in the Victorian typological imagination, as George P. Landow has shown. Whereas Landow's survey of Victorian literature and art distinguishes between "orthodox" and "modern" versions of the Pisgah Sight based on whether they foreground the presence or absence of God, Schreiner's narrative revisions resist classification along these lines.[56] Blinded by "the mist of death," the hunter assures himself that others will benefit from the work he has done in building a set of steps up the mountain. Just before he dies, he is met with an unexpected turn of events:

> Then slowly from the white sky above, through the still air, came something falling, falling, falling. Softly it fluttered down, and dropped onto the breast of the dying man. He felt it with his hands. It was a feather. He died holding it.
>
> (133)

Through its sensuously tactile description of the feather's motion and the man's grasp, this passage portrays Truth's landing as an intimate gesture, one that recalls the biblical tradition of Moses as one who was known by God "face to face" (Deut. 34:10). Moreover, Schreiner's replacement of sight with touch shifts the emphasis of the scene from the distant prospect of the entire Promised Land to the immediate—and fragmentary—presence of truth.

Just before this feather descends, the hunter reflects on his quest as something that exceeds tidy categories of self-abnegation or self-realization. Speculating about those who will follow in his footsteps, up the stairs he has carved, he acknowledges that "they will never know the name of the man who made them," even conceding, "at the clumsy work they will laugh"; nonetheless, he consoles himself with the assurance "but they will mount, and on *my* work; they will climb, and by *my* stair! They will find her, and through me! And no man liveth to himself, and no man dieth to himself" (133). His final words echo the book of Romans, a quotation that is all the more noticeable for the archaisms that are otherwise out of place in the hunter's speech (Rom. 14:7, "For none of us liveth to himself, and no man dieth to himself"). Within the Pauline letter, this statement appears as part of an exhortation to religious community, despite differing customs about dietary restrictions and Sabbath observances among members. So too Schreiner's novel yearns for an expansive understanding of fellowship. Even as *The Story of an African Farm* dwells on finitude and failure, the narrative suggests that wisdom arises from the effort to contribute to a cosmic endeavor that exceeds the scope of any individual. As metafiction, this parable aids in illuminating the combination of futility and possibility figured through the deaths of both Lyndall and Waldo at the novel's conclusion. It thereby hints at the novel's wider intellectual and ethical trajectory, from isolation to incorporation, from authorial privilege to readerly participation.

Novel Endings: From Limitation to Aspiration

Lyndall's last living moments are at once tragic and promising. Her earlier feminist polemic, delivered after she returns to the farm as a young woman in the novel's second part, specifically rejects the Pisgah Sight as an undesirable ending, claiming that "it would be better not to see it" than "to be Moses on the mountain of Nebo, with the land at your feet and no power to enter" (162). However, her deathbed scene recalls the hunter's dying moments and, by extension, this moment in biblical myth. Though weak and delirious in her final hours, she still speaks as a visionary, seeming to intuit this parable's ideas. She claims to see "a poor weak soul striving after good," one who "learnt, through tears and much pain, that holiness is an infinite compassion for others; that greatness is to take the common things of life and walk truly among them" (249). For Lyndall, whose speech ends elliptically, there is no exodus, no ultimate deliverance; nevertheless, the promise of something sacred animates everyday life. Her sense of what is holy aligns with broader Romantic patterns of thought that sought to redefine religion in terms of human feeling and reverence for the ordinary, from Ludwig Feuerbach to Samuel Taylor Coleridge, as discussed in Chapter 3.[57]

Bearing witness to Lyndall's final words is her nurse, the cross-dressing Gregory. As he turns away from the dying young woman in grief, the narrator again invokes the stories of Genesis: "Like Hagar, when she laid her treasure down in the wilderness, he sat afar off" (251). This simile is provocative for both its gendered and its religious implications. Hagar, who bore the child Ishmael with Abraham in her capacity as Sarah's handmaid before being turned away by her jealous mistress, is the mother of the son who did not inherit the blessing given to Isaac, and as such is associated not with Judaism or Christianity but with Islam. And yet, in the passage invoked, God speaks to Hagar, the seeming outsider, telling her not to fear, providing water, and blessing her son.[58] This allusion thickens the novel's challenge to religious exclusivism. Even though Lyndall (unlike Ishmael) perishes and even though Gregory (unlike Hagar) hears no divine voice, Schreiner's inventive recourse to Genesis combines sorrow with a hope that radiates beyond the "chosen people."

Waldo meets death in more prosaic company, yet here again the narrative combines pessimism and possibility. Not long after receiving news of Lyndall's passing, he dies quietly in his sleep from an unexplained ailment, slipping away while reposed on the grounds, as the backyard chickens perch on him. Passing nearby, Em leaves him a glass of milk, thinking, "he will wake soon … and be glad of it." The narrator, however, undercuts this confident assertion with the novel's enigmatic last words, "But the chickens were wiser" (270). Arguably, this scene offers a parody of the interpolated narrative: in place of Truth's glorious feather, readers are left with the antics of common barnyard fowl. And yet, Waldo's last moments of consciousness are his perceptions of these chickens as "those tiny sparks of brother life" (269). This leveling of human/nonhuman hierarchies in the face of mortality once again accords with the third chapter of Ecclesiastes, in its affirmation that all return to dust and its questioning of distinctions between human and animal spirits.[59] Such creature kinship further recalls the ineffable fullness expressed at the end of the "Times and Seasons" chapter: "all is part of a whole, whose beginning and end we know not. The life that throbs in us is a pulsation from it; too mighty for our comprehension, not too small" (118). Schreiner's phrasing echoes Qohelet's claim that God "hath made every thing beautiful in its time: also he hath set the world in their heart, so that no man can find out the work that God maketh from the beginning to the end" (Eccl. 3:11). Even as both Schreiner and Qohelet focus on the vanity of all that is done under the sun, they uphold the prospect of a meaningfulness that lies at the limits of what can be articulated.

This novel's seemingly cynical ending, then, becomes ambiguously hopeful. In the face of death, Schreiner advances no doctrine of resurrection or reincarnation. Rather, she marshals metaphors derived from biblical wisdom literature to grapple with unanswered and even unanswerable questions. Her penultimate chapter, entitled "Dreams"—the very title that Schreiner later re-used for her collection of short allegories that included a reprinting of the story of the hunter, published by T. Fisher Unwin in 1890—self-reflexively comments on both the impossibility of arriving at satisfying interpretations and the necessity of seeking them. As Waldo meditates before the fire, he entertains a series of potential ideas about eternity, beginning with the literal notions about heaven and hell expressed by "the Christian, the true Bible Christian," followed by a universalist vision of resurrection for all advanced by "the nineteenth-century Christian, deep into whose soul modern unbelief and thought have crept, though he knows it not" (256–7). Finally, Waldo hears "the Transcendentalist's high answer": that the flesh will perish but the spirit will endure. Although Schreiner's own admiration for Emerson's Transcendentalism would seem to suggest that this third answer should be the true one, the narrator goes on to describe it as "the offering of jewels to the hungry, of gold to the man who dies for bread" (258). Schreiner's readiness to turn a critical eye on the philosophy that she herself held in high regard aligns with her overall emphasis on the limits of all knowledge, and the terms of this rejection emphasize her esteem for concrete, embodied realities. After vehemently rejecting these fantasies—"all dreams and lies! No ground anywhere"—Waldo has his own vision. He achieves something akin to peace through his mystic affirmation of universal unity, though the narrator maintains a level of critical distance from Waldo's position, concluding, "Our fathers had their dream; we have ours; the generation that follows will have its own. Without dreams and phantoms man cannot exist" (260). Without endorsing any one vision above the rest, this statement simply affirms that human beings are meaning-seeking creatures.

Rather than advance a straightforward narrative of progress by which humankind gradually evolves from superstition to enlightenment, Schreiner's reflections on the intellectual shifts of the nineteenth century underscore the limits and possibilities of various paradigms. In so doing, she provides a potentially productive model for the self-reflexive task of "owning up to our religiousness" that Lori Branch proposes as a vital part of a postsecular approach. Such an approach might lead to new directions in literary criticism, provided that readers have the courage "to go into the symptom of our uncertainty, to refuse to reinscribe the secular/religious divide, and to say to ourselves, this condition of believing in the midst of imperfect knowledge is the human, linguistic condition of being in the world."[60] As Branch sees it, such is the pathway to pluralism. Although *The Story of an African Farm* stops short of realizing this pluralism, the novel's insistent challenge to religious exclusivism and its experimentation with a more flexible use of religious symbolism invites readers to follow in these footsteps. Appreciating Schreiner's religious revisionism might help Victorian studies to move beyond a reductive concept of religion according to a faith/doubt dichotomy and pursue more robust explorations of religious discourse for both its tensions and its many-sided textures.

A Hidden Design: Revelation, Concealment, and Wisdom Literature

In her adaptation of the formal patterns of biblical wisdom literature, Schreiner participates creatively in the work of nineteenth-century higher critics. An unsigned translator's preface to an early English translation of Renan's *Vie de Jésus* (dated December 8, 1863) positioned this scholarship as an attempt not to repudiate but to reframe Christianity's sacred texts. As the translator put it, "the great problem of the present age is to preserve the religious spirit, whilst getting rid of the superstitions and absurdities that deform it, and which are alike opposed to science and common sense."[61] He further identified both Renan's work and *Essays and Reviews* as recent examples of scholarly work that attempts to intervene within this dilemma. Benjamin Jowett's "On the Interpretation of Scripture," the final piece in *Essays and Reviews*, used similar terms to invite his readers to keep an open mind and cultivate nuanced reading practices. Jowett, an ordained Anglican minister, claimed that the end result of harmonizing these texts with higher critical findings would be not to empty Christianity's sacred texts of their power but to revitalize them in a manner more congruent with the spirit of the gospel. Protesting against the unthinking preservation of dogmatic claims about the Bible's divine inspiration, Jowett declared "that in the present day the great object of Christianity should be, not to change the lives of men, but to prevent them from changing their opinions, that would be a singular inversion of the purposes for which Christ came into the world."[62] While Jowett may not have gone as far as Schreiner in deeming Jesus "a freethinker," he nevertheless recognized the provocative power of the parables.[63] Even as Jowett's essay advocates for reading texts within their historical contexts, he calls attention to "the inwardness of the words of Christ" as requiring a reflective, introspective method of reading that cannot be easily reduced to historical-critical scrutiny.[64] He singles out texts including Job, Ecclesiastes, and the gospel parables as containing "a depth and inwardness of which require a measure of the same qualities in the interpreter himself."[65] By implication, then, the wisdom tradition has an important role to play within efforts to re-read the Bible not as dogma but as literature.

This point might be extended by drawing on the resources offered by subsequent developments in biblical hermeneutics, including Ricoeur's discussion of how wisdom literature embeds a distinctive model of religious revelation. Much of this wisdom literature, in Ricoeur's words, emphasizes "the silence and absence of God" and thus "brings to light the overwhelming question of the sense or nonsense of existence."[66] This obscurity, however disquieting, has important theological implications, as Ricoeur proposes: "to say that the God who reveals himself is a hidden God is to confess that revelation can never constitute a body of truths which an institution may boast of or take pride in possessing."[67] The dialectical model of revelation and concealment encoded by wisdom literature, then, provides a subtle yet potent corrective to dogmatic claims about the meaning of sacred texts, including those advanced by narrowly literalist exegesis. Schreiner shows a keen awareness of the extent to which religious discourse might be subject to authoritarian uses, as exemplified in her satirical portrait of Bonaparte's fire-and-brimstone sermon. And yet, her own biblical rewritings unleash a broader range of imaginative possibilities, moving away from fundamentalist uses of religious discourse and toward more pluralistic ones. Ricoeur's discussion of the variety of genres within biblical texts similarly opens toward multiplicity: he suggests that this variety of discourses results in both a "polycentric" understanding of the self and a "plural naming of God." Whereas the books of the law designate God as "the source of the imperative" and the prophets signify him as "divine I doubling the human I," wisdom literature "searches for him as the meaning of the meaningful"—an attempt at renaming that underscores the ongoing nature of this interpretive process. For Ricoeur, this rereading of the Bible as a polyphonic text "leaves open" a new problem, namely, that of "knowing how this religious consciousness, informed by the biblical Great Code, could be open to other religious consciousnesses, informed by other scriptural codes."[68] While he does not address this issue at length, he suggests that a reading of the biblical tradition that recognizes its fragmentation and multiplicity might provide the gateway to a greater, inter-religious hospitality. Again, attending carefully to wisdom literature promises to contribute meaningfully to this endeavor, given that this genre addresses itself less to a chosen people than to all humankind. Several biblical scholars have highlighted wisdom literature's cosmic scope, remarking that its insistent reach beyond the covenant made with Israel means that wisdom literature can serve as "the open door in an otherwise closed canon."[69] This genre distinguishes itself as eminently concerned not only with the task of interpretation, as Ricoeur highlights, but also with literary craftsmanship, as Alter has shown.[70]

Schreiner's literary engagement with wisdom texts and traditions challenges readers to be self-reflexive, dialectical thinkers as they too participate in this art of interpretation. Within *The Story of an African Farm*, her embedded parable arises in response to Waldo's handiwork, which is at once described from a perspective of critical distance (the narrator remarks that it "was by no means lovely," deeming it "almost grotesque") and celebrated for its ambition (122–1). The quest narrative that results from the stranger's attempts to translate the carving into words engages creatively, even appreciatively, with a variety of literary and mythic precursors, without exalting any of them as a final authority. Prior to his journey through the wilderness and up the mountains, the Hunter builds a net that entraps three beautiful birds, who sing three enchanting songs—"A human-God!" "Immortality!," and "Reward after Death!"—all of whom he believes are true until Wisdom tells him that he is mistaken (125). For Schreiner, wisdom resides in acknowledging that truth can never be fully grasped while simultaneously refusing to abandon its pursuit. Her readiness not only to question but also to overturn inherited traditions distinguishes her, to be sure, from writers such Elizabeth Barrett Browning and George MacDonald, whose artistic responses to these biblical traditions firmly adhere to a Christological framework. Moreover, Schreiner goes further than either John Ruskin or George

Eliot in exposing the limitations and customary abuses of religious discourse. Yet all of these writers turn to wisdom literature both to respond to the higher critical developments that put pressure on received traditions about the Bible's literal truth and to pursue personal, affective encounters with sacred texts that go beyond the bounds of a historically minded criticism.

Schreiner's creative interpretations within *The Story of an African Farm* anticipate the ideas about literary form and religious revelation that she articulated in a later letter to Lloyd, the Presbyterian minister who nevertheless admired her freethinking work:

> Except in my own language of parables, I cannot express myself. If I say that in a stone in the road, in the thoughts in my brain, in the corpuscles in a drop of blood under my microscope, in a railway engine rushing past me in the velt, I see God, shall I not only be darkening counsel with words?[71]

Self-reflexively acknowledging the poverty of her own phrasing, Schreiner nevertheless advances a series of arresting metaphors for divine immanence. Echoing God's speeches in the book of Job—which open with the rebuke, "who is this who darkeneth counsel by words without knowledge?" (Job 38:2)—she emphasizes that words function not only to express meaning, but, sometimes, to obscure it. A similar emphasis emerges in *The Story of an African Farm*: questioning the idea of divinely dictated truth, Schreiner suggests that revelation and concealment occur together, through imperfect yet artistic human words. At once skeptical and imaginative, her religious revisionism probes the wisdom tradition for all its depths. She, like the other Victorian writers discussed in this book, turns to wisdom literature not to restrict or contain ideas about righteousness and truth but to catalyze an ongoing process of spiritual searching.

Notes

1 Joyce Avrech Berkman, *The Healing Imagination of Olive Schreiner: Beyond South African Colonialism* (Amherst: University of Massachusetts Press, 1989), 12–14, 51–2.

2 Olive Schreiner to Havelock Ellis, November 3, 1888, ll. 34–5. National English Literary Museum, Grahamstown, Olive Schreiner Letters Project transcription, *The Olive Schreiner Letters Online*, 2012. All transcriptions replicate Schreiner's writing as closely as possible, including notations for additions and deletions.

3 Canon MacColl, "An Agnostic Novel": Review of *The Story of an African Farm*" [*The Spectator* (August 13, 1887)], in *Olive Schreiner*, ed. Cherry Clayton

(Johannesburg: McGraw-Hill, 1983), 72. For more recent studies that highlight Schreiner's agnosticism, see Mike Kissack and Michael Titlestad, "Olive Schreiner and the Secularization of the Moral Imagination," *English in Africa* 3, no. 1 (2006): 29–34; see also Matthew Fike, "Anima and Psychic Fragmentation in Olive Schreiner's *The Story of an African Farm*," *English in Africa* 42, no. 1 (2015): 83–96. On Schreiner's reading of Spencer, see Berkman, *The Healing Imagination*, 20.

4   *The Bible: Authorized King James Version with Apocrypha* (Oxford: Oxford University Press, 2008). All biblical quotations are cited parenthetically in text. Rights in the Authorized (King James) Version in the UK are vested in the Crown. Reproduced by permission of the Crown's patentee, Cambridge University Press.

5   Higher critical studies that offer brief but telling commentary on the parables include Charles Hennell's *Inquiry Concerning the Origin of Christianity* and David Friedrich Strauss's *Das Leben Jesu* (*Life of Jesus*), as discussed in my book's third chapter. More recent biblical scholarship on the gospel parables as wisdom literature includes Ronald A. Piper, *Wisdom in the Q-Tradition: The Aphoristic Teaching of Jesus* (Cambridge: Cambridge University Press, 1989), Ben Witherington, *Jesus the Sage: The Pilgrimage of Wisdom* (Philadelphia: Fortress Press, 1994), and Charles W. Hedrick, *The Wisdom of Jesus: Between the Sages of Israel and the Apostles of the Church* (Eugene: Cascade Books, 2014).

6   Wilhelm Martin Leberecht De Wette, *A Critical and Historical Introduction to the Canonical Scriptures of the Old Testament*, trans. Theodore Parker, 2 vols. (Boston: Rufus Leighton Jr., 1859), 2: 548; Robert Alter, *The Wisdom Books: Job, Proverbs, and Ecclesiastes: A Translation with Commentary* (New York: Norton, 2010), 337.

7   Roland E. Murphy, "The Sage in Ecclesiastes and Qoheleth the Sage," in *The Sage in Israel and the Ancient Near East*, ed. John G. Gammie and Leo G. Perdue (Indiana: Winona Lake, 1990), 263.

8   Richard Hess, *The Old Testament: A Historical, Theological, and Critical Introduction* (Grand Rapids: Baker Academic, 2016), 408.

9   De Wette, *A Critical and Historical Introduction*, 2: 547, 551.

10 Thomas Kelly Cheyne, *Job and Solomon, or the Wisdom of the Old Testament* (New York: Thomas Whittaker, 1889), 256, 242–3.

11 Ibid., 242, 246.

12 Olive Schreiner, *The Story of an African Farm* (Oxford: Oxford University Press, 1992), 115, 118. All subsequent references to Schreiner's novel refer to this edition and are cited parenthetically by page numbers.

13 Alter, *The Wisdom Books*, 340.

14 For a discussion of Schreiner's activity in these circles, see Berkman, *The Healing Imagination*, 59.

15 Ruth First and Ann Scott, *Olive Schreiner* (New York: Schocken Books, 1980), 58; Kissack and Titestlad, "Olive Schreiner," 33.

16 Berkman, *The Healing Imagination*, 43.
17 Olive Schreiner to John T. Lloyd, October 29, 1892, ll. 103–4, 135–6. NLSA Cape Town, Special Collections, Olive Schreiner Letters Project Transcription, *The Olive Schreiner Letters Online*, 2012.
18 Olive Schreiner to Adela Villiers Smith nee Villiers, April 9, 1908, ll. 6–7. NLSA Cape Town, Special Collections, Olive Schreiner Letters Project Transcription, *The Olive Schreiner Letters Online*, 2012; Olive Schreiner to Betty Molteno, May 23, 1900, UCT Manuscripts & Archives, Olive Schreiner Letters Project Transcription, *The Olive Schreiner Letters Online*, 2012.
19 Olive Schreiner to Havelock Ellis, April 19, 1884, ll. 31–2. Harry Ransom Research Center, University of Texas at Austin, Olive Schreiner Letters Project Transcription, *The Olive Schreiner Letters Online*, 2012.
20 Olive Schreiner to Karl Pearson, June 12, 1886, ll. 77–8. University College London Library, Special Collections, Olive Schreiner Letters Project Transcription, *The Olive Schreiner Letters Online*, 2012.
21 On Schreiner's admiration for Emerson, see Berkman, *The Healing Imagination*, 75. On the biblical symbolism of the "pen of iron," see Jer. 17:1 and Job 19:24.
22 Gerald Monsman, *Olive Schreiner's Fiction: Landscape and Power* (New Brunswick: Rutgers University Press, 1991), 79–80.
23 Ibid., 59.
24 Cheyne, *Job and Solomon*, 246.
25 Carol T. Christ, "'The Hero as Man of Letters': Masculinity and Victorian Nonfiction Prose," in *Victorian Sages and Cultural Discourse: Renegotiating Gender and Power*, ed. Thaïs E. Morgan (New Brunswick: Rutgers University Press, 1991), 19; John Holloway, *The Victorian Sage: Studies in Argument* (London: Macmillan, 1953), 1–10; George P. Landow, *Elegant Jeremiahs: The Sage from Carlyle to Mailer* (Ithaca: Cornell University Press, 1986), 40–3.
26 Thomas Carlyle, *Sartor Resartus* (Oxford: Oxford University Press, 1999), 22.
27 Patricia Murphy, "Timely Interruptions: Unsettling Gender through Temporality in *The Story of an African Farm*," *Style* 32, no. 1 (1998): 80–1.
28 Galia Ofek, "'Reviewing the Rites Proper to Canonization': New Woman Novels and New Conceptions of Canonicity," *Victorian Literature and Culture* 38, no. 1 (2010): 177.
29 Ibid., 166–7.
30 Simon Lewis, "The Transnational Circulation of Dissent: Olive Schreiner and the Colonial Counter-Flows of Unitarian Freethinking," *Safundi* 14, no. 1 (2013): 12.
31 Timothy Larsen, *Contested Christianity: The Political and Social Contexts of Victorian Theology* (Waco: Baylor University Press, 2004), 72–5.
32 W. T. Stead, "The Book of the Month: The Novel of the Modern Woman," *Review of Reviews* 10 (July 1894): 64.

33 John Kucich, *Imperial Masochism: British Fiction, Fantasy, and Social Class* (Princeton: Princeton University Press, 2007), 87–8.
34 Ann Heilmann, *New Woman Strategies: Sarah Grand, Olive Schreiner, Mona Caird* (Manchester: Manchester University Press, 2004), 126.
35 See Eccl. 7:26-29.
36 Fike, "Anima and Psychic Fragmentation," 94.
37 Ibid., 96; see also Berkman, *The Healing Imagination*, 124.
38 Olive Schreiner to John T. Lloyd, October 29, 1892, ll. 116–17. NLSA Cape Town, Special Collections, Olive Schreiner Letters Project Transcription, *The Olive Schreiner Letters Online*, 2012.
39 J. Jeffrey Franklin, *The Lotus and the Lion: Buddhism and the British Empire* (Ithaca: Cornell University Press, 2008), 27.
40 On Schreiner and imperialism, see Heilman, *New Woman Strategies* 5–6; Kucich, *Imperial Masochism*, 247–57; Anne McClintock, *Imperial Leather: Race, Gender, and Sexuality in the Colonial Conquest* (New York: Routledge, 1995), 259; and Robin Hackett, *Sapphic Primitivism: Productions of Race, Class, and Sexuality in Key Works of Modern Fiction* (New Brunswick: Rutgers University Press, 2004), 42.
41 Ryan Fong, "The Stories outside the African Farm: Indigeneity, Orality, and Unsettling the Victorian," *Victorian Studies* 62, no. 3 (2020): 423, 429–31.
42 Jade Munslow Ong, *Olive Schreiner and African Modernism: Allegory, Empire, and Postcolonial Writing* (New York: Routledge, 2018), 80.
43 Jade Munslow Ong, "Dream Time and Anti-Imperialism in the Writings of Olive Schreiner," *Journal of Postcolonial Writing* 50, no. 6 (2014): 713–14.
44 On this imperialist appropriation of biblical language in the literature and sermons of Victorian Britain, see Eric M. Reisenauer, "Between the Eternal City and the Holy City: Rome, Jerusalem, and the Imperial Ideal in Britain," *Canadian Journal of History* 44, no. 3 (2009): 244–5.
45 See, for instance, Eccl. 7:1-7.
46 William Blake, *The Marriage of Heaven and Hell* (Oxford: Bodleian Library, 2011), 11–12. Blake's statements might be seen as playing subversively with the advice about dealing with fools and the imagery of the straight path in the book of Proverbs (Prov. 4:26-27, 26:4-5). That said, Proverbs itself encompasses its own thought-provoking contradictions. See Peter Hatton, *Contradiction in the Book of Proverbs* (Farham: Ashgate Press, 2008), 3.
47 Cheyne, *Job and Solomon*, 201.
48 Leo G. Perdue, *Wisdom and Creation: The Theology of Wisdom Literature*. (Nashville: Abingdon Press, 1994), 20–1.
49 Monsman, *Olive Schreiner's Fiction*, 61.
50 Lewis, "The Transnational Circulation of Dissent," 4–8.
51 Mt. 25:35.

52 John Milton, "*Areopagitica*," in *Complete Poems and Major Prose*, ed. Merritt Y. Hughes (Indianapolis: Hackett, 2003), 747.
53 Friedrich Schleiermacher, *Hermeneutics and Criticism and Other Writings*, trans. Andrew Bowie (Cambridge: Cambridge University Press, 1998), 24.
54 Ernest Renan, *The Life of Jesus*, trans. John Haynes Holmes (New York: The Modern Library, 1955), 384.
55 Paul Ricoeur, "Biblical Hermeneutics," *Semeia* 4 (1975): 33.
56 George P. Landow, *Victorian Types, Victorian Shadows: Biblical Typology in Victorian Literature, Art and Thought* (New York: Routledge, 1980), 220.
57 On this discussion of Christianity as a religion of feeling, see Ludwig Feuerbach, *The Essence of Christianity*, trans. George Eliot (New York: Harper and Row, 1957), 140.
58 Gen. 21:17-19.
59 Eccl. 3:20-21.
60 Lori Branch, "Postcriticism and Postsecular: The Horizon of Belief," *Religion and Literature* 48, no. 2 (2016): 166.
61 While the translator's identity is uncertain, it may have been Charles Edwin Wilbour, the American journalist and Egyptologist who translated the first American edition of Renan's work, published by Carleton in New York, 1864. This prefatory note, dated December 8, 1863, is included in the front matter of the translation of Renan's work by the American Unitarian biblical scholar John Haynes Holmes, originally published in 1927 and reissued by Modern Library in 1955.
62 Benjamin Jowett, "On the Interpretation of Scripture," in *Essays and Reviews: The 1860 Text and Its Reading*, ed. Victor Shea and William Whitla (Charlottesville: University Press of Virginia, 2000), 502.
63 Olive Schreiner to Betty Molteno, May 23, 1900, UCT Manuscripts & Archives, Olive Schreiner Letters Project Transcription, *The Olive Schreiner Letters Online*, 2012.
64 Jowett, "On the Interpretation of Scripture," 493.
65 Ibid., 505.
66 Paul Ricoeur, "Toward a Hermeneutic of the Idea of Revelation," in *Essays on Biblical Interpretation*, ed. Lewis S. Mudge, trans. David Pellauer (Philadelphia: Fortress Press, 1980), 86.
67 Ibid., 95.
68 Paul Ricoeur, "Experience and Language in Religious Discourse," in *Phenomenology and the Theological Turn: The French Debate*, ed. Dominique Janicaud (New York: Fordham University Press, 2000), 145-6.
69 William P. Brown, *Wisdom's Wonder: Character, Creation, and Crisis in the Bible's Wisdom Literature* (Grand Rapids: William B. Eerdmans, 2014), 3. See also Perdue, *Wisdom and Creation*, 20-1, and Alter, *The Wisdom Books*, xiv.

70 Robert Alter, *The Art of Biblical Poetry* (New York: Basil Books, 1985), 210. See also Alter, "The Poetic and Wisdom Books," in *The Cambridge Companion to Biblical Interpretation*, ed. John Barton (Cambridge: Cambridge University Press, 2006), 234.

71 Olive Schreiner to John T. Lloyd, October 29, 1892, ll. 137–43, 135–6. NLSA Cape Town, Special Collections, Olive Schreiner Letters Project Transcription, *The Olive Schreiner Letters Online*, 2012.

Coda

"Of making many books there is no end; and much study is a weariness of the flesh" (Eccl. 12:12).[1] So concludes the Epilogue appended to the final chapter of Ecclesiastes. This passage, positioned not as the words of the Teacher (or Qohelet) himself but those of one reflecting on his teachings, is generally recognized as a late editorial edition. The summative statement "Fear God and keep his commandments: for this is the whole duty of man" appears to be an amendment by more conservative scribes aiming to bring this seemingly unruly text into alignment with overarching traditions and messages within the Hebrew scriptures (Eccl. 12:13).[2] And yet there are subtle continuities between the ideas expressed in the Epilogue and those put forth in earlier passages. The closing note of weariness reprises the text's overarching motif of vanity. Moreover, the remarks about the futility of scholarly work are in keeping with Qohelet's characteristically ironic and self-reflexive stance: it seems only fitting that this book on wisdom ends by calling into question the very project of wisdom writing itself. Such would appear to be a rather pessimistic conclusion. And yet, to affirm that experiential wisdom exceeds the bounds of academic inquiry need not be to deny that there is value in trying to put it into words. On the contrary, this task's sheer inexhaustibility might, paradoxically, generate its own creative energy.

Both the overt pessimism and the latent hopefulness of Ecclesiastes find an intriguing echo in the commentary on "The Book of Koheleth" published in 1889 by the Victorian biblical critic Thomas Kelly Cheyne, who made a self-conscious attempt to reconcile traditional Christian theology and insights from modern textual scholarship. Cheyne is notably receptive to the higher criticism, though he prefaces his literature review of recent scholarship on Ecclesiastes, including writings by continental scholars such as Johann Gottfried Herder and Ernest Renan, with a subtle cautionary note: "It is not every critic of Ecclesiastes who helps the reader to enjoy the book which is criticized. Too much criticism and too little taste have before now spoiled many excellent books of the Old Testament."[3]

Without naming names, Cheyne's remarks about "too much criticism" warn that works of scholarly explication might do more harm than good. At the same time, his nod to "taste" and the implicit goal "to enjoy the book"—both of which once again align with Ecclesiastes in affirming pleasure—suggest that there might be another way to read this wisdom literature, one that runs counter to prevailing critical practices.[4] Along similar lines, a variety of twentieth and twenty-first-century biblical scholars have remarked that wisdom literature invites and even requires a distinctly meditative approach.[5]

This focus on contemplative, introspective approaches to reading resonates with insights from both postsecular and postcritical approaches to literary studies. These two branches of scholarship might themselves be brought into productive conversation, as Winter Jade Werner and John Wiehl have proposed in a recent double special issue of *LIT: Literature Interpretation Theory*. Werner and Wiehl observe that, insofar as postsecular scholarship has recovered the religious roots of literary studies as a discipline (a history that practitioners have typically been quick to disavow), it has also helped "to identify how a defensively secular and self-avowedly rational literary criticism tries to banish those experiences of reading that seem too closely aligned with the irrationality of religion."[6] Such work would seem to be a potentially strong ally for a postcriticism that aims to find alternatives to reading practices that are narrowly focused on analytical distance and critical detachment. Postsecularism, as Werner and Wiehl emphasize, seeks to show "how commitments and practices that have been labeled 'religious'—belief, enchantment, self-transcendence, ritual and liturgy, prayer, exegesis, spiritual yearning—unavoidably constitute the *seculum*, including our supposedly 'secular' knowledges."[7] Put another way, postsecularism is concerned with dismantling the very logic that would exile from the discipline of literary studies some of the more personal, affective, and reflective modes associated with postcritique.

Overall, postsecular scholarship aims to challenge the reductive readings that result from an "ongoing commitment in some critical circles to uncovering the false ideology of religion rather than engaging with its diversity," as Mark Knight puts it.[8] And, as work by Knight and others has demonstrated, Victorian literature provides rich opportunities for probing this diversity. Nineteenth-century Britain saw the proliferation of many new belief positions—the ongoing ramifications of the "nova effect" that Charles Taylor identifies as arising in the aftermath of eighteenth-century deism.[9] Even within the particular case of Christianity, the spread of the higher criticism underscored that the Bible was itself a composite document, encompassing many different histories, theologies, and genres. As I have suggested, as nineteenth-century thinkers (re)discovered these literary traditions, they anticipated the ideas about the Bible's plurality of genres advanced by later scholars. Crucially, different genres construct the very concept of revelation in various ways. Paul Ricoeur's exposition of this idea throughout his *Essays on Biblical Interpretation* develops the insights that his earlier work had stated in memorably aphoristic form: "the symbol gives rise to thought."[10] Extrapolating from Ricoeur, one might go so far as to say that literary forms and their symbolic contours can help readers to forge pathways into new realms of thinking.

The genre of wisdom literature seems, to my mind, to have at least one potentially promising contribution to make to the postsecular and postcritical project: it might help us, as readers, to come to terms with our own finitude. Experiencing limitation seems to be what much of this wisdom literature is all about, at the level of content, from the "merest breath" observed by Qohelet to the privation suffered by Job, from the humility affirmed in Proverbs to the counter-intuitive inversions of social order that characterize the parables of Jesus.[11] Something similar happens at the level of this tradition's literary form: the poetic dialogue, the aphorism, the parable, the hymn to personified wisdom, and the autobiographical reflection alike serve to take readers to the limits of rational thought. As the previous chapters have suggested, these forms foreground questioning, paradox, metaphor, and self-reflexivity, at once demanding the reader's intensive inquiry and obscuring, delaying, or withholding the object of the search. More than any other genre within the biblical tradition, wisdom literature presents the pursuit of meaning as an artistic process and emphasizes that, despite all attempts to trace it out, the design of the universe remains hidden. More than any other genre, wisdom literature looks beyond the horizon of the covenant made with Israel and toward the vast expanse of creation.

This wisdom literature occupied a crucial place within the Victorian literary imagination, and several nineteenth-century thinkers and writers insisted that these texts carried a special resonance for their own time. Cheyne, for one, claimed that the poetry of Ecclesiastes has an "elemental force" that "appeals to the modern reader in some of his moods more than anything else in the Old Testament except the Book of Job."[12] To Cheyne's ears, Qohelet's musings on vanity, informed as they were by a postexilic and Hellenistic skepticism, reverberated keenly throughout the late Victorian era, with its rising agnosticism and growing disillusionment about ideologies of progress. Yet what Cheyne identifies as quintessentially Victorian might also be understood as much more long-standing. In a special issue of the interdisciplinary journal *Religions* published in 2016, editors Arthur J. Keefer and Katharine J. Dell invited contributors to reflect on the question of "why ancient wisdom matters in the modern world."[13] As Jennie Grillo proposes in her article for this collection, both the exploration of selfhood and the search for meaning as expressed in the book of Ecclesiastes find intriguing echoes within the definitions of "modernity" offered not only by Matthew Arnold, in the nineteenth century, but also by Charles Taylor, in the twenty-first.[14] This emphasis on ongoing relevance is perhaps unsurprising given the unique temporal aspect that wisdom literature occupies: as Ricoeur puts it, this literature is "at once timeless and daily" in its elemental concern with life in the here and now.[15]

How, then, might the creative interpretations of this wisdom literature by Victorian writers continue to signify today? To twenty-first-century readers, the debates about inspiration, revelation, and authority catalyzed by nineteenth-century developments in biblical scholarship might seem oddly remote, if not downright antiquated. However, the underlying philosophical and hermeneutic issues galvanized during this nineteenth-century moment remain alive and well. In his incisive discussion of controversies engendered by *Essays and Reviews* during the 1860s, Jude V. Nixon emphasizes, "the war on literalism is still being fought on all fronts," making connections to the social and political issues faced by the United States at the opening of the twenty-first century.[16] Since Nixon's remarks of twenty years ago, this struggle has continued and intensified. Fundamentalism, religious and otherwise, is anything but a thing of the past. The word *pluralism*, used in the philosophical sense of holding together competing, potentially conflicting ideas, is a product of the late Victorian period, but debates about how such a paradigm might be put into practice remain ongoing.[17]

Literary reinterpretations of biblical texts, I suggest, have much to contribute to broader efforts to navigate conceptual shifts from fundamentalist modes of thinking toward more pluralistic ones. In his analysis of changing attitudes among late Victorian Christians, Daniel L. Pals observes that, by the 1890s, most British scholars and clerics, along with a considerable portion of lay readers, had largely accepted biblical higher criticism's findings and methods. He compares and contrasts this response pattern with the more polarized reactions to the higher criticism that prevailed within late-nineteenth-century American contexts, which he describes as witnessing a "bitter falling-out" between "fundamentalists and liberals." Pals attributes the different patterns observed in Britain, in part, to the many different Victorian "Lives of Christ" published in the preceding decades, which, as my previous chapters have noted, ranged from skeptical to reverent.[18] His discussion underscores that literary reinterpretations play a vital role in the development of broader ways of thinking about inherited religious ideas.

Even for readers seeking to navigate as far away from any religious inheritance as possible, the path for doing so often goes by the way of symbolic renovation. Carol P. Christ's pioneering essay on feminist theology, first published in 1978, "Why Women Need the Goddess," argues persuasively that the power, both political and psychological, of religious symbols means that these symbols cannot be simply discarded but must be actively reformed. Drawing attention to connections between deep-seated misogynistic attitudes and patriarchal stories about Eve, her essay calls on women writers to recreate the Goddess, envisioned expansively across religious traditions, as a necessary part of affirming female embodiment, sexuality, and creativity.[19] Thirty-five years later, Christ returned to these ideas in her reflective piece "Why Women, Men, and Other Living Things Still Need the Goddess." As the updated title suggests, her later work considers the wider ramifications of dualistic and hierarchical paradigms that privilege mind over body, thinking over feeling, and spirit over matter—ideas that several feminist theologians have seen as having important ecological implications.[20] At the time of this essay's publication in 2012, Christ emphasized that the work of changing these thought patterns remains ongoing, insisting that "we have only begun to address the disparagement of nature, the body, and feeling encoded in the Platonic dualism through which God transcendent of the world has been understood."[21] A problem with religious roots requires a religious remedy, to paraphrase Lynn White's conclusion to a groundbreaking exploration of ecology and religion published in 1967. His essay begins by considering how Christian ideologies of transcendence have motivated abuses of the earth and concludes by hailing St. Francis of Assisi as "the patron saint of ecologists."[22] As more recent ventures into religion, ecology, and literature have shown, St. Francis is hardly alone as a promising ecological figure from within the Christian tradition, and the creation theology affirmed throughout biblical traditions might provide fertile ground for reconceptualizing relationships among the earth and its inhabitants.[23] If we as literary scholars choose to ignore or sideline religious texts and reading practices, we do so not only at our peril—that is, at the risk of increasing blind-spots and unwittingly repeating mistakes from the past—but also to our loss—that is, at the risk of overlooking potentially rich resources for both imagination and transformation.

The creative engagements with biblical wisdom literature that I have traced throughout this book are but a few examples of what Victorian literature has to offer on this subject. What these reworkings of wisdom literature have in common is their commitment to dialogue—not just as a manner of speaking, but as a critical orientation. This orientation requires a stance of openness that is anything but easy to obtain. Hans-Georg Gadamer puts it well in his reflections on the distinction between authentic and inauthentic dialogue when he remarks, "contrary to the general opinion, it is more difficult to ask questions than answer them."[24] To create the conditions in which genuine dialogue can flourish may be the most difficult task of all.

All too often, what could become dialogue devolves into a combative exchange focused on winning an argument rather than pursuing knowledge and justice. Despite its many and vital functions, critique can become unfortunately "weaponized," used as a stick for beating those who think differently and as "an excuse to immunize ourselves from the same level of scrutiny that we direct elsewhere," to quote Knight's remarks about the negative experiences that postcritical approaches seek to circumvent.[25] Reductive readings not only distort the object of study but also turn us into caricatures of ourselves. As a strategy for getting past such coercive approaches, Knight proposes a two-part shift: a recognition of one's own interpretive fallibility and a willingness to suspend judgment on other readers.[26] What is needed, I would add, is a reorientation toward the possibilities that holding together a diverse range of interpretive practices might have in shedding light on the existential condition of partial knowledge that all human beings share and yet each experiences differently.

The road to such a revitalized reading practice begins, I believe, by reckoning with enduring questions about value. Such questions have seen a resurgence within twenty-first-century literary studies. Rita Felski's *The Limits of Critique*, the book that catalyzed the reflections on postcritical reading practices in the *LIT* special issue cited previously, opens by remarking the recent proliferation of critical titles that proclaim to address the question of why literature matters. Felski attributes this trend to a surge of anxieties about the role of the humanities, both within academic contexts and in broader public spheres, and suggests that, though the practice of critique has effectively equipped literary scholars to interrogate ideological constructions of value, it sometimes leaves them strangely ill-prepared to articulate their own sense of purposefulness.[27] Put another way, the discourse of critique can make it easier to say what one is arguing *against* than what one is writing *for*. Her proposal for a "postcritical reading" method that would encompass both the tools of critique and other, less suspicious approaches to texts might be seen as a continuation of the project begun in her earlier *Uses of Literature*, which aims to recuperate a many-sided concept of "usefulness" that, in Felski's words, brings together "analysis and attachment, criticism and love."²⁸ Here again, it can be helpful to turn to the Victorians, who wrestled with related questions of use value in their responses to the rising tide of utilitarianism.

Consider, for instance, Thomas Carlyle's *Sartor Resartus* (1833–4), which Cheyne singled out for its "fine adaptation" of the imagery in Ecclesiastes, and which engages self-reflexively with the project of re-imagining religious symbols.²⁹ Permeated as it is with literary and biblical allusions, this extended meditation on British and German philosophy playfully foregrounds the task of interpretation: Carlyle's philosophical discussion presents itself as the fragmentary writings of the fictitious Professor Diogenes Teufelsdröckh (God-Breathed Devil's-Dung), punctuated by the remarks of an unnamed Editor who translates this work into English and frequently comments on the difficulties of this project. This metacommentary calls attention to the interpretive dilemmas and economic metaphors that animate the book of Ecclesiastes, with its opening question, "What profit hath a man of all his labour which he taketh under the sun?" (Eccl. 1:3). Or, as Carlyle's Editor reframes it, "many a British reader" must surely be asking, "Where to does all this lead; or what use is in it?" He responds by attempting to redefine the concept of usefulness itself. First, he concedes, "in the way of replenishing thy purse ... it leads to nothing, and there is no use in it." But then, he adds that, if Teufelsdröckh's writings have allowed the reader to perceive "that thy daily life is girt with Wonder," then the reader has assuredly "profited beyond money's worth."³⁰ Such statements underscore Carlyle's resistance to the utilitarian philosophies of his time, at the same time that they echo Ecclesiastes, which similarly uses the metaphor of monetary profit to evoke that which cannot be quantified.

These reflections on instrumental versus inherent value are promising because they locate an element of hopefulness within what would otherwise seem to be a futile task. The variety of interpretive methods that postcritical theory demands might, in practice, be difficult to align in a perfectly tailored fit—to adapt Carlyle's sartorial metaphor. But these imperfections need not foreclose on attempts to explore this tension productively, especially if one takes seriously the idea that imperfection itself is a sign of both beauty and vitality, as memorably suggested by Carlyle's admirer John Ruskin, who likewise took issue with utilitarian attitudes and aspired to a more capacious view of human happiness, capability, and flourishing.³¹ It does not take much observation to see that the ongoing turbulence of natural disasters, diseases, and wars makes people inclined to fearful, reactionary behavior: to dig in their heels, retrench, and retreat into a false sense of certitude. It is difficult to hold on to a sense of wonder when the very capacity for enchantment seems, with the earth itself, to be eroding away. But that is precisely what wisdom literature invites readers to do: to forge a pathway through the *terra incognita* of fractured, incomplete knowledge, seeking not simply to discard the weight of inherited traditions but, rather, to transform them productively.

Such work would require substantial acts of reimagination regarding the very practice of reading, as an individual and a communal experience. Reflecting on Felski's *The Limits of Critique*, Alan Jacobs suggests that decentering critique would demand nothing less than "to re-narrate the Primal Scene of Reading in such a way that is not merely and always a site of contestation."[32] His allusion to the Primal Scene is a reference to Freudian theory and, more specifically, to this theory's account of a child's initial observation of or fantasy about their parents' sexual intercourse, construed by the child as a scene of violence. As Jacobs sees it, such renarration requires a rethinking of the experience of pleasure, beyond dominance/submission—not only within the erotic sphere but also in terms of textual pleasures akin to friendship or gift-giving. What new horizons might open up as a result of re-imagining reading as an opportunity for edification and enjoyment with other readers?

Perhaps this prospect sounds like a vague utopic notion. Or perhaps it sounds like an accurate descriptor of the kind of fellowship that already exists, at least in some circles. Talia Schaffer's *Communities of Care: The Social Ethics of Victorian Fiction* discusses "care communities" as both a significant relational structure within the nineteenth-century novel and an important means of reconfiguring the work of research, teaching, and service for the twenty-first century. Care, as Schaffer emphasizes, is not a matter of vague sentimental feelings but a commitment to intentional action.[33] What is at stake is a structure of reciprocity that involves genuine attention to the other. Developments in critical, digital, and feminist pedagogy have likewise advocated for moving beyond traditional teacher/student roles in favor of more fluid, multi-directional, and collaborative experiences of learning. Such concerns have been thoughtfully and practically discussed in a recent special issue of *Nineteenth-Century Gender Studies* on "'Teaching to Transgress' in the Emergency Remote Classroom" which responds to both the pioneering work of bell hooks and the challenges posed by the global pandemic.[34] At a time when many educators are reconsidering their strategies for facilitating inclusive and effective teaching, it seems worthwhile to return to wisdom literature, a broadly didactic genre driven by open-ended questioning.

Pursuing such a reciprocal, dialogic mode of inquiry would require a profound reorientation to the experience of limitation. To cultivate a reading practice that assembles and values many competing and even conflicting interpretive prospects, we would need to change the ways we are typically taught to regard the experience of being mistaken—or, at least, of not being entirely correct. This work, I suggest, would involve an imaginative act akin to what Jacobs has proposed. His turn to psychoanalytic theory invites further reconsideration of the formative images and ideas that, if only on an unconscious level, orient an individual's sense of self, as an embodied, desiring, hungering, meaning-seeking creature. Here again, religious discourse presents both formidable challenges and potential solutions. At its worst, religious language might bolster the model of reading as a power struggle. Indeed, this discourse can be all too easily twisted such that it escalates from what Jacobs calls "contestation" into fantasies of condemnation—from forecasts of Armageddon and sermons on hellfire to everyday expressions of exclusion and judgment. Dire portents such as the writing on the wall loom large within the apocalyptic imagination, and regardless of whether or not they have a conscious recollection of stories such as the warning delivered at King Belshazzar's feast, I suspect that many readers, like myself, have a deep-seated fear of being weighed in the balance and found wanting.[35] However, the threats and denunciations of the prophetic jeremiad are by no means the only imaginative resources that biblical texts have to offer. What about genres and forms that facilitate thinking beyond the terms of judgment? Wisdom literature supplies a wealth of possibilities for re-imagining communal joy. Ecclesiastes, for one, says little about the end times, and refrains from speculation about what happens after death. Rather, Qohelet exhorts readers to make the most of their fleeting time on earth, as *memento mori* gives rise to *carpe diem*.[36] In the book of Job, the voice from the whirlwind blatantly ignores the entire question of rewards and punishments, redirecting attention to the terrifying yet majestic creation of which humankind is but one part.[37] And Proverbs venerates Wisdom herself as a beautiful and beneficent force, present from the laying of the earth's foundations, more desirable than precious metals and responsive to those who seek her.[38]

For a succinct and compelling expression of this shift from condemnation to celebration, we need look no further than the parable of the prodigal son. When the erring young man returns to his father, having squandered his inheritance in reckless living, he counts himself no longer worthy of inclusion in the family, hoping only to be offered a position as a hired servant. But then his father welcomes him with open arms and throws him a loud and lavish party.[39] True to the form that Susan E. Colón identifies as characteristic of biblical parables, this story hinges on a gesture of extravagance that contravenes readerly expectations.[40] In addition to provoking the reader's response, this parable provides a memorable example of the resisting reader—that is, the elder brother, who has served his father faithfully and becomes angered by this turn of events. As his complaints illustrate, the radical generosity of this story's ending might well upset a sense of fairness. By rights, perhaps the wayward youth should have been relegated to the servants' quarters. But, as the father reminds his frustrated firstborn son, the tidy economy of rewards and punishments has no way of accounting for miraculous possibilities such as the dead made alive, the lost become found.

If we imagine the event of reading as an occasion not of contestation or condemnation but of celebration, the fear of being wrong might be replaced with the delight of being taken by surprise. After all, the experience of surprise is integral to both the pleasure and the educative power of figurative language, at least as Ricoeur explains it. Extrapolating from Aristotle, Ricoeur remarks that one of metaphor's key functions is "to instruct by suddenly combining elements that have not been put together before," thus redescribing and even recreating reality.[41] This work begins at the metaphorical level, but it is anything but a retreat into abstraction. At their best, metaphors are not attempts to escape embodied realities but efforts to reinhabit them. Take, for example, Ruskin's creative recourse to the economic parables of the synoptic gospels, an artistic strategy that informs not only his revision of the parable of the workers in the vineyard throughout the four essays comprising *Unto This Last*, as noted in previous chapters, but also his discussion of the parable of the talents in his lectures on "The Political Economy of Art."[42] Here, Ruskin challenges what he sees as the prevailing interpretive tendency to spirit away the sense of the story. Protesting against what he identifies as the most popular reading—"that the story doesn't mean money, it means wit, it means intellect, it means influence in high quarters, it means everything in the world except itself"—he counters, "the first and most literal application is just as necessary a one as any other—that the story does very specially mean what it says—plain money." His purpose for invoking this story is to challenge attitudes of entitlement resulting from a Protestant work ethic.[43] His manner of so doing illuminates a fully orbed reading practice that revitalizes even the literal sense of the word, not as something that binds the text but as that which might help readers to come to terms with their materiality—whatever is solid, practical, and grounded in ordinary realities. As Ruskin's exegesis underscores, sometimes the simplest readings prove, at the end of the day, to be the most richly rewarding ones.

Even today, literary scholars might profitably turn to the Victorians for nuanced examples of the many forms that religious revisionism might take. Written in the aftermath of the nineteenth century's polarizing controversies, their imaginative work can illuminate pathways for navigating the challenging conversations that arise when talking about religion in the twenty-first century. Taken together, the creative interpretations of biblical wisdom literature advanced by writers such as Elizabeth Barrett Browning, George MacDonald, George Eliot, John Ruskin, and Olive Schreiner provide models for what such dialogue might look like. As they wrestle with wisdom literature's abiding tension between finitude and fullness, they extend this unending search toward their readers. They remind us that there is a time to interrogate and a time to uphold, a time to search and a time to savor, a time to criticize and a time to create.

Notes

1   *The Bible: Authorized King James Version with Apocrypha* (Oxford: Oxford University Press, 2008). All biblical quotations are cited parenthetically in text. Rights in the Authorized (King James) Version in the UK are vested in the Crown. Reproduced by permission of the Crown's patentee, Cambridge University Press.
2   See Robert Alter, *The Wisdom Books: Job, Proverbs, and Ecclesiastes: A Translation with Commentary* (New York: Norton, 2010), 390.
3   Thomas Kelly Cheyne, *Job and Solomon, or the Wisdom of the Old Testament* (New York: Thomas Whittaker, 1889), 242.
4   For examples of this book's affirmation of pleasure, see, for instance, Eccl. 2:24 ("There is nothing better for a man, than that he should eat and drink, and that he should make his soul enjoy good in his labour") and Eccl. 8:15 ("Then I commend mirth, because a man hath no better thing under the sun, than to eat, and to drink, and to be merry").
5   Roland E. Murphy, *The Tree of Life: An Exploration of Biblical Wisdom Literature* (Grand Rapids: William B. Eerdmans, 1990), 7; Ben Witherington, *Jesus the Sage: A Pilgrimage of Wisdom* (Minneapolis: Fortress Press, 1994), 3; and Mary E. Mills, *Reading Ecclesiastes: A Literary and Cultural Exegesis* (Farham: Ashgate, 2003), 5–7.
6   Winter Jade Werner and John Wiehl, "Chasing David Copperfield's Memory of a Stained Glass Window: Or, Meditations on the Postsecular and Postcritical," *LIT: Literature Interpretation Theory* 31, no. 1 (2021): 3–4.
7   Ibid., 3–4.
8   Mark Knight, *Good Words: Evangelicalism and the Victorian Novel* (Columbus: Ohio State University Press, 2019), 5–6.
9   Charles Taylor, *A Secular Age* (Cambridge: Harvard University Press, 2007), 377.
10 Paul Ricoeur, *The Symbolism of Evil*, trans. Emerson Buchanan (New York: Harper and Row, 1967), 349.

11 The biblical quotation is from the translation offered by Alter, *The Wisdom Books*, 346. On the counterintuitive social order of the gospel parables and their connection to the biblical wisdom tradition, see Robert Funk, *A Credible Jesus: Fragments of a Vision* (Salem: Polebridge Press, 2002), 135.
12 Cheyne, *Job and Solomon*, 246.
13 Arthur J. Keefer and Katharine J. Dell. "Introduction to the Special Issue: 'The Wayfinders': Why Ancient Wisdom Matters in the Modern World," *Religions* 7, no. 7 (2016): n.pag.
14 Jennie Grillo, "Qohelet and the Masks of Modernity: Reading Ecclesiastes with Matthew Arnold and Charles Taylor," *Religions* 7, vol. 6 (2016): n.pag.
15 Paul Ricoeur, "Experience and Language in Religious Discourse," in *Phenomenology and the Theological Turn: The French Debate*, ed. Dominique Janicaud (New York: Fordham University Press, 2000), 142.
16 Jude V. Nixon, "'Kill[ing] Our Souls with Literalism': Reading *Essays and Reviews*," in *Victorian Religious Discourse*, ed. Jude V. Nixon (New York: Palgrave Macmillan, 2004), 74.
17 See the discussion of this etymology offered by Stephen Prickett, *Narrative, Religion, and Science: Fundamentalism Versus Irony* (Cambridge: Cambridge University Press, 2002), 6.
18 Daniel L. Pals, *The Victorian "Lives" of Jesus* (San Antonio: Trinity University Press, 1982), 152–3. Among the works that Pals discusses are John Seeley's *Ecce Homo* (1865), F. W. Farrar's *The Life of Christ* (1874), Henry James Coleridge's *The Public Life of Our Lord* (1874), G. S. Drew's *The Son of Man* (1875), and John Cunningham Geikie's *The Life and Words of Christ* (1877). These studies offered a devotional yet thoughtful response to the skeptical and historical precedents set by David Friedrich Strauss and Ernest Renan.
19 Carol P. Christ, "Why Women Need the Goddess," *Heresies: The Great Goddess Issue* 2, no. 1 (1978): 9–12.
20 Carol P. Christ, "Why Women, Men, and Other Living Things Still Need the Goddess: Remembering and Reflecting 35 Years Later," *Feminist Theology* 20, no. 3 (2012): 242–55. For related reflections on ecofeminist spirituality, see Elizabeth A. Johnson, *Ask the Beasts: Darwin and the God of Love* (New York: Bloomsbury, 2014), and Rosemary Radford Ruether, "Ecology and Theology: Ecojustice at the Center of the Church's Mission," *Interpretation: A Journal of Bible and Theology* 65, no. 4 (2011): 354–63.
21 Christ, "Why Women, Men, and Other Living Things Still Need the Goddess," 255.
22 Lynn White Jr., "The Historical Roots of Our Ecological Crisis," in *The Ecocriticism Reader: Landmarks in Literary Ecology*, ed. Cheryll Glotfelty and Harold Fromm (Athens: University of Georgia Press, 1996), 13.
23 See, for instance, Richard Bauckham, *The Bible and Ecology: Rediscovering the Community of Creation* (Waco: Baylor University Press, 2010); Emma Mason,

Christina Rossetti: Poetry, Ecology, Faith (Oxford: Oxford University Press, 2018); and Joshua King, "Revelatory Beasts: Christina Rossetti on the Apocalypse and Creation's Worship," *Christianity and Literature* 70, no. 4 (2021): 382–403.

24 Hans-Georg Gadamer, *Truth and Method*, 2nd edn., trans. Joel Weinsheimer and Donald G. Marshall (New York: Continuum, 1975), 356.

25 Mark Knight, "Natural Theology and the Revelation of *Little Dorrit*," *LIT: Literature Interpretation Theory* 31, no. 1 (2021): 13.

26 Ibid., 21.

27 Rita Felski, *The Limits of Critique* (Chicago: University of Chicago Press, 2015), 14–15.

28 Rita Felski, *Uses of Literature* (Oxford: Blackwell, 2008), 22.

29 Cheyne, *Job and Solomon*, 246.

30 Thomas Carlyle, *Sartor Resartus* (Oxford: Oxford University Press, 1999), 204.

31 John Ruskin, "The Nature of Gothic," in *The Works of John Ruskin*, ed. E. T. Cook and Alexander Wedderburn (London: George Allen, 1903–12), X: 180–269.

32 Alan Jacobs, "Vulnerabilities and Rewards," *Religion and Literature* 48, no. 2 (2016): 177.

33 Talia Schaffer, *Communities of Care: The Social Ethics of Victorian Fiction* (Princeton: Princeton University Press, 2021), 20–2.

34 Kimberly Cox, Shannon Draucker, and Doreen Thierauf, Introduction to the Special Issue "'Teaching to Transgress' in the Emergency Remote Classroom", *Nineteenth-Century Gender Studies* 17, no. 1 (Spring 2021): 1–11; see also bell hooks, *Teaching to Transgress: Education as the Practice of Freedom* (New York: Routledge, 1994).

35 Dan. 5:1-31.

36 Eccl. 9:10.

37 Job 38–41.

38 Prov. 8:1-11.

39 Lk. 15:11-31.

40 Susan E. Colón, *Victorian Parables* (London: Continuum, 2012), 16.

41 Ricoeur, *The Rule of Metaphor: Multidisciplinary Studies in the Creation of Meaning in Language*, trans. Robert Czerny, with Kathleen McLaughlin and John Costello (Toronto: University of Toronto Press, 1977), 33.

42 Mt. 20:1-16, 25:14-30.

43 John Ruskin, "The Political Economy of Art," in *The Works of John Ruskin*, ed. E. T. Cook and Alexander Wedderburn (London: George Allen, 1903–12), XVI: 99.

Bibliography

Aikin, Lucy. *Epistles on Women, Exemplifying Their Character and Condition in Various Ages and Nations: With Miscellaneous Poems*. London: J. Johnson and Co, 1810.

Albritton, Vicky, and Frederick Albritton Jonsson. *Green Victorians: The Simple Life in Ruskin's Lake District*. Chicago: University of Chicago Press, 2016.

Alter, Robert. *The Art of Biblical Narrative*. New York: Basil Books, 1981.

Alter, Robert. *The Art of Biblical Poetry*. New York: Basil Books, 1985.

Alter, Robert. "The Poetic and Wisdom Books." In *The Cambridge Companion to Biblical Interpretation*, edited by John Barton, 226–41. Cambridge: Cambridge University Press, 1998.

Alter, Robert. *The Wisdom Books: Job, Proverbs, and Ecclesiastes: A Translation with Commentary*. New York: Norton, 2010.

Anger, Suzy. *Victorian Interpretation*. Ithaca: Cornell University Press, 2005.

Arnold, Matthew. "The Function of Criticism at the Present Time." 1864. In *Essays in Criticism: First Series*, 1–44. London: Macmillan and Co., 1903.

Arnold, Matthew. *Literature and Dogma: An Essay towards a Better Apprehension of the Bible*. 1873. London: Macmillan and Co., 1895.

Asad, Talal. *Formations of the Secular: Christianity, Islam, Modernity*. Stanford: Stanford University Press, 2003.

Atkins, Gareth. "'Strauss-Sick?' Jesus and the Saints of the Church of the Future." In *The Figure of Christ in the Long Nineteenth Century*, edited by Elizabeth Ludlow, 227–41. London: Palgrave Macmillan, 2020.

Auerbach, Erich. "Figura." In *Scenes from the Drama of European Literature*, 11–76. Manchester: Manchester University Press, 1984.

Auerbach, Erich. *Mimesis: The Representation of Reality in Western Literature*. Translated by Willard R. Trask. Princeton: Princeton University Press, 1953.

Augustine. *The Confessions, the City of God, on Christian Doctrine*. Translated by J. F. Shaw. Chicago: William Benton, 1952.

Bacon, Francis. *The Advancement of Learning*. 1605. Edited by Joseph Devy. New York: P. F. Collier and Son, 1905.

Baker, William. *George Eliot and Judaism*. Salzburg: Institut für Englische Sprache und Literatur, Universität Salzburg, 1975.

Bakhtin, Mikhail M. *The Dialogic Imagination: Four Essays*. Edited by Michael Holquist, translated by Caryl Emerson and Michael Holquist. Austin: University of Texas Press, 1981.

Batchelor, John. *John Ruskin: A Life*. New York: Carroll and Graf, 2000.
Battles, Kelly E. "George Eliot's *Romola*: A Historical Novel 'Rather Different in Character.'" *Philological Quarterly* 88, no. 3 (2009): 215–37.
Bauckham, Richard. *The Bible and Ecology: Rediscovering the Community of Creation*. Waco: Baylor University Press, 2010.
Beer, Gillian. *Darwin's Plots: Evolutionary Narrative in Darwin, George Eliot, and Nineteenth-Century Fiction*. Cambridge: Cambridge University Press, 1983.
Berkman, Joyce Avrech. *The Healing Imagination of Olive Schreiner: Beyond South African Colonialism*. Amherst: University of Massachusetts Press, 1989.
The Bible. Authorized King James Version with Apocrypha. Oxford: Oxford University Press, 2008.
Birch, Dinah. "Lecturing and Public Voice." In *The Cambridge Companion to John Ruskin*, edited by Francis O'Gorman, 201–15. Cambridge: Cambridge University Press, 2015.
Birch, Dinah. "Ruskin, Myth, and Modernism." In *Ruskin and Modernism*, edited by Giovanni Cianni and Peter Nicholls, 32–47. New York: Palgrave, 2001.
Birch, Dinah. *Ruskin's Myths*. Oxford: Clarendon Press, 1988.
Birch, Dinah. "'Who Wants Authority?': Ruskin as a Dissenter." *The Yearbook of English Studies* 36, no. 2 (2006): 65–77.
Blair, Kirstie. *Form and Faith in Victorian Poetry and Religion*. Oxford: Oxford University Press, 2012.
Blake, William. "Appendix to the Prophetic Books." In *Poetical Works*, edited by John Sampson, 435–36. Oxford: Oxford University Press, 1913.
Blake, William. *The Marriage of Heaven and Hell*. 1790. Edited by Michael Phillips. Oxford: Bodleian Library, 2011.
Bloomfield, Morton. "The Tradition and Style of Biblical Wisdom Literature." In *Biblical Patterns in Modern Literature*, edited by David H. Hirsch and Nehama Aschkensay, 19–30. Atlanta: Scholars Press, 1972.
Blumberg, Ilana M. "Sympathy or Religion? George Eliot and Christian Conversion." *Nineteenth-Century Literature* 74, no. 3 (2019): 360–87.
Bonaparte, Felicia. *The Triptych and the Cross: The Central Myths of George Eliot's Poetic Imagination*. New York: New York University Press, 1979.
Branch, Lori. "Postcriticism and Postsecular: The Horizon of Belief." *Religion and Literature* 48, no. 2 (2016): 160–7.
Branch, Lori, and Mark Knight. "Why the Postsecular Matters: Literary Studies and the Rise of the Novel." *Christianity and Literature* 67, no. 3 (2018): 493–510.
Brotton, Melissa J. "'"Lost Angel in the Earth": Ecotheodicy in Elizabeth Barrett Browning's 'A Drama of Exile.'" In *Ecotheology in the Humanities: An Interdisciplinary Approach to Understanding the Divine and Nature*, edited by Melissa J. Brotton, 209–28. Minneapolis: Lexington Books, 2015.
Brown, William P. *Wisdom's Wonder: Character, Creation, and Crisis in the Bible's Wisdom Literature*. Grand Rapids: William B. Eerdmans, 2014.

Browning, Elizabeth Barrett. *The Works of Elizabeth Barrett Browning*. Edited by Sandra Donaldson, Rita Patteson, Marjorie Stone, and Beverly Taylor, 5 vols. London: Pickering and Chatto, 2010.

Browning, Robert. "Christmas-Eve." In *Robert Browning: The Poems*, edited by John Pettigrew, vol. 1, 464–96. New Haven: Yale University Press, 1981.

Bubel, Katharine. "Knowing God 'Other-Wise': The Wise Old Woman Archetype in George MacDonald's *The Princess and the Goblin*, *The Princess and Curdie*, and *The Golden Key*." *North Wind* 25 (2006): 1–17.

Budge, Gavin. "Rethinking the Victorian Sage: Nineteenth-Century Prose and Scottish Common Sense Philosophy." *Literature Compass* 2, no. 1 (2005): 1–11.

Bultmann, Rudolf. *The History of the Synoptic Tradition*. Translated by John Marsh. New York: Harper and Row, 1963.

Bundock, Christopher M. *Romantic Prophecy and the Resistance to Historicism*. Toronto: University of Toronto Press, 2016.

Burd, Van Akin. Introduction to *The Winnington Letters: John Ruskin's Correspondence with Margaret Alexis Bell and the Children and Winnington Hall*. Edited by Van Akin Burd, 19–88. Cambridge: Harvard University Press, 1969.

Carlyle, Thomas. "Characteristics." 1831. In *Critical and Miscellaneous Essays by Thomas Carlyle*, 296–309. New York: D. Appleton, 1871.

Carlyle, Thomas. *Sartor Resartus*. 1836. Oxford: Oxford University Press, 1999.

Carpenter, Mary Wilson. *George Eliot and the Landscape of Time: Narrative Form and Protestant Apocalyptic History*. Chapel Hill: University of North Carolina Press, 1986.

Carpenter, Mary Wilson. "The Trouble with *Romola*." In *Victorian Sages and Cultural Discourse: Renegotiating Gender and Power*, edited by Thaïs E. Morgan, 105–28. New Brunswick: Rutgers University Press, 1991.

Carroll, David. *George Eliot and the Conflict of Interpretations: A Reading of the Novels*. Cambridge: Cambridge University Press, 1992.

Chapman, Alison. *Networking the Nation: British and American Women's Poetry and Italy, 1840–1870*. Oxford: Oxford University Press, 2015.

Chatterjee, Ronjaunee, Alicia Mireles Christoff, and Amy R. Wong. "Introduction: Undisciplining Victorian Studies." *Victorian Studies* 62, no. 3 (2020): 369–91.

Cheeke, Stephen. *Transfiguration: The Religion of Art in Nineteenth-Century Literature before Aestheticism*. Oxford: Oxford University Press, 2016.

Chesterton, G. K. Introduction to *George MacDonald and His Wife*. Edited by Greville MacDonald, 1–18. London: George Allen and Unwin, 1924.

Cheyne, Thomas Kelly. *Job and Solomon, or the Wisdom of the Old Testament*. New York: Thomas Whittaker, 1889.

Chrétien, Jean-Louis. *Under the Gaze of the Bible*. Translated by John Marson Dunaway. New York: Fordham University Press, 2015.

Christ, Carol P. "Why Women, Men, and Other Living Things Still Need the Goddess: Remembering and Reflecting 35 Years Later." *Feminist Theology* 20, no. 3 (2012): 242–55.

Christ, Carol P. "Why Women Need the Goddess." *Heresies: The Great Goddess Issue* 2, no. 1 (1978): 8–13.
Colenso, John William. *The Pentateuch and the Book of Joshua Critically Examined*. London: Longman, 1862.
Coleridge, Samuel Taylor. *The Collected Works of Samuel Taylor Coleridge. Vol. 6: Lay Sermons*. Edited by R. J. White. Princeton: Princeton University Press, 1972.
Coleridge, Samuel Taylor. *The Collected Works of Samuel Taylor Coleridge. Vol. 7: Biographia Literaria*. Edited by James Engell, and Walter Jackson Bate. Princeton: Princeton University Press, 1983.
Coleridge, Samuel Taylor. *The Collected Works of Samuel Taylor Coleridge. Vol. 9: Aids to Reflection*. Edited by John Beer. Princeton: Princeton University Press, 1995.
Coleridge, Samuel Taylor. *The Collected Works of Samuel Taylor Coleridge. Vol. 11: Shorter Works and Fragments II*. Edited by H. J. Jackson, and J. R. de J. Jackson. Princeton: Princeton University Press, 1995.
Colón, Susan E. *Victorian Parables*. London: Continuum, 2012.
Coté, Amy. "Parables and Unitarianism in Elizabeth Gaskell's Mary Barton." *Victorian Review* 40, no. 1 (2014): 59–76.
Cox, Kimberly, Shannon Draucker, and Doreen Thierauf. "Introduction: 'Teaching to Transgress' in the Emergency Remote Classroom." *Nineteenth-Century Gender Studies* 17, no. 1 (2021): n.pag.
Crenshaw, James L. *Old Testament Wisdom: An Introduction*. 3rd edition. Louisville: John Knox Press, 2010.
Crenshaw, James L. *Prophets, Sages, and Poets*. St. Louis: Chalice Press, 2006.
De Wette, Wilhelm Martin Leberecht. *A Critical and Historical Introduction to the Canonical Scriptures of the Old Testament*. Translated by Theodore Parker, 2 vols. 3rd edition. Boston: Rufus Leighton Jr., 1859.
Dieleman, Karen. "Ecotheological Relationships in Elizabeth Barrett Browning's *A Drama of Exile*." *Christianity and Literature* 69, no. 3 (2020): 418–38.
Dieleman, Karen. "A Politics of Just Memory: Elizabeth Barrett and the Greek Christian Poets." *The Journal of Browning Studies* 3 (2012): 5–28.
Dieleman, Karen. *Religious Imaginaries: The Liturgical and Poetic Practices of Elizabeth Barrett Browning, Christina Rossetti, and Adelaide Proctor*. Columbus: Ohio University Press, 2012.
Docherty, John. "The Sources of *Phantastes*." *North Wind: A Journal of George MacDonald Studies* 9 (1990): 38–53.
Dubois, Martin. "Sermon and Story in George MacDonald." *Victorian Literature and Culture* 34, no. 3 (2015): 577–87.
Dupré, Louis. *The Quest of the Absolute: Birth and Decline of European Romanticism*. Notre Dame: University of Notre Dame Press, 2013.
Dwor, Richa. *Jewish Feeling: Difference and Affect in Nineteenth-Century Jewish Women's Writing*. London: Bloomsbury Academic, 2015.

Eliot, George. *Adam Bede*. 1859. Peterborough: Broadview Press, 2005.
Eliot, George. *The George Eliot Letters*. Edited by Gordon S. Haight, 9 vols. New Haven: Yale University Press, 1954.
Eliot, George. "Introduction to Genesis." In *Essays of George Eliot*, edited by Thomas Pinney, 255–60. London: Routledge and Keagan Paul, 1963.
Eliot, George. *Middlemarch: A Study of Provincial Life*. 1871–72. Peterborough: Broadview Press, 2004.
Eliot, George. *Romola*. 1862–63. London: Penguin Books, 2005.
Eliot, George. "Thomas Carlyle." In *Essays of George Eliot*, edited by Thomas Pinney, 212–5. London: Routledge and Kegan Paul, 1963.
Felski, Rita. *The Limits of Critique*. Chicago: University of Chicago Press, 2015.
Felski, Rita. *Uses of Literature*. Oxford: Blackwell, 2008.
Feuerbach, Ludwig. *The Essence of Christianity*. Translated by George Eliot. 1854. New York: Harper and Row, 1957.
Fike, Matthew. "Anima and Psychic Fragmentation in Olive Schreiner's *The Story of an African Farm*." *English in Africa* 42, no. 1 (2015): 77–101.
First, Ruth, and Ann Scott. *Olive Schreiner*. New York: Schocken Books, 1980.
Fong, Ryan D. "The Stories outside the African Farm: Indigeneity, Orality, and Unsettling the Victorian." *Victorian Studies* 62, no. 3 (2020): 421–32.
Franklin, J. Jeffrey. *The Lotus and the Lion: Buddhism and the British Empire*. Ithaca: Cornell University Press, 2008.
Franklin, J. Jeffrey. *Spirit Matters: Occult Beliefs, Alternative Religions, and the Crisis of Faith in Victorian Britain*. Ithaca: Cornell University Press, 2018.
Frei, Hans. *The Eclipse of Biblical Narrative: A Study in Eighteenth- and Nineteenth-Century Hermeneutics*. New Haven: Yale University Press, 1974.
Frye, Northrop. *The Great Code: The Bible and Literature*. New York: Harcourt Brace Jovanovich, 1982.
Funk, Robert. *A Credible Jesus: Fragments of a Vision*. Salem: Polebridge Press, 2002.
Gaarden, Bonnie. "George MacDonald's *Phantastes*: The Spiral Journey to the Goddess." *The Victorian* Newsletter 96 (1999): 6–14.
Gabelman, Daniel. *George MacDonald: Divine Carelessness and Fairytale Levity*. Waco: Baylor University Press, 2013.
Gadamer, Hans-Georg. *Truth and Method*. 1960. 2nd edition. Translated by Joel Weinsheimer, and Donald G. Marshall. New York: Continuum, 1975.
Gray, F. Elizabeth. *Christian and Lyric Tradition in Victorian Women's Poetry*. New York: Routledge, 2010.
The Greek New Testament. Edited by Kurt Aland et al. 3rd edition. United Bible Societies: West Germany, 1983.
Greiner, Rae. "Sympathy Time: Adam Smith, George Eliot, and the Realist Novel." *Narrative* 17, no. 3 (2009): 291–311.
Grillo, Jennie. "Qohelet and the Masks of Modernity: Reading Ecclesiastes with Matthew Arnold and Charles Taylor." *Religions* 7, no. 6 (2016): n.pag.

Habermas, Jürgen. "Notes on Post-Secular Society." *New Perspectives Quarterly* 25, no. 4(2008): 17–29.

Hackett, Robin. *Sapphic Primitivism: Productions of Race, Class, and Sexuality in Key Works of Modern Fiction.* New Brunswick: Rutgers University Press, 2004.

Hair, Donald S. *Fresh Strange Music: Elizabeth Barrett Browning's Language.* Montreal: McGill-Queen's University Press, 1915.

Harding, Anthony John. *Coleridge and the Inspired Word.* Montreal: McGill-Queen's University Press, 1985.

Harrison, Roland Kenneth. *Introduction to the Old Testament.* Grand Rapids: William B. Eerdmans, 1969.

Hatton, Peter. *Contradiction in the Book of Proverbs: The Deep Waters of Counsel.* Farham: Ashgate Press, 2008.

Hedrick, Charles. *The Wisdom of Jesus: Between the Sages of Israel and the Apostles of the Church.* Eugene: Cascade Books, 2014.

Heilmann, Ann. *New Woman Strategies: Sarah Grand, Olive Schreiner, Mona Caird.* Manchester: Manchester University Press, 2004.

Hennell, Charles. *Inquiry Concerning the Origin of Christianity.* 1838. 2nd edition. London: Trübner and Company, 1870.

Henry, Nancy. *The Cambridge Introduction to George Eliot.* Cambridge: Cambridge University Press, 2008.

Herbert, Christopher. *Evangelical Gothic: The English Novel and the Religious War on Virtue from Wesley to Dracula.* Charlottesville: University of Virginia Press, 2019.

Herder, Johann Gottfried. *The Spirit of Hebrew Poetry.* Translated by James Marsh, 2 vols. Burlington: Edward Smith, 1833.

Hess, Richard S. *The Old Testament: A Historical, Theological, and Critical Introduction.* Grand Rapids: Baker Academic, 2016.

Hewison, Robert. "'Paradise Lost': Ruskin and Science." In *Time and Tide: Ruskin and Science*, edited by Michael Wheeler, 29–44. Yelvertoft: Pilkington Press, 1996.

Hoagwood, Terence Allan. "Biblical Criticism and Secular Sex: Elizabeth Barrett Browning's 'A Drama of Exile' and Jean Ingelow's 'A Story of Doom.'" *Victorian Poetry* 42, no. 2 (2004): 165–80.

Hodgson, Peter C. *The Mystery beneath the Real: Theology in the Fiction of George Eliot.* Philadelphia: Fortress Press, 2000.

Holloway, John. *The Victorian Sage: Studies in Argument.* London: Macmillan, 1953.

Holmes, John. *Darwin's Bards: British and American Poetry in the Age of Evolution.* Edinburgh: Edinburgh University Press, 2013.

Houston, Gail Turley. *Victorian Women Writers, Radical Grandmothers, and the Gendering of God.* Columbus: Ohio State University Press, 2013.

hooks, bell. *Teaching to Transgress: Education as the Practice of Freedom.* New York: Routledge, 1994.

Jacobs, Alan. "Vulnerabilities and Rewards." *Religion and Literature* 48, no. 2 (2016): 173–9.

Jaffe, Audrey. *Scenes of Sympathy: Identity and Representation in Victorian Fiction*. Ithaca: Cornell University Press, 2000.

Jasper, David. "Biblical Hermeneutics and Literary Theory." In *The Blackwell Companion to the Bible in English Literature*, edited by Rebecca Lemon et al., 22–389. Chichester: Wiley Blackwell, 2009.

Jeffrey, David Lyle. "Wisdom." In *A Dictionary of Biblical Tradition in English Literature*, edited by David Lyle Jeffrey, 832–7. Grand Rapids: William B. Eerdmans, 1992.

Johnson, Elizabeth. *Ask the Beasts: Darwin and the God of Love*. New York: Bloomsbury, 2014.

Jowett, Benjamin. "On the Interpretation of Scripture." 1860. In *Essays and Reviews: The 1860 Text and Its Reading*, edited by Victor Shea and William Whitla, 477–536. Charlottesville: University Press of Virginia, 2000.

Kaufman, Michael W. "The Religious, the Secular, and Literary Studies: Rethinking the Secularization Narrative in Histories of the Profession." *New Literary History* 38, no. 4 (2007): 607–28.

Keefer, Arthur J. and Katharine J. Dell. "Introduction to the Special Issue: "The Wayfinders": Why Ancient Wisdom Matters in the Modern World." *Religions* 7, no. 7 (2016): n.pag.

Keirstead, Christopher M. *Victorian Poetry, Europe, and the Challenge of Cosmopolitanism*. Columbus: Ohio State University Press, 2011.

Kelley, Philip, Ronald Hudson, and Scott Lewis, editors. *The Brownings' Correspondence*, 29 vols. to date. Winfield: Wedgestone Press, 1984–2023.

Kelly, Sean P. *The Wisdom Books of the Bible: Proverbs, Job, Ecclesiastes, Ben Sira, Wisdom of Solomon: A History of Their Interpretation*. Lewiston: Edward Mellen, 2012.

Kierkegaard, Søren. "For Self-Examination [First series]." 1851. *The Essential Kierkegaard*. Edited and translated by Howard V. Hong, and Edna H. Hong, 393–402. Princeton: Princeton University Press, 2000.

King, Joshua. "Revelatory Beasts: Christina Rossetti on the Apocalypse and Creation's Worship." *Christianity and Literature* 70, no. 4 (2021): 382–403.

King, Joshua, and Winter Jade Werner. Introduction to *Constructing Nineteenth-Century Religion: Literary, Historical, and Religious Studies in Dialogue*. Edited by Joshua King, and Winter Jade Werner, 1–24. Columbus: Ohio State University Press, 2019.

Kissack, Mike, and Michael Titlestad. "Olive Schreiner and the Secularization of the Moral Imagination." *English in Africa* 3, no. 1 (2006): 23–46.

Knight, Mark. *Good Words: Evangelicalism and the Victorian Novel*. Columbus: Ohio State University Press, 2019.

Knight, Mark. "Natural Theology and the Revelation of *Little Dorrit*." *LIT: Literature Interpretation Theory* 31, no. 1 (2021): 10–23.

Knight, Mark, and Emma Mason. *Nineteenth-Century Literature and Religion: An Introduction*. Oxford: Oxford University Press, 2006.

Kreglinger, Gisela H. *Storied Revelations: Parables, Imagination, and George MacDonald's Christian Fiction*. Cambridge: Lutterworth Press, 2014.

Kucich, John. *Imperial Masochism: British Fiction, Fantasy, and Social Class*. Princeton: Princeton University Press, 2007.

Landow, George P. *The Aesthetic and Critical Theories of John Ruskin*. Princeton: Princeton University Press, 1971.

Landow, George P. *Elegant Jeremiahs: The Sage from Carlyle to Mailer*. Ithaca: Cornell University Press, 1986.

Landow, George P. *Victorian Types, Victorian Shadows: Biblical Typology in Victorian Literature, Art and Thought*. New York: Routledge, 1980.

LaPorte, Charles. "Romantic Cults of Authorship." In *Constructing Nineteenth-Century Religion: Literary, Historical, and Religious Studies in Dialogue*, edited by Joshua King and Winter Jade Werner, 246–61. Columbus: Ohio State University Press, 2019.

LaPorte, Charles. "Victorian Literature, Religion, and Secularization." *Literature Compass* 10, no. 3 (2013): 277–87.

LaPorte, Charles. *Victorian Poets and the Changing Bible*. Charlottesville: University of Virginia Press, 2011.

LaPorte, Charles, and Sebastian Lecourt. "Introduction: Nineteenth-Century Literature, New Religious Movements, and Secularization." *Nineteenth-Century Literature* 73, no. 2 (2018): 147–60.

Larsen, Timothy. *Contested Christianity: The Political and Social Contexts of Victorian Theology*. Waco: Baylor University Press, 2004.

Larsen, Timothy. *Crisis of Doubt: Honest Faith in Nineteenth-Century England*. Oxford: Oxford University Press, 2006.

Larsen, Timothy. *George MacDonald in the Age of Miracles: Incarnation, Doubt, and Re-enchantment*. Westmont: InterVarsity Press Academic, 2018.

Larsen, Timothy. *A People of One Book: The Bible and the Victorians*. Oxford: Oxford University Press, 2011.

Lecourt, Sebastian. *Cultivating Belief: Victorian Anthropology, Liberal Aesthetics, and the Secular Imagination*. Oxford: Oxford University Press, 2018.

Levine, Caroline, and Mark W. Turner, editors. *From Author to Text: Re-reading George Eliot's* Romola. Burlington: Ashgate, 1998.

Levine, George. *Darwin Loves You: Natural Selection and the Re-enchantment of the World*. Princeton: Princeton University Press, 2006.

Levine, George. "Ruskin, Darwin, and the Matter of Matter." *Nineteenth-Century Prose* 35, no. 1 (2008): 223–49.

Lewis, C. S. *Surprised by Joy: The Shape of My Early Life*. 1955. New York: Barnes and Noble, 2002.

Lewis, Linda M. *Dickens, His Parables, and His Reader*. Columbia: University of Missouri Press, 2011.

Lewis, Linda M. *Elizabeth Barrett Browning's Spiritual Progress: Face to Face with God*. Columbia: University of Missouri Press, 1998.

Lewis, Simon. "The Transnational Circulation of Dissent: Olive Schreiner and the Colonial Counter-Flows of Unitarian Freethinking." *Safundi* 14, no. 1 (2013): 1–15.

Lloyd, Jennifer M. "Raising Lilies: Ruskin and Women." *Journal of British Studies* 34, no. 3 (1995): 325–50.

Lowth, Robert. *Lectures on the Sacred Poetry of the Hebrews.* 1787, 2 vols. Hildesheim: Georg Olms Verlag, 1969.

Ludlow, Elizabeth. *Christina Rossetti and the Bible: Waiting with the Saints.* London: Bloomsbury, 2014.

Ludlow, Elizabeth, editor. *The Figure of Christ in the Long Nineteenth Century.* London: Palgrave Macmillan, 2020.

Lukács, Georg. *The Theory of the Novel: A Historico-Philosophical Essay on the Forms of Great Epic Literature.* Translated by Anna Bostock. London: Merlin, 1978.

MacColl, Canon. "An Agnostic Novel": Review of *The Story of an African Farm.*" [*The Spectator* (August 13, 1887)]. In *Olive Schreiner*, edited by Cherry Clayton, 72–4. Johannesburg: McGraw-Hill, 1983.

MacDonald, George. "Browning's 'Christmas Eve.'" *The Monthly Christian Spectator* 3, no. 5 (May 1853): 261–73.

MacDonald, George. *An Expression of Character: The Letters of George MacDonald.* Edited by Glenn Edward Sadler. Grand Rapids: William B. Eerdmans, 1994.

MacDonald, George. "The Fantastic Imagination." In *A Dish of Orts: Chiefly Papers on the Imagination* and *On Shakespeare*, 313–22. London: Edwin Dalton, 1908.

MacDonald, George. "The Higher Faith." In *Unspoken Sermons: First Series*, 50–65. London: Longmans, Green, & Co., 1887.

MacDonald, George. "The Imagination: Its Functions and Its Culture." In *A Dish of Orts: Chiefly Papers on the Imagination and on Shakespeare*, 1–42. London: Edwin Dalton, 1908.

MacDonald, George. *Phantastes.* 1858. Edited by John Pennington, and Roderick McGillis. Hamden: Winged Lion Press, 2017.

MacDonald, George. "The Voice of Job." In *Unspoken Sermons: Second Series*, 207–51. London: Longmans, Green, & Co, 1885.

MacDonald, Greville. *George MacDonald and His Wife.* London: George Allen and Unwin, 1924.

MacDuffie, Allen. *Victorian Literature, Energy, and the Ecological Imagination.* Cambridge: Cambridge University Press, 2014.

Madsen, Deborah L. *Rereading Allegory: A Narrative Approach to Genre.* New York: Palgrave Macmillan, 1994.

Martin, Carol A. *George Eliot's Serial Fiction.* Columbus: Ohio State University Press, 1994.

Mason, Emma. *Christina Rossetti: Poetry, Ecology, Faith.* Oxford: Oxford University Press, 2018.

Mason, Emma. "Considering the Lilies: Christina Rossetti's Ecological Jesus." In *The Figure of Christ in the Long Nineteenth Century*, edited by Elizabeth Ludlow, 149–61. London: Palgrave Macmillan, 2020.

Mazaheri, John H. *Essays on Religion in George Eliot's Early Fiction*. Cambridge: Cambridge Scholars Publishing, 2018.

McClintock, Anne. *Imperial Leather: Race, Gender, and Sexuality in the Colonial Contest*. New York: Routledge, 1995.

McCrie, George. *The Religion of Our Literature: Essays upon Thomas Carlyle, Robert Browning, Alfred Tennyson, etc*. London: Hodder and Stoughton, 1875.

McKelvy, William R. *The English Cult of Literature: Devoted Readers, 1774–1880*. Charlottesville: University of Virginia Press, 2007.

McLean, B. H. *Biblical Criticism and Philosophical Hermeneutics*. Cambridge: Cambridge University Press, 2012.

Melnyk, Julie. "'Mighty Victims': Women Writers and the Feminization of Christ." *Victorian Literature and Culture* 31, no. 1 (2003): 131–47.

Mermin, Dorothy. *Elizabeth Barrett Browning: The Origins of a New Poetry*. Chicago: University of Chicago Press, 1989.

Millett, Kate. "The Debate over Women: Ruskin versus Mill." *Victorian Studies* 14, no. 1 (1970): 63–82.

Mills, Mary E. *Reading Ecclesiastes: A Literary and Cultural Exegesis*. Farham: Ashgate, 2003.

Milton, John. *Areopagitica*. 1644. In *Complete Poems and Major Prose*, edited by Merritt Y. Hughes, 716–49. Indianapolis: Hackett, 2003.

Milton, John. *Paradise Lost*. 1674. In *John Milton: Complete Poems and Major Prose*, edited by Merritt Y. Hughes, 211–470. Indianapolis: Hackett, 2003.

Mitchell, Rebecca N. *Victorian Lessons in Empathy and Difference*. Columbus: Ohio State University Press, 2011.

Moltmann, Jürgen. "God's Kenosis in the Creation and Consummation of the World." In *The Work of Love: Creation as Kenosis*, edited by John Polkinghorne, 137–51. Grand Rapids: William B. Eerdmans, 2001.

Monsman, Gerald. *Olive Schreiner's Fiction: Landscape and Power*. New Brunswick: Rutgers University Press, 1991.

Morgan, Thaïs E., editor. *Victorian Sages and Cultural Discourse: Renegotiating Gender and Power*. New Brunswick: Rutgers University Press, 1990.

Morrison, Kevin A. "Myth, Remembrance, and Modernity: From Ruskin to Benjamin via Proust." *Comparative Literature* 60, no. 2 (2008): 125–41.

Murphy, Patricia. "Timely Interruptions: Unsettling Gender through Temporality in *The Story of an African Farm*." *Style* 32, no. 1 (1998): 80–101.

Murphy, Roland E. "The Sage in Ecclesiastes and Qoheleth the Sage." In *The Sage in Israel and the Ancient Near East*, edited by John G. Gammie, and Leo G. Perdue, 263–74. Eisenbrauns: Penn State University Press, 1990.

Murphy, Roland E. *The Tree of Life: An Exploration of Biblical Wisdom Literature*. Grand Rapids: William B. Eerdmans, 1990.

Nash, David. "Reassessing the 'Crisis of Faith' in the Victorian Age: Eclecticism and the Spirit of Moral Inquiry." *Journal of Victorian Culture* 16, no. 1 (2011): 65–82.

Newsom, Carol A. *The Book of Job: A Contest of Moral Imaginations*. Oxford: Oxford University Press, 2003.

Nixon, Jude V. "'Kill[ing] Our Souls with Literalism': Reading *Essays and Reviews*." In *Victorian Religious Discourse*, edited by Jude V. Nixon, 51–82. New York: Palgrave Macmillan, 2004.

Nurbhai, Saleel, and K. M. Newton. *George Eliot, Judaism, and the Novels*. New York: Palgrave, 2002.

Ofek, Galia. "'Reviewing the Rites Proper to Canonization': New Woman Novels and New Conceptions of Canonicity." *Victorian Literature and Culture* 38, no. 1 (2010): 165–98.

O'Gorman, Francis. "Ruskin, Science, and the Miracles of Life." *The Review of English Studies New Series* 61, no. 249 (2010): 276–8.

Olive Schreiner Letters Transcription Project. *The Olive Schreiner Letters Online*. University of Edinburgh and Leeds Beckett University. www.oliveschreiner.org. 2012.

Olsen, Trenton B. *Wordsworth and Evolution in Victorian Literature: Entangled Influence*. London: Routledge, 2020.

Ong, Jade Munslow. "Dream Time and Anti-Imperialism in the Writings of Olive Schreiner." *Journal of Postcolonial Writing* 50, no. 6 (2014): 704–16.

Ong, Jade Munslow. *Olive Schreiner and African Modernism: Allegory, Empire, and Postcolonial Writing*. New York: Routledge, 2018.

Orr, Marilyn. *George Eliot's Religious Imagination: A Theopoetics of Evolution*. Evanston: Northwestern University Press, 2018.

Pals, Daniel L. *The Victorian "Lives" of Jesus*. San Antonio: Trinity University Press, 1982.

Pannenberg, Wolfhart. *Jesus, God and Man*. 2nd edition. Translated by Lewis L. Wilkins, and Duane A Priebe. Louisville: Westminster Press, 1977.

Perdue, Leo G. *Wisdom and Creation: The Theology of Wisdom Literature*. Nashville: Abingdon Press, 1994.

Perkin, J. Russell. *Theology and the Victorian Novel*. Montreal: McGill-Queen's University Press, 2009.

Piper, Ronald A. *Wisdom in the Q-Tradition: The Aphoristic Teaching of Jesus*. Cambridge: Cambridge University Press, 1989.

Plourde, Aubrey. "George MacDonald's Doors: Suspended Telos and the Child Believer." *Victorian Literature and Culture* 49, no. 2 (2021): 231–58.

Poe, Edgar Allan. Review of *A Drama of Exile and Other Poems*. *The Broadway Journal* (January 4, 1845): 17–20. Reprinted in *The Brownings' Correspondence*, vol. 9, edited by Philip Kelley, Ronald Hudson. and Scott Lewis, 349–51. Winfield: Wedgestone Press, 1991.

Price, Leah. "George Eliot and the Production of Consumers." *NOVEL: A Forum on Fiction* 30, no. 2 (1997): 145–69.

Prickett, Stephen. "Fictions and Metafictions: *Phantastes*, Wilhelm Meister, and the Idea of the Bildungsroman." In *The Gold Thread: Essays on George MacDonald*, edited by William Raeper, 109–25. Edinburgh: Edinburgh University Press, 1990.

Prickett, Stephen. "The Idea of Tradition in George MacDonald." In *Rethinking George MacDonald: Contexts and Contemporaries*, edited by Christopher MacLachlan, John Patrick Pazdziora, and Ginter Stelle, 1–17. Glasgow: Scottish Literature International, 2013.

Prickett, Stephen. *Narrative, Religion, and Science: Fundamentalism versus Irony*. Cambridge: Cambridge University Press, 2002.

Prickett, Stephen. *Words and the Word: Language, Poetics, and Biblical Interpretation*. Cambridge: Cambridge University Press, 1986.

Reisenauer, Eric. M. "Between the Eternal City and the Holy City: Rome, Jerusalem, and the Imperial Ideal in Britain." *Canadian Journal of History* 44, no. 3 (2009): 237–60.

Renan, Ernest. *The Life of Jesus*. Translated by John Haynes Holmes. New York: The Modern Library, 1955.

Review of *Phantastes*. *The Athenaeum* (6 November 1858): 560. In *Phantastes*, edited by John Pennington and Roderick McGillis, 200–203. Hamden: Winged Lion Press, 2017.

Review of *Phantastes*. *The British Quarterly Review* 29 (January 1859): 296–7. In *Phantastes*, edited by John Pennington and Roderick McGillis, 208–9. Hamden: Winged Lion Press, 2017.

Review of *Phantastes*. *The Spectator* (4 December 1858): 1286. In *Phantastes*, edited by John Pennington and Roderick McGillis, 204–5. Hamden: Winged Lion Press, 2017.

Ricoeur, Paul. "Biblical Hermeneutics." *Semeia* 4 (1975): 29–148.

Ricoeur, Paul. "Experience and Language in Religious Discourse." In *Phenomenology and the Theological Turn: The French Debate*, edited by Dominique Janicaud, 127–46. New York: Fordham University Press, 2000.

Ricoeur, Paul. *Freud and Philosophy: An Essay on Interpretation*. Translated by Denis Savage. New Haven: Yale University Press, 1970.

Ricoeur, Paul. *The Rule of Metaphor: Multidisciplinary Studies in the Creation of Meaning in Language*. Translated by Robert Czerny, with Kathleen McLaughlin, and John Costello. Toronto: University of Toronto Press, 1977.

Ricoeur, Paul. *The Symbolism of Evil*. Translated by Emerson Buchanan. New York: Harper and Row, 1967.

Ricoeur, Paul. "Toward a Hermeneutic of the Idea of Revelation." In *Essays on Biblical Interpretation*, edited by Lewis S. Mudge, translated by David Pellauer, 73–118. Philadelphia: Fortress Press, 1980.

Ruether, Rosemary Radford. "Ecology and Theology: Ecojustice at the Center of the Church's Mission." *Interpretation: A Journal of Bible and Theology* 65, no. 4 (2011): 354–6.

Ruskin, John. *The Winnington Letters: John Ruskin's Correspondence with Margaret Alexis Bell and the Children and Winnington Hall*. Edited by Van Akin Burd. Cambridge: Harvard University Press, 1969.

Ruskin, John. *The Works of John Ruskin*. Edited by E. T. Cook, and Alexander Wedderburn, 39 vols. London: George Allen, 1903-12.

Sawyer, Paul. "Ruskin and the Matriarchal Logos." In *Victorian Sages and Cultural Discourse: Renegotiating Gender and Power*, edited by Thaïs E. Morgan, 129-41. New Brunswick: Rutgers University Press, 1990.

Sawyer, Paul. *Ruskin's Poetic Argument: The Design of the Major Works*. Ithaca: Cornell University Press, 1985.

Scarry, Elaine. *On Beauty and Being Just*. Princeton: Princeton University Press, 1999.

Schaffer, Talia. *Communities of Care: The Social Ethics of Victorian Fiction*. Princeton: Princeton University Press, 2021.

Scheinberg, Cynthia. *Women's Poetry and Religion in Victorian England*. Cambridge: Cambridge University Press, 2002.

Schifferdecker, Kathryn. *Out of the Whirlwind: Creation Theology in the Book of Job*. Cambridge: Harvard University Press, 2008.

Schleiermacher, Friedrich. *A Critical Essay on the Gospel of St. Luke*. 1817. Translated by Connop Thirlwall. London: John Taylor, 1825.

Schleiermacher, Friedrich. *Hermeneutics and Criticism and Other Writings*. 1838. Translated by Andrew Bowie. Cambridge: Cambridge University Press, 1998.

Schreiner, Olive. *The Story of an African Farm*. 1883. Oxford: Oxford University Press, 1992.

Schreiner, Susan. *Where Shall Wisdom Be Found? Calvin's Exegesis of Job from Medieval and Modern Perspectives*. Chicago: University of Chicago Press, 1994.

Shaffer, E. S. "The Hermeneutic Community: Coleridge and Schleiermacher." In *The Coleridge Connection: Essays for Thomas McFarland*, edited by Richard Gravil, and Molly Lefebure, 200-232. New York: Macmillan, 1990.

Shaw, W. David. *Secrets of the Oracle: A History of Wisdom from Zeno to Yeats*. Toronto: University of Toronto Press, 2009.

Shea, Victor, and William Whitla, editors. *Essays and Reviews: The 1860 Text and Its Reading*. Charlottesville: University of Virginia Press, 2000.

Shelley, Percy Bysshe. *A Defence of Poetry*. Indianapolis: The Bobbs-Merrill Company, 1904.

Sinni, Ryan. "Wise Women and Strange Men: The Book of Proverbs in 'Goblin Market.'" *Victorian Poetry* 60, no. 1 (2022): 71-86.

Smith, Adam. *The Theory of Moral Sentiments*. 1759. Amherst: Prometheus Books, 2000.

Spenser, Edmund. *The Faerie Queene*. 1590. Edited by J. C. Smith. Oxford: Clarendon Press, 1909.

Stead, W. T. "The Book of the Month: The Novel of the Modern Woman." *Review of Reviews* 10 (July 1894): 64-74.

Stern, David. *Midrash and Theory: Ancient Jewish Exegesis and Contemporary Literary Studies*. Evanston: Northwestern University Press, 1996.

Stone, Marjorie. *Elizabeth Barrett Browning*. Hampshire: Macmillan, 1995.
Stone, Marjorie. "A Heretic Believer: Victorian Religious Doubt and New Contexts for Elizabeth Barrett Browning's 'A Drama of Exile,' 'The Virgin Mary,' and 'The Runaway Slave at Pilgrim's Point.'" *Studies in Browning and His Circle* 26, no. 2 (2006): 7–39.
Stone, Marjorie. "Lyric Tipplers: Elizabeth Barrett Browning's 'Wine of Cyprus,' Emily Dickinson's 'I taste a liquor,' and the Transatlantic Anacreontic Tradition." *Victorian Poetry* 54, no. 2 (2016): 123–54.
Strauss, David Friedrich. *Life of Jesus, Critically Examined*. Translated by George Eliot. 1846. London: Swan Sonnenschein & Co., 1898.
Styler, Rebecca. *Literary Theology by Women Writers of the Nineteenth Century*. Farham: Ashgate, 2010.
Taylor, Barbara. *Eve and the New Jerusalem: Socialism and Feminism in the Nineteenth Century*. London: Virago Press, 1983.
Taylor, Charles. *A Secular Age*. Cambridge: Harvard University Press, 2007.
Taylor, Charles. *Sources of the Self: The Making of a Modern Identity*. Cambridge: Harvard University Press, 1989.
Tertullian. "The Apparel of Women." In *Disciplinary, Moral, and Aesthetical Works*, translated by Rudolph Arbesman, Sister Emily Joseph Daly, and Edwin A. Quain, 111–52. New York: Fathers of the Church, 1959.
Thomas, Terence. "The Impact of Other Religions." In *Religion in Victorian Britain. Volume II. Controversies*, edited by Gerald Parsons, 280–98. Manchester: Manchester University Press, 1980.
Thompson, Andrew. *George Eliot and Italy*. New York: Macmillan, 1998.
Tucker, Herbert. "An Ebbigrammar of Motives; or, Ba for Short." *Victorian Poetry* 44, no. 4 (2006): 445–62.
Vance, Norman. *Bible and Novel: Narrative Authority and the Death of God*. Oxford: Oxford University Press, 2013.
Waco, Armstrong Browning Library. Browning Collections.
Waco, Armstrong Browning Library. A2020. Schleiermacher, Friedrich Daniel Ernest. *Schleiermacher's Introductions to the Dialogues of Plato*. Translated by W. Dobson. London, 1836.
Waco, Armstrong Browning Library. MS D0216. Elizabeth Barrett Browning. *A Drama of Exile*. 1844.
Waco, Armstrong Browning Library. L0128.1. John Kenyon. Criticism on EBB's *A Drama of Exile*. No date.
Waco, Armstrong Browning Library. L0128.2. John Kenyon. Criticism on EBB's *Poems*. No date.
Weil, Simone. *Gravity and Grace*. Translated by Arthur Wills. Lincoln: University of Nebraska Press, 1997.
Weltman, Sharon Aronofsky. "Mythic Language and Gender Subversion: The Case of Ruskin's Athena." *Nineteenth-Century Literature* 52, no. 3 (1997): 350–71.

Werner, Winter Jade. *Missionary Cosmopolitanism in Nineteenth-Century British Literature*. Columbus: Ohio State University Press, 2020.

Werner, Winter Jade, and John Wiehl. "Chasing David Copperfield's Memory of a Stained Glass Window: Or, Meditations on the Postsecular and Postcritical." *LIT: Literature Interpretation Theory* 31, no. 1 (2021): 1–9.

Werner, Winter Jade, and Mimi Winick. "How to See Global Religion: Comparativism, Connectivity, and the Undisciplining of Victorian Studies." *Modern Language Quarterly* 83, no. 4 (December 2022): 499–520.

White Jr., Lynn. "The Historical Roots of Our Ecological Crisis." In *The Ecocriticism Reader: Landmarks in Literary Ecology*, edited by Cheryll Glotfelty, and Harold Fromm, 3–13. Athens: University of George Press, 1996.

Wilde, Oscar. "The Critic as Artist." 1891. In *The Artist as Critic: Critical Writings of Oscar Wilde*, edited by Richard Ellmann, 341–408. New York: Random House, 1969.

Wilde, Oscar. "English Poetesses." 1888. In *The Complete Works of Oscar Wilde*, vol. 14, edited by Robert Ross, 110–20. London: Dawsons of Pall Mall, 1969.

Williams, Wendy. *George Eliot, Poetess*. Burlington: Ashgate, 2014.

Witherington, Ben. *Jesus the Sage: A Pilgrimage of Wisdom*. Minneapolis: Fortress Press, 1994.

Wörn, Alexandra M. B. "'Poetry Is where God Is': The Importance of Christian Faith and Theology in Elizabeth Barrett Browning's Life and Work." In *Victorian Religious Discourse: New Directions in Criticism*, edited by Jude V. Nixon, 232–52. New York: Palgrave Macmillan, 2004.

Wright, T. R. *The Religion of Humanity: The Impact of Comtean Positivism on Victorian Britain*. Cambridge: Cambridge University Press, 1986.

Author Biography

Denae Dyck is Assistant Professor of English at Texas State University. Her publications include articles in *Victorian Poetry, Victorian Review, European Romantic Review,* and *Christianity and Literature*.

Index

aestheticism 1, 3
agnosticism 144, 166 n.3, 175
Aikin, Lucy 44
allegory 65–7, 90–1, 96–7, 105, 123
Alter, Robert 9–10, 51, 63, 99–100, 145–6, 165
Anger, Suzy 2, 100
Anglicanism 2, 16, 199, 120
aphorism 4, 60–3, 68, 93–4, 106, 175
apocalyptic 98, 133, 156, 181
apocrypha 22, 116, 131, 151
apostasy 100, 120–1, 147–8 (*See also* loss of faith)
application 5, 62, 71, 107–8
Ariadne 104, 109
Aristotelian philosophy 107, 109, 135
Arnold, Matthew 9, 17, 103, 121–2, 176
Arts and Crafts Movement 116, 120, 137
Athena 115–17, 121, 124–36
Atkins, Gareth 103
Auerbach, Erich 65, 99, 130
Augustine 43, 65, 71
authority 4, 8–9, 13, 40, 118, 135–6

Bacon, Francis 64, 68
Baker, William 112 n.24
Bakhtin, Mikhail 24 n.4, 38
Batchelor, John 116
Battles, Kelly E. 111 n.16
beauty 3, 42, 116, 128, 135
Beer, Gillian 1
belief 6–9, 11, 81, 120, 174
Bell, Margaret Alexis 119, 122
Berkman, Joyce Avrech 166 n.1, 167 n.3, 168 n.21
Bible (*See also* biblical interpretation)
    1 Corinthians 70, 74
    1 John 74
    2 Corinthians 64
    2 Samuel 184 n.47
    Acts 127
    Ecclesiastes 3, 9, 15, 19, 63, 78, 144–6, 152, 155–6, 158, 162, 173–6, 179
    Genesis 32, 36, 45–6, 50
    Isaiah 49
    James 71–2
    Job 3, 9, 15, 19, 32–3, 36–8, 42, 46, 48–9, 59, 121, 166
    John 3
    Luke 94, 181–2
    Matthew 92, 130, 148
    Philippians 33, 49, 133
    Proverbs 3, 9, 41, 60–3, 79, 116, 123, 155, 169 n.46, 174, 181
    Psalms 9, 36, 141 n.41
    Revelation 156
    Romans 160
    Song of Songs 9, 79
biblical higher criticism (*See under* higher criticism)
biblical interpretation
    Bible as literature 10–11, 14–15, 34–6, 103, 164
    nineteenth-century developments 2–3, 11–15, 34, 71–2 (*See also* higher criticism)
    patristic exegesis 34, 43–5, 56 n.38, 65, 71, 107, 145, 153
    twentieth and twenty-first-century developments 9–10, 20, 38, 92, 164–5
bildungsroman 60, 144, 149, 150
Birch, Dinah 118, 135 n.7
Blair, Kirstie 35
Blake, William 9, 44, 49, 63, 148, 155, 169 n.46
Bloomfield, Morton 82 n.16
Blumberg, Ilana 87
Bonaparte, Felicia 88, 96–7, 98
Bradlaugh, Charles 6, 25 n.18
Branch, Lori 6, 163
Brotton, Melissa J. 56 n. 46
Browning, Elizabeth Barrett
    Aurora Leigh 31, 47
    and biblical interpretation 32–6, 38–9, 42–7

and Congregationalism 40, 52
and cosmopolitanism 52
A Drama of Exile 31–3, 37, 40–52
and feminist criticism 32–3, 44–8
The Seraphim 31
Browning, Robert 34, 74–5
Brown, William P. 82 n.10, 170 n.69
Bubel, Katharine 79
Buddhism 126, 154
Budge, Gavin 9
Bultmann, Rudolf 92
Bundock, Christopher M. 26 n.29
Bunyan, John 65
Burd, Van Akin 139 n.10, 142 n.49

canonicity 13, 130–1, 150, 165
Carlyle, Thomas
  and Romanticism 121, 136
  Sartor Resartus 149–50, 179
  Victorian sage 9, 40, 62, 98
Carpenter, Mary Wilson 97, 98
Carroll, David 89, 103
Carroll, Lewis 66
Catholicism 16, 24 n.6, 89, 102, 111 n.11
certitude 80, 94, 123–9
Chapman, Alison 52, 54 n.13
Chatterjee, Ronjaunee 25 n.19
Cheeke, Stephen 120
Chesterton, G. K. 63
Cheyne, Thomas Kelly 3, 38, 145, 149, 155, 173–4
children's literature 79–80
Chrétien, Jean-Louis 71
Christ, Carol P. 177
Christmas 74–5, 103
Christology 21–2, 29 n.80, 48–50, 74–6, 131–2
Colenso, John William 13, 98, 117, 119, 122, 126, 155
Coleridge, Samuel Taylor 12, 21, 35, 60–1, 64–7, 71, 80, 106
Colón, Susan 20, 90, 105, 108, 181
comparative religion 13, 115, 126–7
Comte, August 91, 96–8, 111 n.11
Congregationalism 7, 40, 52, 59
conversion 100–2, 107, 126
Cornhill Magazine 88–90, 121, 136
cosmology 33, 40–4
cosmopolitanism 7, 52, 126–7
Coté, Amy 112 n.29
covenant 130, 133, 165, 175

Cox, Kimberly 185 n.34
creation 33, 36–8, 50, 65, 133 (*See also* nature)
Crenshaw, James 10, 24 n.6
crisis of faith 2, 7–8, 147 (*See also* apostasy)

Darwin, Charles 1, 2, 124, 154
Dell, Katharine J. 176
devil 44, 143, 155 (*See also* Lucifer)
De Wette, Wilhelm Martin Leberecht 145
dialogue 32, 37–40, 118, 134, 155, 158, 178
  (*See also* Socratic dialogue)
Dickens, Charles 74, 93
didacticism 59, 64, 92, 109, 117
Dieleman, Karen 32, 34, 40
dissenting Protestantism 2–3, 7, 16, 33, 52, 64
Docherty, John 66, 73
doubt 2, 4, 80–1, 92, 144, 163
Draucker, Shannon 185
Dupré, Louis 106
Dwor, Richa 8, 112 n.24

ecocriticism 47, 125, 177
ecotheology 45, 48, 56 n.46, 57 n.47
Eichhorn, Johann Gottfried 12, 32
Eliot, George
  Adam Bede 89, 108
  and biblical interpretation 87–8
  Middlemarch 108
  and religion 87, 91–2, 103
  Romola 88–90, 94–8, 100–2, 103–9
  translations of the higher criticism 14, 87, 90–1
Ellis, Havelock 143, 148
Emerson, Ralph Waldo 148–9, 157, 162, 168 n.21
Essays and Reviews 2, 12, 19, 98, 119, 121, 124, 163–4
Eucharist 106
evangelicalism 7, 16, 47, 81 n.2
Eve 32, 40, 43–7
evolution 1, 48, 124
exile 43

faith 2, 7–8, 79–80, 163 (*See also* loss of faith)
felix culpa 43
Felski, Rita 17, 28 n.64, 178–9, 180
feminist criticism 8, 32, 129–30, 150, 177
feminist theology 8, 177, 184 n.30

Feuerbach, Ludwig 14, 49, 87, 100, 102–3, 106–7, 161
Fike, Matthew 153
First, Ruth 147
Fong, Ryan D. 154
fragment 3, 37–40, 93, 144, 150, 160
Francis of Assisi 177
Franklin, J. Jeffrey 139 n.2, 154
freethought 6, 103, 143, 147–8, 157
Frei, Hans 18
Frye, Northrop 10
fundamentalism 16, 90, 105, 164, 176
Funk, Robert 108, 184 n.11
futility 150, 152, 160, 173 (*See also* vanity)

Gaarden, Bonnie 75–6
Gabelman, Daniel 71
Gadamer, Hans-Georg 17, 28 n.65, 39, 107
Gaskell, Elizabeth 93
Good Words 59, 81 n.2
Gothic 90, 97, 105, 137
Gray, F. Elizabeth 8
Gregory Nazianzen 153
Greiner, Rae 113 n.48
Grillo, Jennie 176

Habermas, Jürgen 6, 17, 28 n.65
Hackett, Robin 169 n.40
Hair, Donald S. 42
Harding, Anthony John 26 n.42
Harrison, Roland Kenneth 55 n.24
Hatton, Peter 63, 169 n.46
Hebrew language 15, 21, 36, 64, 145, 146
Hedrick, Charles W. 27 n.54, 112 n.22
Heilmann, Ann 151, 169 n.40
hell 59, 162
Hennell, Charles 92
Hennell, Sara Sophia 14, 103
Henry, Nancy 88
Herbert, Christopher 88–9, 105
Herder, Johann Gottfried 12, 18, 32, 36–7, 38, 42, 46, 51
hermeneutics 2–4, 16–19, 39, 77, 99–100, 107, 118, 159, 164
Hess, Richard S. 26 n.41, 167 n.8
heuristic 20, 62, 67–8, 122
Hewison, Robert 141 n.29
higher criticism (*See also* biblical interpretation)
    historical scholarship 2, 11–15, 64, 119–20
    on literary forms and genres 18–19, 34–6, 91–3
    lives of Jesus 13–15, 87–8, 103, 148
historical novel 88, 94
Hoagwood, Terence Allan 32
Hodgson, Peter C. 87, 103, 108
Holloway, John 8–9, 40, 149
Holmes, John 170 n.61
hooks, bell 180
hope 47, 166, 175, 179
Hopkins, Gerard Manley 16
Houston, Gail Turley 8, 141 n.44
Hughes, Arthur 79
humility 47, 48–9, 68, 133, 175
hymn 4, 48, 116, 133

incarnation 21, 43, 72–5, 100, 103, 106–7, 131 (*See also* theology)
Inklings 59, 61
imagination 59–66
immanence 48–50, 75, 106, 131–3, 148, 168
imperialism 6–7, 13, 116, 125–6, 146–7, 154–5
inspiration 2–3, 11–12, 21, 61, 64–5, 92, 132, 164
irony 63, 97–8, 108, 145, 148–9, 157
Italy 94

Jacobs, Alan 180–1
Jaffe, Audre 113 n.48
Jasper, David 28 n.62
Jeffrey, David Lyle 15
Jesus (*See also* Christology)
    debates about divinity 13–14, 25, 109–10, 148
    incarnation theology 75, 103, 131
    moral teachings 87–8, 92, 94, 154
Jewish traditions 9, 15, 25 n.35, 50, 92, 93, 112 n.24, 130
Johnson, Elizabeth A. 184 n.20
Jowett, Benjamin 2, 12, 19–20, 121, 124, 163–4

Kaufman, Michael W. 28 n.61
Keats, John 125
Keefer, Arthur J. 176
Keirstead, Christopher M. 52
kenosis 33, 48–9
Kenyon, John 39
Kierkegaard, Søren 71–2

kingdom of God 90–1, 94–5, 102, 104, 106, 108
King, Joshua 5, 185 n.23
Kissack, Mike 147, 167 n.3
Knight, Mark 5, 6, 16, 81 n.2, 174, 178
Knight, Richard Payne 119
Kreglinger, Gisela H. 64
Kucich, John 151

Landow, George P. 8–9, 11, 40, 118, 123, 136–7, 149–50, 159
LaPorte, Charles 2, 16, 18, 35, 103
Larsen, Timothy 8, 11, 74, 113 n.39
Lecourt, Sebastian 103, 126
lectio divina 71, 134
Lessing, Gotthold Ephraim 13, 32, 98
Levine, Caroline 88
Levine, George 1, 124
Lewis, C. S. 59, 61, 81 n.1
Lewis, Linda 32, 54 n.13
Lewis, Simon 151
literalism 13, 21, 35, 61, 64, 121, 176
Lloyd, Jennifer 141 n.42
Lloyd, John T. 148, 166
loss of faith 7–8, 87, 120
love
    divine love 47–9, 72–4, 107
    among humankind 70, 77–9, 104, 153, 156
Lowth, Robert 18, 35–6, 46, 51
Lucifer 37, 43–4
Ludlow, Elizabeth 27 n.55, 29 n.80
Lukács, Georg 5

MacColl, Canon 166 n.3
MacDonald, George
    At the Back of the North Wind 79
    and biblical interpretation 64–5, 74–5
    and Congregationalism 52, 59
    "The Fantastic Imagination" 60, 67, 77
    "The Imagination: Its Functions and Its Culture" 62, 63, 77, 81
    Phantastes 60–1, 68–71, 72–3, 75–80
    The Princess and the Goblin 79, 80
    Unspoken Sermons 59, 79
MacDuffie, Allen 141 n.34
Madsen, Deborah L. 66
Main, Alexander 93
Martin, Carol A. 111 n.8
Mason, Emma 15–16, 47

Maurice, F. D. 59, 81 n.2, 126
Mazaheri, John H. 87
McClintock, Anne 169 n.40
McCrie, George 81
McKelvy, William R. 5
McLean, B. H. 28 n.35
Melnyk, Julie 47
Mermin, Dorothy 32
metaphor 18, 20–21, 77, 122, 124, 133, 182
Millett, Kate 129
Mill, John Stuart 129, 135–6, 158
Mills, Mary E. 183 n.5
Milton, John 32, 43–4, 158
missionaries 7, 126–7, 143, 147, 151
Mitchell, Rebecca 113 n.48
Moltmann, Jürgen 50
Monsman, Gerald 148–9, 156
Morgan, Thaïs E. 9
Morrison, Kevin A. 139 n.7
Morris, William 116, 125, 137
Moses 10, 93, 158, 160, 161
Müller, Friedrich Max 115, 117, 132, 135, 139 n.2
Murphy, Patricia 150
Murphy, Roland E. 20
music 69, 76–9
mystery 62, 80
mysticism 34, 106–7, 148, 153–4
mythmaking 115–6, 118, 123–5
mythology 88, 93, 94, 115, 123–5, 132, 135

Nash, David 8
nature 42, 48, 124–5, 128–9, 132–3, 154 (*See also* ecocriticism)
Newman, John Henry 16, 153
Newsom, Carol A. 38
Newton, K. M. 112 n.24
New Woman 150, 151, 153
Nixon, Jude V. 176
Nurbhai, Saleel 112 n.24

Ofek, Galia 150
O'Gorman, Francis 138
Olsen, Trenton B. 1
Ong, Jade Munslow 154–5
Orr, Marilyn 87
Oxford Movement 16, 34–5

Pals, Daniel 14, 27 n.47, 176, 184 n.18
Pannenberg, Wolfhart 57 n.52

parable 20, 87–8, 90–3, 99, 105, 108, 136, 158–60, 166, 181–2
paradox 95, 107, 138, 175
parallelism 18, 36, 51, 63, 79
Pearson, Karl 147, 148
pedagogy 180
Perdue, Leo G. 18, 20, 133, 155
periodical press 2, 33, 54 n.10, 66
Perkin, J. Russell 5, 110 n.1
personification 8, 21, 66, 128–30
philology 13–14, 115, 126, 135
Piper, Ronald A. 27 n.54
Pisgah Sight 159–60
Plourde, Aubrey 80
Poe, Edgar Allan 52
poetics 20, 35, 121–2, 124–5
positivism 96–8
postcritical scholarship 16–17, 23, 138, 174–5, 178
postsecular scholarship 5–6, 17, 23, 138, 163, 174–5
preaching (*See under* sermon)
Price, Leah 112 n.30
Prickett, Stephen 18, 36, 71
progress 1, 96–8, 116, 150, 175
prophecy 8–10, 40, 63, 97–9, 133, 149–50, 155–7
Pygmalion 68

reader response 23, 67–8, 70–1, 90–1, 133–5, 159
realist novel 20, 105, 108
Reimarus, Hermann Samuel 13
Reisenauer, Eric. M. 164 n.44
religion (*See also* theology)
    comparative religious study 13, 115–16, 119, 126–7
    and literary criticism 5–8, 174–5, 182–3
    and poetry 34–5, 121–2
    Victorian controversies 1–2, 7–8, 34, 119, 124, 163–4
religious exclusivism 158, 161, 163
religious syncretism 13
religious symbolism 4, 163, 18, 177
Renan, Ernest 1–2, 13–14, 15, 109, 122, 131, 148, 159, 163
revelation 10, 23, 34, 63, 71, 99–100, 164–6
rhetoric 20, 122, 136–7
Rhodes, Cecil 154

Ricoeur, Paul
    biblical interpretation 4, 10–11, 33–4, 42, 49, 164–5, 176
    hermeneutics 17–18, 99, 108, 175
    metaphor 77, 133, 182
    parables 90, 95, 159
    poetics 20, 62, 68, 122, 124
    The Symbolism of Evil 4, 18
Risorgimento 94
Ruether, Rosemary Radford 184 n.20
Romanticism 9, 60, 63–5, 80, 106, 121, 132
Rossetti, Christina 3, 15–16, 27 n.55, 47
Rossetti, Dante Gabriel 116
Ruskin, John
    and biblical interpretation 115–16, 117–20, 127, 131
    The Ethics of the Dust 134
    Modern Painters 116, 128
    The Queen of the Air 115–17, 123–5, 127–8
    and religion 120–21
    Sesame and Lilies 134
    The Stones of Venice 137–8
    Unto this Last 90, 117, 135–6
    as Victorian sage 118, 133, 136

satire 156–7
Savonarola, Girolamo 88–90, 94–5, 99, 100–9
Sawyer, Paul 115, 123, 129, 132
Scarry, Elaine 135
Schaffer, Talia 180
Scheinberg, Cynthia 8, 26 n.35, 43
Schifferdecker, Kathryn 56 n.47
Schleiermacher, Friedrich 19, 38–9, 67, 70, 92, 100, 107, 134, 159
Schreiner, Olive
    and biblical interpretation 143, 148, 156–8, 159–60
    Dreams 158, 162
    And feminism 151–4
    and freethought 143, 147–8
    and imperialism 154–5
    The Story of an African Farm 144–7, 149, 150–63, 165–6
    Trooper Peter Halket of Mashonaland 154
science 64, 118, 124–5
Scott, Ann 147
secularization 1–2, 5–8, 87, 163, 174
self-reflexivity 23, 60, 105, 117, 136

sermon 59, 94–5, 106, 127
Sermon on the Mount 95, 106, 148
Shaffer, E. S. 34
Sharples, Eliza 44, 129
Shaw, W. David 3, 24 n.9
Shelley Percy Bysshe 60, 125
sin 43–4, 148
Sinni, Ryan 27 n.55
skepticism 63, 107, 110, 139, 145, 155
Smith, Adam 102
Socratic dialogue 3, 68, 134
Solomon 145
source criticism 12, 26 n.41, 38, 150, 155
Spencer, Herbert 144, 157, 167 n.3
Spenser, Edmund 66, 128
Spurgeon, Charles 33
Stanton, Elizabeth Cady 150
Stead, W. T. 151
Stern, David 92
Stone, Marjorie 31, 34, 43
Strauss, David Friedrich 14, 19, 35, 65–6, 87–8, 92, 98, 103, 118, 122, 131, 148
Styler, Rebecca 8
subversion 9, 63, 152, 155, 158
suffering servant 49, 57 n.53, 103, 113 n.48
surprise 72–6, 182
symbolism 66, 97, 130, 148, 159, 163
sympathy 99, 102–3, 107
synaesthesia 21, 41
synoptic gospels 64, 92, 157, 182

Taylor, Barbara 56 n.44
Taylor, Charles 5–6, 7–8, 106, 174
Temple, Frederick 98, 119
Tertullian 65
theodicy 43
theology
    creation theology 50–1, 56 n.47, 133, 155–6, 177
    incarnation theology 21, 43, 72–5, 100, 103, 106–7, 118, 131
    Johannine theology 74–5
    kenotic theology 33, 48–9, 57 n.52, 107, 132 (*See also kenosis*)
    natural theology 124, 141 n.29
    Pauline theology 48–9, 64, 199, 127
    trinitarian theology 153
Thierauf, Doreen 185 n.34
Thomas, Terence 141 n.35
Thompson, Andrew 112 n.32
Titlestad, Michael 147, 167 n.3

Tractarianism (*See under* Oxford Movement)
truth 3, 52, 65, 72, 123–5, 158–60
Turner, Mark W. 88
typology 10–11, 15, 49, 123, 130–1, 159

uncertainty 4, 80, 163
Unitarians 75, 84 n.53, 91–2, 170 n. 61
universalism 126–7
utilitarianism 135–6, 179

value 178–9
Vance, Norman 5, 25 n.18, 26 n.39
vanity 146, 162, 173 (*See also* futility)
Victorian gender ideologies 108, 118, 129, 153
Victorian imperialism 6–7, 13, 116, 125–6, 146–7, 154–5
Victorian religious controversies 1–2, 7–8, 34, 119, 124, 163–4
Victorian sage 8–9, 40, 63, 98, 118, 134–6, 149–50
visual arts 11

Weil, Simone 107
Werner, Winter Jade 5, 7, 141 n.39, 174
Westminster Review 14, 27 n.49, 87, 92–3
White Jr., Lynn 177
Wiehl, John 174
Wilde, Oscar 1, 3, 13
Williams, Wendy 103
Winick, Mimi 141 n.39
wisdom
    as a biblical genre 3–5, 9–10, 31–2, 164–5, 175
    and biblical higher criticism 15–16, 22–3, 92, 145, 155, 159
    and Christology 15, 21, 133
    in classical traditions 107, 135
    and divine design 10, 42, 164–5
    and ecology 48–51, 133, 177
    and embodiment 5, 20–2, 41, 131
    and literary form 4, 20–3, 60, 63–4, 68, 92–3
    personified 75, 115–16, 127, 130–1
    and Victorian literature and culture 3, 15–16, 175
Witherington, Ben 21, 49
wonder 51, 59, 62, 68, 80, 106
Wong, Amy R. 25 n.19
Wörn, Alexandra M. B. 32
Wright, T. R. 111 n.11

www.ingramcontent.com/pod-product-compliance
Lightning Source LLC
Chambersburg PA
CBHW052112300426
44116CB00010B/1641